# GHOSTS

## OF

# HONOLULU

# GHOSTS

## — OF —

# HONOLULU

### A JAPANESE SPY, A JAPANESE AMERICAN SPY HUNTER, AND THE UNTOLD STORY OF PEARL HARBOR

## MARK HARMON

## LEON CARROLL, JR.

Harper Select

ISBN 978-1-4003-3701-9 (hardcover)
ISBN 978-1-4003-3704-0 (softcover)
ISBN 978-1-4003-3703-3 (audiobook)
ISBN 978-1-4003-3658-6 (ePub)
ISBN 978-1-4003-4127-6 (B&N signed ed.)

**Library of Congress Control Number: 2023937628**

*Printed in the United States of America*
24 25 26 27 28 LBC 5 4 3 2 1

# CONTENTS

# INTRODUCTION

The Naval Criminal Investigative Service is close to our hearts, and we've always felt an obligation to represent the NCIS in a realistic way. It's sobering to google "NCIS" and see that the first dozen returns are about our shows. The casts and crews bend over backward to get procedural details correct, from uniforms to weapons to lingo. It's one way we pay respect to the real NCIS agents, analysts and support staff who work there.

In the years ahead, we plan on using that same dedication to explore the roots of NCIS and the forgotten players who made the service what it is today. There are many stories to be told, true tales of the men and women who drove great events from their shadowy positions. This book is the first step in the journey through the *sub-rosa* history of people who value stealth over glory.

Combine our fascination with Hawaii and our love of NCIS history, and you get *Ghosts of Honolulu*. This true story covers the city's clandestine history before, during and after the attack on Pearl Harbor in 1941, seen mostly through the eyes of a naval intelligence special agent named Douglas Wada.

You may wonder how NCIS is related since it wasn't created until the 1990s, but it's fitting that we begin with a World War II story. In 1939, President Franklin Roosevelt ordered the Navy to investigate domestic threats of espionage and sabotage, sowing the seeds of what would eventually grow to become NCIS.

Some readers will recognize that NCIS can trace its roots deeper than that. Navy Department General Order 292 established the Office of Naval Intelligence (ONI) in 1882 to collect information on foreign vessels, chart foreign bodies of water and tour overseas defense and industrial facilities. ONI expanded into spy cases during World War I and covert operations (in New York) in 1916. But these efforts were largely dismantled after the Great War ended. With the rise of the Japanese Empire and looming war, the Navy rediscovered the value of counterespionage operations.

When FDR directed that the ONI handle the investigation of Navy cases relating to sabotage, espionage and subversive activities in '39, he put criminal investigations back on the menu. And civilians would be at the heart of the effort—in 1940 reservists started to be called up for duty with the Naval Intelligence Service. ("NIS" is a term that included a cadre of agents in naval stations and ships at sea, along with the entire ONI and a division within the Office of the Chief of Naval Operations.) They proved their worth: in 1943 alone, NIS personnel investigated 97,000 cases.

NCIS sprung from the NIS, as we'll explain at the book's conclusion (see Appendix A). That places the World War II experiences of naval counterintelligence agents firmly at the very foundations of the modern NCIS. And no one may have a more unique perspective on the war and its aftermath than Douglas Wada, the son of a Honolulu Shinto shrine builder, a naval reservist and the only Asian American who worked inside the ONI in Hawaii or anywhere else during the war.

The television franchise focuses on death investigations—perfect for a procedural drama—but the agency is about much more than that, including counterintelligence and counterespionage, which are the focus of this book. The answer to how NCIS became involved with domestic counterespionage usually comes in just two words: "Pearl Harbor." The true story, only told in the shadows, is more complex.

And for the current generation of NCIS agents facing their own unique challenges, we can only hope this story serves them as an entertaining morale boost with a reminder attached: your quiet work matters and is not forgotten.

**MARK HARMON AND LEON CARROLL**
**APRIL 2023**

# PROLOGUE

## DIAMOND HEAD BEACH, HONOLULU
## DECEMBER 7, 1941

"What the hell is that?" asks Douglas Wada, spotting smoke curling into the sky behind the bluff above. "That's too dark to be a cane field fire, isn't it?"

It's Sunday morning, and for Wada that means fishing. The thirty-one-year-old usually goes with his wife, Helen, but today he's recruited two friends from his Japanese-dominated Kapalama neighborhood instead. The trio are ready to cast into the surf of Diamond Head Beach, on the rock-strewn southern edge of Oahu. There's hardly a beach here to speak of, just an irregular ribbon of sand deposited on top of water-pitted sandstone. The shore ends in sheer cliffs, lush with overgrowth and the occasional intrepid palm tree. There's been a lighthouse atop those heights since 1899, and the beach affords a full picturesque view of the Coast Guard's tower, Fresnel beacon and keeper's residence.[1]

As a lifelong resident of Honolulu, Wada knows all the best fishing spots. It was an easy drive in his Chevrolet from his home downtown to this remote spot, a paradise seemingly created for fishermen on bright Sunday mornings.

But now the three men pause baiting their hooks to gaze at the mysterious plume. "Some kind of training thing, maybe?" one of Wada's friends asks. "Shooting real stuff."

The nearest military facility is the airfield at Bellows Field. Perhaps a plane crashed? But Wada remains doubtful, watching mutely as the smoke continues to thicken.

---

1. In 2007, the Diamond Head Lighthouse would be featured on a US stamp.

A voice from the bluffs suddenly commands their attention. It's the keeper of the Diamond Head Lighthouse, racing down to the beach in a near panic. (Inside, Coast Guard radio operator Melvin Bell is frantically warning civilian vessels to steer clear of Oahu's ports.)

"Don't you people know we're at war?" the lighthouse keeper cries when he gets close enough. It's clear that he wasn't expecting to confront three Japanese men near his lighthouse mere minutes into a shooting war.

Wada withdraws his US Navy identification and shows it to the man. The badge doesn't say so, but he works with the Office of Naval Intelligence in downtown Honolulu. He cut his teeth on undercover work, including surveilling Japanese ships coming into the harbor, but Wada's forte these days is translation and analysis. That puts him into contact with tapped phone conversations, local Japanese language newspapers, intercepted radio transmissions, purloined documents and subjects in interrogation rooms.

"What war?" he asks the lightkeeper. "No one told me about it."

The man points northwest. "The base is under attack," he says. "You better get back, right away."

That's how Douglas Wada, America's only Japanese American naval intelligence agent, found out that Japan launched a surprise air raid on Pearl Harbor Naval Base.[2]

---

2. On March 21, 2002, Ted Tsukiyama and Jim Tanabe conducted a comprehensive interview with Douglas Wada, which is a vital source for this book. The Military Intelligence Veterans of Honolulu conducted the interview and shared it with the Japanese Cultural Center of Hawaii. According to Mary Campany, librarian at the JCCH: "This interview was conducted by the MIS Veterans Club of Hawaii for inclusion in the Library of Congress's American Folklife Center's Veterans History Project. It seems that they did not submit the interview for inclusion in that collection."

# PART 1

# THE BOY FROM HONOLULU

# THE BOY FROM HONOLULU

## MAUNAKEA STREET, HONOLULU
## DECEMBER 5, 1922

Kazumasa Wada pumps the bicycle pedals in a steady rhythm, coaxing as much horsepower as possible from his fourteen-year-old legs. In Honolulu, bike rides can become passports to tropical vistas and favorite ocean fishing spots. Today, he hopes the bike can deliver him to his three o'clock class at the nearby Japanese language school. He's still building speed as he crosses Beretania Street.[1]

J. W. Lamb, behind the wheel of an oil truck, is turning onto Beretania from Maunakea Street when his passenger, Clinton Carroll, screams, "Look out!"

There's a small form on a bike entering the intersection, with seemingly no intention of slowing down. Lamb blares the horn and will later recall seeing the kid's feet working the pedals right up until the moment the truck's grill hit him.[2]

Kazumasa lies injured in the street and is taken to the hospital by a stranger in a nearby car. The child dies later that day, leaving his family bereaved. His younger brother, eleven-year-old Douglas Toshio Wada, falls physically ill for days. The pair had been steady companions, partners in exploring their island home, especially on bicycles.[3]

It's also a staggering blow to the child's parents, Hisakichi and Chiyo

---

1. *Nippu Jiji*, December 7, 1922.
2. *The Honolulu Advertiser*, April 6, 1923.
3. MIS Veterans Club of Hawaii interview. When Wada speaks of the truck, even years later, he can't help but spit out, "Damn thing."

Wada. Unlike most of the hundred thousand Japanese immigrants who came to Hawaii, the family doesn't work in sugar plantations.[4] The pair came to Hawaii from Yamaguchi Prefecture in 1902, when Hisakichi was hired by banker Samuel Mills Damon to build a Shinto shrine and two-story traditional Japanese tea house in Moanalua Gardens.[5]

Hisakichi is a *miyadaiku* carpenter, one who specializes in building and repairing Shinto shrines and Buddhist temples. The islands of Japan lack iron, so architects and artisans devised ways to construct buildings without using any metal, including nails.

A *miyadaiku* carpenter uses tools developed thousands of years ago: thin-bladed saws that cut on the pull stroke, rather than a push; planes shaped with tapering blades and an array of chisels designed by long-dead masters. The sole use of wood, the reliance on ancient tools and the spiritual, nearly ceremonial ways of working makes such carpenters revered in Japan and a rare commodity among the tens of thousands of pious Buddhist and Shinto Japanese in Hawaii.[6]

Hisakichi Wada also worked as contract carpenter for the city's public transportation system—there was a lot of woodworking involved in a network that depended on mule-drawn cars. The Wadas' home on Robello Lane has a livery barn; Hisakichi still makes money servicing the animals. Chiyo works as a dressmaker, aided by her daughter Itoyo, nineteen. The youngest member of the family is daughter Hanako, age nine.

Kazumasa's death changes the trajectory of the Wada family. They sue for damages and receive a $10,000 award the next year.[7] (Adjusted for inflation, that's equal to about $175,000 in 2023.) Hisakichi Wada

---

4. In 1920, more than 109,000 Japanese immigrants constituted forty-three percent of Hawaii's population.
5. Damon established Moanalua Gardens in 1898 on forty acres bequeathed to him in the will of the last living member of the House of Kamehameha. Damon died in 1924; the estate is managed by his trustees.
6. *The Honolulu Advertiser*, August 12, 1961.
7. Hisakichi Wada v. Associated Oil Co., 27 Haw. 671 (1924). The amount is challenged in appeals, with arguments over how to calculate the net loss of a human life, and the final tally may have been higher. Travel records show that Hisakichi, his wife, Chiyo, his daughters and his son-in-law also made trips to visit family in Japan after the accident. Their uncle is listed as their contact in Japan.

moves the family to a plot of land on Kama Lane, a Japanese-dominated street in the Kapalama district of Honolulu, adjacent to Chinatown.

The neighborhood is an enclave for working-class Chinese, rural Hawaiian, Korean and—above all—Japanese residents. There is poverty and desperation, but also well-tended home gardens, businesses, dance halls and health-care services. "The whites neither conduct business nor live in this district," reads one survey of Kapalama.[8] The exceptions are occasional groups of *haoles*[9] who haunt the speakeasies and gambling dens.

The elder Wada is joining the handful of other Japanese families who are building on the undeveloped land on Kama Lane, each plot built with main homes flanked by separate *ohana* buildings. These properties are known as "camps," making the family move the founding of the "Wada Camp" on Kama Lane. The family opens a store, run by Chiyo, catering to Japanese customers in Kapalama.

Douglas Wada grows up in Honolulu, steadily Americanized by the allure of his bicycle, fishing and sports. It's easy to be an active youth on Oahu, but he's also a social one. He's an enthusiastic Cub Scout, well-liked by his fellows in Den 13. He enjoys football despite his small size but discovers a true aptitude for baseball.

The sport anchors his identity when he is old enough to attend McKinley High School. The school's predominantly Japanese student body earns it the moniker, inside and out, of "Tokyo High." His interest in studying fades before the appeal of playing second base and a new obsession with cars.

His parents are doing their best to keep him tied to the family's culture and Shinto religion.[10] The children of Japanese immigrants born in the United States are called *Nisei*; their parents are called *Issei*. Nisei make up three-fourths of the Japanese population in Hawaii, and

8. "A Sociological Study of Palama District Along King Street from Liliha St. to Pua Lane," Romanzo Adams Social Research Laboratory Records, 1929.
9. Non-Hawaiians, but also slang for any Caucasian.
10. MIS Veterans Club of Hawaii interview. "He was strict, real strict," Douglas Wada will later describe his father.

they're adopting American ways with a passion that disturbs many Issei, including Hisakichi Wada.

Like many Nisei in Hawaii, Douglas Wada attends Japanese language school classes a couple times a week after public school ends. His is run by a Shin Buddhist association called the West Hongwanji. They teach him more than just idioms and syntax—students study subjects from Japan's national curriculum to its culture.

For many outsiders, these schools look like indoctrination centers for the Empire of Japan. However, most teachers were born in America and studied in Japan, a group known as the *Kibei*. Those who attend classes know better than most that these are not havens of nationalism, but traditionalism.[11]

The language classes do little to stem the tide of Americanization of the Nisei, certainly not Douglas Wada. The older he gets, the more his strict parents fret over his seeming lack of direction. By the time he's a senior at McKinley in 1928, they're ready to intervene with some help from the West Hongwanji.

Chiyo Wada lures him in with an early graduation present: two steamship tickets to Japan. "I am taking you to see the coronation," she says.

She doesn't have to explain further. Emperor Taisho died in 1926, passing the throne to his son, Shōwa. Now after two years of preparatory rites, he's finally ready to be officially enthroned in a Shinto ceremony at the Imperial Palace in Kyoto.

Japan's new Emperor may be Shōwa, but English speakers more often refer to him by his personal name: Hirohito.

Shinto predates the formation of even the earliest Japanese state, but emperor worship has become a potent political force in Japan since the government adopted the religion in the late 1800s. Since then, emperor veneration has become more than the formality of Shinto ceremonies at state functions. Now the government glorifies traditional Japanese virtues to the violent exclusion of Western influences, while neighbors

---

11. Sadaichi Kubota, interview by Tom Ikeda, July 1, 1998, Densho Visual History Collection, Honolulu, HI.

in Asia are labeled as equally inferior. Under State Shinto, expansionist foreign policy has the fervor of a crusade, and a coronation doubles as an ascension to government-mandated godhood.

For the Wada family, venturing to see Hirohito enthroned is not a political act but a religious pilgrimage. This is a major moment for Shintoists, given the divine nature of the emperor's position. The new Emperor's birthday, April 29, will now be celebrated across the world, and crowds will flock to Shinto shrines to post their hopes for the next year on paper notes.

On April 6, 1928, Douglas and Chiyo Wada wave from the deck of the *Shinyo Maru*, receiving cheers from fifty of his fellow Scouts gathered at the pier to send him off.[12] He's nearly bursting with pride, but the teenager is oblivious to what's really happening. The Emperor won't be crowned until November; Douglas's parents have arranged for him to study abroad at a school run by the West Hongwanji. He isn't heading to Japan as a tourist, but as an unwitting transplant.[13]

Despite Douglas's shock and eventual realization that he's meant to stay there, Kyoto proves a marvel for the young man. He has endless curiosity for the city, impressed with its sheer size—more than double Honolulu's population—and its dogged retention of traditional religion, architecture and culture.[14] With no port, it's been spared from the blights of modern industry. There are Buddhist temples that leave him awestruck, winding streets lined with the shops of master artisans, the splendors of the Shogun-haunted Nijo Palace and public parks clustered with people meditating and practicing martial arts. Apprentice carpenters and craftsmen from across Japan maintain religious buildings or build new ones and return home to use the techniques.

Kyoto is a massive medieval Japanese city, preserved in time, except for one modern fascination: baseball.

---

12. *The Honolulu Advertiser*, April 15, 1928. The newspaper covered the event in a brief, adding: "No departing scout left behind him a sadder group of friends than Scout Wada."
13. MIS Veterans Club of Honolulu interview.
14. Population in 1930: 765,142 in Kyoto versus 368,300 in Honolulu.

Missionaries and language teachers from America introduced the sport to Japan in 1872, and the first organized team, the Shimbashi Athletic Club, formed in 1878. Since then, baseball has become Japan's undisputed favorite pastime, its public fixated on the pros, regional leagues, university tournaments and even high-school rivalries.[15]

As a baseball powerhouse in Kyoto, Heian Middle School welcomed Wada's infielder skills (and advanced age) on the roster. His skills developed and his nerves hardened during high-pressure games. He spent a month in 1932 on a playing tour of Formosa and even took the field in an exhibition game in Kyoto against some retired American players, including Ty Cobb.[16]

Wada envisions staying in Japan after graduation from Heian and playing ball for Waseda University. He is even accepted by the school, and the team's coach has agreed to play him. But one threat clouds that future: the fear of being conscripted into the Japanese Army.

Since 1927, all Japanese men were required to report for examination at age twenty. Those selected for military duty were obliged to serve for two years and remained eligible for active duty until age forty.

Being drafted these days likely means going overseas. In September 1931, Japanese forces invaded Manchuria, hypocritically citing "more than 120 cases of infringement of rights and interests" of Japanese and Korean residents there. After five months of fighting, Japan established the puppet state of Manchukuo. The reaction from Russia, Britain, France and the United States is unsurprisingly bellicose.

Wada had renounced his dual citizenship in 1928 before leaving Hawaii, thinking this would clear up his legal status.[17] But as the

---

15. In America, amateur ball clubs formed in the 1830s and the first professional leagues sprung up in the 1870s. The first pro leagues formed in Japan in the 1930s.

16. "Wada was the only American who played on the Japanese side, which lost five to four." Tom Coffman, *Inclusion: How Hawai'i Protected Japanese Americans from Mass Internment, Transformed Itself, and Changed America* (Honolulu: University of Hawaii Press, 2021).

17. Before 1924, Japan considered American children born of Issei as its citizens. The Nisei were thus dual citizens. In 1924, Japan changed its law. Issei parents now had to register their infant within fourteen days of birth to obtain Japanese citizenship for the child.

Imperial Army scooped up his friends and teammates, he sensed they wouldn't care about technicalities. Even getting paperwork to return to Hawaii could invite what recipients call the *akagami*, a red-colored paper delivered overnight, ordering him to serve.[18]

Baseball becomes his way out. When ballplayers from the United States visit Kyoto and play Heian Middle School, Wada is delighted to see McKinley High School graduates among them. They create a "vacancy" on the team.[19]

When the McKinley team leaves Kyoto, they have Douglas Wada with them to help with the gear. It was an easy escape, except Wada isn't able to recover his travel documents, including his passport and certificate of citizenship (required of all Japanese Americans travelling abroad). He doesn't return to Hawaii with the team but instead stays in Yokohama with his uncle, Iwaichi Wada, until securing passage home and making his escape back to the land of his birth and away from the rapidly expanding Imperial Army.

# CHICHIBU MARU

## HONOLULU HARBOR
## APRIL 27, 1933

Wada takes in the skyline of Honolulu from the deck of the 560-foot passenger liner *Chichibu Maru*, feeling overwhelming relief.[20] The city's welcome, familiar terrain is marked with a new skyline; there are new hotels on the oceanfront and tall office buildings downtown. There are

18. MIS Veterans Club of Hawaii interview. "I expatriated in 1928, before I went to Japan. But then, they didn't care about those things."
19. Dick McDonald and Dick Patterson, "Douglas Wada Remembers." Wada also gives a version of this story in the MIS Veterans Club of Hawaii interview.
20. US Arriving and Departing Passenger and Crew Lists, 1900–1959, Honolulu Hawaii, NARA, *Records of the Immigration and Naturalization Service*, 1787–2004; Record Group Number: RG 85, Roll Number: 188. See Appendix B to learn the vessel's tragic fate.

also more berths for cruise ships in the harbor than he's even seen before, especially beneath the welcoming Aloha Tower at Pier 9.[21]

The twenty-two-year-old has spent the last five years in Japan, with only one trip back to Hawaii in 1930. During his visit, his family seemed impressed by his language skills and, back then, he was eager to return to Japan. If he only knew then how his next trip would end—by slipping the Japanese government authorities to escape back to the United States.

The *Chichibu Maru* sidles up next to its pier and Wada prepares to disembark. He's anticipating a cold homecoming—he tells teammates that his parents will be "mad as hell."[22]

Before he can worry about the reunion, though, he must face American immigration officials without his documents. It takes until the next day, after an uncomfortable night in a detention cell, for the issue to be sorted out. Douglas Wada then heads to Kama Lane, where his family is waiting.

The Wada Camp is busier than ever. Chiyo manages the store, while fourteen-year-old Hanako helps out. The Americanization of the youngest Wada child is undeniable; she's started to sometimes go by the names "Hannah" and "Edith."

The family's eldest daughter, twenty-five-year-old Itoyo, was also born in Hawaii but is not quite as enamored of it as her sister. The diminutive woman, standing just five foot tall, left school after sixth grade and can't read or write in English. She married salesman and legal Japanese alien Katsuke Yamamoto in 1924, which forced Itoyo to renounce her US citizenship. The couple has two daughters, Katsuko at age eight and Takeko at age five, all living with the family in one crowded Kama Lane house; the property's *ohana* home is being rented to two young, single boarders.[23]

The biggest change on Kama Lane is the Shinto shrine that's opened

---

21. The Hawaii Tourist Bureau's Annual Report for 1930 says, "Hawaii tourists have left $75 million here in the past ten years." More than two thousand visitors arrived annually and spent an average of around five hundred dollars. The Great Depression and a maritime strike helped sink the numbers. James Mak, "Creating Paradise of the Pacific," University of Hawaii Economic Research Organization, University of Hawaii at Manoa, February 3, 2015.
22. MIS Veterans Club of Hawaii interview.
23. 1930 Federal Census, along with *The Honolulu Advertiser*, August 12, 1961.

next door to the Wada Camp. In 1931, the Kotohira Jinsha bought more than 57,000 square feet of land at 1045 Kama Lane for their third, and grandest, Shinto complex in Honolulu. The bulk of the money came from fundraisers like movie viewings organized by volunteers. Hisakichi Wada donated his skills to carve a Kompira shrine, dedicated to sailors and seafaring, now prominently displayed.

The plans for the grounds are not solely cosmetic—construction of a community center, a *kyudo* archery range, an outdoor theater, a *renbujo* for the martial art *kendo* and a *sumo* ring is even now underway. When fully completed, it'll be able to host events involving hundreds of participants and spectators.[24]

Shinto is an ancient religion that can be traced back to the Yayoi culture from the third or second century BCE. The earliest writings about Shinto appear from the eighth century. It's a polytheistic religion that revolves around the worship of spirits called *kami*, which inhabit all things and are worshiped within households and public shrines called *jinsha*. The religion has no single doctrine, but the ceremonies center on purity rituals meant to appease various local *kami*. Shinto is often lumped in with Buddhism, but the basic tenants are very different. Buddhists don't worship *kami* and aspire to transcend the suffering cosmos, while Shintoists more pragmatically adapt to the world around them.

The Kotohira Jinsha was started under the auspices of another Japanese Shinto shrine by Rev. Hitoshi Hirota, who moved to Hawaii with his wife and daughter in 1917. The thirty-six-year-old cleaved off his own sect just two years after his arrival, establishing a new shrine with him as its head *guji*, or chief priest. The shrine is sort of an umbrella of worship to several spirits, each with a separate reverence club attached, but the one *kami* that all Kotohira members share is Kompira, the god of merchant sailors. The broad code of ethics at the core of Kompira worship makes worship easy common ground.

Kotohira is sanctioned in Japan as a legitimate branch of a famous

---

24. "History of the Shrine," Hawaii Kotohira Jinsha, http://www.e-shrine.org/history.html.

shrine in Kagawa-ken. As of 1924, the Kotohira Jinsha has also been acknowledged by the Hawaiian territorial government as a nonprofit church.

Ties between the Wada family and the shrine go deep. On June 24, 1924, the influential Reverend Hirota performed the marriage ceremony for Itoyo Wada despite his suffering from an advancing illness. He died the next year at age forty-two. The Rev. Misao Isobe is now in charge, and he's leading the shrine to new heights in Honolulu.

One ancient celebration that the Kotohira Shrine no longer commemorates is the Japanese emperor's birthday. Kama Lane used to be the epicenter of these activities in Hawaii, but in 1930, the Japanese Consulate insisted on taking over. Hardly anyone even stops by the Kotohira Shrine on April 29 to venerate Hirohito.[25] A flight from the authorities was certainly not the kind of immersive experience Hisakichi Wada envisioned when he sent his son to Japan. Yet the overall purpose of the trip is a success. Douglas Wada is now steeped in Japanese traditions and the Shinto religion. He also now speaks fluent Japanese, something that eludes even those Hawaiian Nisei who study at local language schools.

Most importantly, there's a new worldliness and sense of purpose that travel has imbued into his previously frivolous son. He's been seasoned by his experiences abroad, sobered by the world beyond Hawaii. If Hisakichi's goal was to have Japan shape Douglas as he became a man, it's an absolute victory.

## HONOLULU STADIUM

### HONOLULU
### APRIL 13, 1936

Douglas Wada steps to the plate and takes a moment to stare down the opposing pitcher, Ray Uchimura. He tries to tune out the noise of the two

---

25. Kotohira Jinsha v. McGrath, 90 F. Supp. 892 (D. Haw. 1950).

12

thousand spectators in the stands at Honolulu Stadium, his teammates watching from the dugout, as well as the runners standing on each base. There's only the next pitch.

It's the second inning of the scoreless Americans of Japanese Ancestry championship game, played before a packed house. AJA games have been a staple of Hawaiian sports since 1909, and starting for a team is a high-profile position for the university student. Sunday games are major events in Honolulu; most draw about a thousand fans who pay a quarter each to watch. Since the stadium costs just one hundred dollars to rent, profits are guaranteed. There's even more action to be found in the illegal (but tolerated) betting pools that spring up in and around the stadium.

Today's game is more than a typical matchup. Wada plays for the Wahiawas, who haven't won a championship in the twelve years of the league's existence, and today they're squaring off against their rivals, the Palamas.

The AJA League is a very public, popular expression of Nisei pride. There's an outcry in 1936 when the Japanese American owner of the Asahis team appoints Neal "Rusty" Blaisdell as coach. "The Asahis have always been the only strictly one-race team," writes *Hawaii Hochi* sports reporter Percy Koizumi. "The Asahis have a tradition to uphold. You might pass this up as a lot of hocus-pocus entertained by fossil-headed fans, but you'd be surprised to see how empty the stands will be if these fossil-heads decide to keep away."[26] (Blaisdell kept the job.)

Behind the Wahiawas-Palamas rivalry is intra-Nisei racial tension. After some hand-wringing, the AJA League leadership allowed mixed-race players, provided that they have the proper Japanese surnames of their fathers. Not every team holds to the same rules: the Palamas are a mixed-race team, while the Wahiawas are not.[27]

Uchimura settles into his posture on the mound, and Wada crouches

---

26. Percy Koizumi, as quoted in Karleen C. Chinen, "Hawaii's AJAs Play Ball—Part 1," *Discover Nikkei*, March 2, 2016, https://discovernikkei.org/en/journal/2016/3/2/hawaii-aja-1.
27. Chinen, "Hawaii's AJAs Play Ball—Part 1." The crucial chronicler of Hawaiian baseball is Rev. Chimpei Goto, author of *The Japanese Balldom of Hawaii* in 1919.

in anticipation. The pitcher seems rattled, and now he's got no room for a mistake after giving up a single to start the inning and then walking two hitters. Wada swings, feeling the satisfying, solid impact of the bat on the ball. He's already moving toward first as the ball streaks into left field, the men on base rushing into motion as the ball plunks into the grass. The Wahiawas on second and third race home—two RBIs for Wada—and the last man scores when the leftfielder bobbles the ball.

The Palamas won't fill this deficit, and the Wahiawas win the championship, 8 to 4. The *Honolulu Star Bulletin* reporter John Fukao writes that the team "finally realized their dream" when they "drubbed the Palamas" in the championship. The victorious team receives a massive silver trophy donated by Genbei Watanabe, owner of the local Seikosha watch store.[28]

Amid the celebration is worry for the twenty-two-year-old Wada. He's currently in the final semester of his senior year at the University of Hawaii, where he also plays baseball, but he doesn't see a future for himself on the field. He's already dropped his demanding major in agricultural science and switched to physical administration—a "duck soup" business and economics major, Wada admits—that enables him to focus on sports.

With an easier major, his grades improve. Wada's even a participating member of the H Club, restricted to accomplished students who have earned athletic awards. He's also the one-time winner of the Know Your University trivia contest and its reward of tickets to the King Theater to see the play *Richard of Bordeaux*.

Playing baseball for the university team is true to his American roots, but by taking the field with the AJA he's also able to use baseball to showcase his Japanese identity. It's been a tug-of-war throughout his college years at the University of Hawaii, and he finds himself accruing many names. He uses the name "Toisho" in yearbooks and public records. Most haole students and professors, like the sport press covering AJA

---

28. *Honolulu Star-Bulletin*, April 13, 1936.

League, call him "Douglas." Some of his teammates call him "Chicken" or its derivative, "Chick."

Graduation is looming this May, and the only thing he can think to do is go to graduate school. But those plans are about to change.

# KAGAWA PREFECTURE

## SHIKOKU, JAPAN
## NOVEMBER 10, 1936

Ensign Takeo Yoshikawa steps out of the Imperial Navy's Regional Headquarters and takes the first deep breath of his new life. His old one, so full of promise, ended in disappointment. Now he's being given a second chance to fulfill what he always felt was an important destiny.

Yoshikawa's youth on Shikoku Island was defined by the pursuit of excellence, as demanded by his physically abusive father. Learning to swim in a river encapsulated the relationship, as the man dragged the boy to deep water and pushed him away to sink or swim. Now that he's older, Takeo recognizes the cruelty but also appreciates the results. He's an excellent, fearless open-water swimmer and has tested himself along miles of Shikoku's ragged coast.[29]

Yoshikawa was an active youth but had a scare when he lost the tip of his middle finger in an "accident." He never discloses how. Despite the injury, during high school he became a champion at *kendo*, the martial art of bamboo armor (*bōgu*) and swords (*shinai*).

Yoshikawa was being primed for a military career, replacing the firm hand of his father with that of the Japanese Empire. He's been instilled with what he calls a "firm and abiding belief in *bushido*—the unquestioning and absolute loyalty of the samurai." He's also a Zen Buddhist. He admires the faith because its "teachings center around the single

---

29. Takeo Yoshikawa, *Japan's Spy at Pearl Harbor* (Jefferson, NC: McFarland, 2020).

concept of self-discipline evolving into loyalty and devotion beyond self." It's no bad philosophy for a soldier, he figured.

By 1933 Yoshikawa was an honor student at the Imperial Japanese Naval College. There he'd been instructed that "the Navy stood for [a] southward advance and war against the United States; while the Army stood for northward expansion and war with Russia." Yoshikawa recalled debates over ways to win a war with America; they all looked upon one as "inevitable."[30]

There was an introductory training cruise on a battleship and a short submarine deployment before Yoshikawa started pilot training in 1934. He was building the résumé of a promising career, and no one knew this more than Yoshikawa. Despite his philosophy of selflessness, he formed a strong ego. He told people his coming career was to be "stellar" and considered himself "the envy of [his] classmates."

But after a few months of flight training, coming back from a practice sortie, the confident young man was struck down by severe abdominal pains and ordered to the hospital. He was sidelined from active duty, designated as physically unfit and shunted into a frustrating netherworld that he endured month after month.

As he languished, things in Japan got more serious. In 1936, officials in the Imperial Army murdered the Imperial advisor Makoto Saito, Army General Jotaro Watanabe and Finance Minister Korekiyo Takahashi and attempted to assassinate many others who opposed their expansionist plans. Tensions with China flared again, and Japan was squaring off against great global powers.

On the cusp of such historic events, Yoshikawa was forced to just watch. In 1936, the Imperial military finally retired him, leaving the youth "in great shock, since all my plans and hopes were bound up with the Navy." He even contemplated suicide.

That was just two months ago. But with the change of the season came hope, when a captain from the regional headquarters summoned

---

30. Yoshikawa, *Japan's Spy at Pearl Harbor.*

him for today's meeting. The man's words are still ringing in his ears: "There is still a place for you in the Navy, if you forgo any hope of advancement and return to active duty as an agent in naval intelligence."[31]

He had entered the building with no prospects and left with a mission. No longer on a path to become an officer, it's a far cry from his former ambition but it's one with a future serving the Emperor.

Yoshikawa's job will begin on the intelligence staff of the Imperial Navy's Third Division, and his areas of study include the US Pacific Fleet and its bases in Guam, Manila, and Hawaii.

# UNIVERSITY OF HAWAII

### HONOLULU
### MAY 4, 1937

The students collect their notebooks at the conclusion of Professor Yukio Uyehara's advanced Japanese language class. Douglas Wada strolls out of the classroom with fellow classmate Ken Ringle.

The University of Hawaii is a haven for Japanese American academics, one of the few places in the United States where their careers are fostered. Its Japanese language program is part of the school's overall push to pursue Asia-Pacific studies; the biggest commitment is founding the University of Hawaii's "Oriental Institute" in 1935.[32]

Uyehara is a pioneer, as one of only a handful of American-educated scholars of Japanese ancestry in the United States pursuing a career in higher education. He's a graduate of the University of Hawaii and a published author; in 1933, at age twenty-eight, the school appointed him as a language instructor. Uyehara used his position to build bridges between Japanese and American students, planning cultural events and directing the school's Oriental Literature Society. He balanced these civic

---

31. Yoshikawa, *Japan's Spy at Pearl Harbor*.
32. Now the East-West Center.

pursuits with teaching, revising textbooks and working toward a master's degree, which he received early this year.

Wada registers for Japanese classes as a senior because he needs a language credit to graduate, and this is the easiest option. Uyehara knows he's more advanced than the rest of the class—at their first encounter, he made Wada translate a copy of the Japanese political magazine *Bungei Shunjū*. It's no problem, and the professor then makes a deal: "When I can't conduct a class, you take over for me. And I'll want you to do some extra library work for me, besides." It's a good bargain.

One of Wada's fellow students is Kenneth Ringle. He's a bit of a curiosity, being ten years older than Wada and auditing the college class for his own seeming self-improvement. He and Wada sit alongside each other and fall into talking baseball. They soon discover they both lived in Japan. After weeks of friendly contact, Wada accepts an invitation to come to Ringle's home on a Saturday to meet his wife, Margaret, and two-year-old, Sally.

Wada finds himself charmed by Margaret's fearless personality. She grew up driving cattle on her uncle's plantation on Avery Island, Louisiana, and attended the Philadelphia Academy of Art. She and Ringle met during a horseback ride and picnic in Portugal when his destroyer arrived on a port of call. Margaret was visiting her sister, whose husband did business there, and they met when uniformed sailors attempted to impress the local bachelorettes in a public display of peacockery. He arrived in Louisiana the next year to seek her hand.[33]

Ringle brags on his wife by telling how she drove across the continental United States with nothing but a spare tire and pistol for company. "How else am I supposed to catch up with my husband when his ship goes coast to coast?" she asks with mock innocence.[34]

---

33. Kenneth Ringle Jr., interview with authors. He describes his parents as extremely sociable and says they frequently threw small parties and invited guests over to the house. This is pertinent, given the nature of Ringle's true work and his growing idea that Wada could become part of it.
34. "Obituary: Margaret Avery Ringle Struble, Navy Wife," *Washington Post*, March 23, 1999, https://www.washingtonpost.com/archive/local/1999/03/23/obituaries/b8f180fd-8b3f-4ea8-87fd-efda84d3bcdf/.

Margaret takes Sally away and leaves the pair to talk. The older man asks tactful but insightful questions about the reaction to Japan's increasing militarism among the American transplants to Hawaii and their Nisei children. Wada tells him what he sees—that most of his peers have no lingering loyalty to Japan. The pair share revulsion for the militarism they witnessed in Japan.

But mostly the men discuss football. Wada has insider insights on the University of Hawaii squad from his role as the team water boy, a less glorious part of his academic major. It's a pleasant afternoon spent with an interesting classmate, and Wada soon puts it out of his mind.

Weeks later, the university's athletic director, Ted "Pump" Searle, pulls him aside for a quiet word.[35] "A couple FBI guys came by my office," he says. "Sat me down for an interview, and all the questions were about you."

This is a curious development, possibly related to his time studying in Kyoto. As tension with Japan rises, the FBI has been on alert for subversive elements in the domestic Japanese population. One group the investigators eye with particular suspicion are Americans who studied in Japan, just as Douglas Wada did. The Japanese government's cooperation in bringing language school students to Japan, once a cultural exchange, is now seen as a method of infiltration.

As the days pass, more people have whispered conversations with Wada over meetings with the two feds. They interview teammates, neighbors, teachers and the ROTC sergeant on campus, most of whom come to their subject to tell him. Even Otto Klum tells Wada the FBI men spoke to him—the famed UH football coach being asked about the loyalty of the team's water boy.

Now that some intensive investigation is clearly afoot, he's wondering if the scrutiny has been caused by his student trip, the newspaper headlines about a looming Pacific war or someone he's met. When it comes to mysterious people in his life, the list is short. At the top is Ken

---

35. Theodore Searle is one of the "Four Horsemen of Manoa." He scored 110 points in six games while playing on the "Wonder Teams" of 1924 and 1925.

Ringle. He never discussed work, current or previous, and Wada found it polite not to pry. But there's something else—they shouldn't have met to begin with. Uyehara always seats his classes in alphabetical order, but Ringle took the chair to Wada's right and a girl named Suzuki sat to his left. Why would the professor put a "W" between "R" and "S" except to engineer a meeting? Or had these FBI interviews made him paranoid?[36]

Just after his June 1937 graduation, after returning from another fruitless job interview, his sister Hanako greets him at the door. "The Navy called," she says skeptically. "They want to see you for a job interview on Friday."

"Are you sure?" he responds. "I don't even know anyone in the Navy."

This cryptic offer is intriguing. Although he's deeply skeptical of the military—he even declined the advanced ROTC training offered at the university—getting a job is the first step to saving money for grad school. And Wada must admit that he doesn't have many other prospects. So, on Friday, he finds himself standing outside the Federal Building, bow tie firmly fixed in place and suit freshly pressed.[37]

The building is an anthill of government workers and uniformed military personnel. He steadies his nerves and heads to the second floor, seeking room 221. The door says Department of Information. What does *that* mean?

There's a total of four men inside the office, seated at tables since there's only one desk. Ken Ringle stands to greet him, smiling. He's wearing a white Navy uniform and, from the shoulder boards, Wada can tell he's an officer.

"What the hell am I getting into?" Wada asks before he can help himself.

His classmate is revealed as Lieutenant Commander K. D. Ringle, assistant district officer for the 14th Naval District Intelligence. He's already a seasoned officer with an impressive résumé. Born in Kansas on September 30, 1900, he graduated from the US Naval Academy in 1923

---

36. MIS Veterans Club of Hawaii interview.
37. His attire is based on ID photos taken of him, admittedly later in life.

and served on the USS *Mississippi*. His time in Tokyo, from 1928 to 1931, was spent as a naval attaché at the US Embassy. Part of his training was to move to Beppo and live with a family there, an immersive experience meant to hone his language and cultural acumen.

Ringle was fascinated with what he saw. He learned the language variants spoken by different classes of Japanese citizens—one for the elites, another for the street and one used exclusively by females. He put this last to the test at tea houses in Beppo, where geishas were taken with the Westerner's language skills and respectful, naval university–inspired demeanor. This contrasted with the boorish behavior of Japanese military officials who also frequented the establishments. They frequently got drunk and handsy, bragging about their destiny to take over the world, the women told him. Ringle dutifully wrote reports on these telling conversations, his first interaction with the US naval intelligence community.[38]

Life and career proceeded. He served as a gunnery officer on the USS *Chester* after he returned from Japan, and he married Margaret Johnston Avery in 1932. Ringle moved into naval intelligence in July 1936, when the couple relocated to Honolulu. He continued taking Japanese language classes to hone his skills and to scout for talent.[39] Ringle knew just how rare Japanese linguistic skills were within the Navy, and those who understood Japanese culture were even rarer. For intelligence gathering, these lapses were potentially fatal.

His solution is Douglas Wada. The recruitment of Wada is among the earliest moves of the intelligence officer's career. It's a bold one, given the rising tide of mistrust of Japanese immigrants and their children, especially traditionally minded ones like those in the Wada family.[40]

Ringle introduces his recruit to Captain Walter Kilpatrick, who will

---

38. Kenneth Ringle Jr., interview with authors.
39. Kenneth Ringle Jr. interview. Ringle's son adds: "My father's assignment essentially was to get to know as many Japanese Americans as he could. And he was very friendly with them."
40. Kenneth Ringle Jr. interview. Military intelligence and the FBI both regard Shinto shrines and Buddhist temples as outposts of Japanese government propaganda, at the very least. Ringle saw past this. "He and Ma always made a distinction between culture and doctrine, between culture and religion. He always judged every man as an individual. He resisted, to his dying day, judging any kind of group identity. He just didn't believe in that."

conduct his job interview. The pair enter an adjacent room and sit down at opposite sides of a table. "You saw the door? Well, we're not the Department of Information," Kilpatrick says. "We're Naval Intelligence."[41]

This small office, a satellite of the district headquarters at the base at Pearl Harbor, is the 14th District Intelligence Office, focusing on counterintelligence. Since the 1920s, the Navy has been fixated only on Japan's rising capabilities at sea. More recently, concern has shifted to subversives and radicals at home. The 14th DIO's job in Hawaii is to monitor the local population and gauge the threat they could pose to the Navy in the event of a war. The agents here are expected to sniff out sympathizers, spies and saboteurs.

Kilpatrick is desperate for help translating the reams of Japanese language sources that his office must monitor. That includes clandestinely collected materials, but also newspapers, literature and other publicly available barometers of the mood of Japanese people overseas and here in Honolulu.

"We need a language specialist," Kilpatrick shares. "Ken tells me that you're fluent, and trustworthy. And we need your help. If we accept and you still want it, you'd be the first Japanese American agent working within naval intelligence anywhere in the world."

Wada doubts he'll be allowed to join the Navy, which does not accept Japanese Americans into the service.[42] He doesn't mind this, since it opens the door to an easier escape if he doesn't like this job. As a civilian, he figures he can just quit.

The preliminaries taken care of, Kilpatrick pivots to current events. "Let's talk about the war in the Far East," he says. "Japan has taken Mongolia already, and no one thinks they have any intention on stopping. They'll invade again, and not just in China. So, that leaves us with a question. On which side is your bread buttered?"

Wada blinks for a second, wondering if he's heard correctly. He wants to say, "I don't know what the hell you mean," but then it hits him.

---

41. Kenneth Ringle Jr. interview. Wada recalled these details of his job interview with the MIS Veterans Club of Hawaii interviewers.
42. The US Army does, and some Territorial National Guard units formed in Hawaii have a majority of Nisei as members.

"My loyalty is with the United States. I was raised here, went to school here, my family is here," Wada says. "Except for five years, I have only lived in Hawaii. It is my only home." He pauses and it's clear the captain wants more. "There are not too many expatriated Japanese citizens, and I renounced my Japanese citizenship in 1928. That wasn't so easy to do back then."

"Oh, we know more about you than you know," says Kilpatrick simply, the closest thing to appreciation for the FBI that he's able to summon. The agency doesn't even have a field office here, and mainland agents are assigned to do background checks. "You can assume we would not be talking if we found any reason whatsoever for us not to."

Douglas Wada has defended his loyalty but hasn't accepted Kilpatrick's proposition. He's at a crossroads, not only in career paths, but between his dueling identities. He has a chance to serve his nation and also protect the city he loves from foreign meddling. The Japanese Empire wants to turn Nisei against their homeland, and the idea angers him. He also hopes there's a way for him to help separate the harmless Issei, like his father, from those who may actively support the Japanese regime. His service may mean something more to his nation and his city than just the job—it'll be proof of his community's loyalty. He'd be a civilian recruit, but there's no mistake he'd be with the Navy now.

"Well," Wada says, "I'll serve any time the government asks me to."

"Good, because we need you," Kilpatrick says. "We need you tomorrow, but we can't get that. We need permission from Washington to make this official. For now, we would like for you to work for us on a part-time basis. Any time you feel like coming in, come in. We'll pay you fifteen dollars every two weeks, thirty dollars a month."

It's not bad pay for what sounds like simple office work. And then Kilpatrick says, "In the meantime, could you find work within the Japanese community?"[43]

---

43. While dramatized, the job interview is based on Wada's recollections of it, described during the MIS Veteran's Club of Honolulu interview. His response upon accepting the position and the request to go undercover in Honolulu are direct quotes from the conversation that he supplied.

# OFFICES OF *NIPPU JIJI*

### HONOLULU
### JULY 7, 1937

"Another island-born lad makes good!" Douglas Wada types, reaching for a catchy lead for his newspaper article on the exploits of a former Honolulu baseball star, Chikaki "Ed" Honda, a product of McKinley High School.

In ways, the athlete's biography is Wada's life if he hadn't left Japan. Both were baseball stars at McKinley who attended school at Heian, but Honda stayed in Kyoto to attend university. He has since played in championship games before one hundred thousand screaming spectators. "Nothing like it is ever seen in Honolulu," Wada notes in the piece. He interviews Honda while the baseball player is visiting his parents before returning to Japan in August.[44]

In private conversations, off the record, Honda is concerned about being drafted into the Army. Despite this, he's heading back to Japan. In the end, he knows on which side his bread is buttered, to borrow Kilpatrick's phrase.[45]

The article, like Wada's job as a cub reporter and translator for the *Nippu Jiji* newspaper, has a double purpose. On one hand, it's a nice profile of a prominent local Nisei, which fits the interests of the English-language newspaper's core Japanese readership. But it's also a chance to question an American resident of Japan, one who can provide firsthand information on the mood of the population there. And the unwitting subject of the interview is also providing a window into the views of a

---

44. *Nippu Jiji*, July 9, 1937, accessed via Hoji Shinbun Digital Collection, https://hojishinbun .hoover.org.
45. Honda renounced his US citizenship in 1941, serving with the Civilian Intelligence Corps and interrogating famed pilot Gregory "Pappy" Boyington. Wada later in life expressed some sympathy with Honda, saying he'd been compelled to serve: "They could have conscripted [me]. They were strict, really strict. Like, there was another Nisei there, Chik Honda. He was taken." Decades later, the fellow ballplayer was on Wada's mind.

prominent Hawaiian Nisei who is trending away from the US, the nation where he was born.

Honda has no idea he's been interviewed by an aspiring naval intelligence agent. Douglas Wada, part-time employee of the 14th District Intelligence Office, is on his first undercover assignment.

Wada's got dues to pay. This fieldwork is more than just a display of his language skills—it'll show he's got the temperament for the lifestyle that comes with this shadowy work. Wada must demonstrate he's got the character expected of a special agent. As the ONI training manual notes, "Any display of vanity, boastfulness, carelessness, officiousness or ignorance of technical matters, brands the Operative as personally incompetent."[46] Instead, the Navy intelligence men are finding him reliable, discreet, charming and committed. In other words, he knows how to be a team player.

Now on the inside of the military intelligence apparatus, some of Wada's illusions about the work are being dispelled. Despite his early immersion into undercover work, there is a lot less cloak-and-dagger work than expected, or even hoped. The ONI's training manual proves discouraging: "Only a rank amateur will attempt to employ sensational methods of the dime-novel order. Each investigation should be regarded as a scientific problem, requiring careful analysis, logical reasoning and the practical demonstration of facts." Having said that, there are chapters on running informants, interviewing techniques, ways to scour public records for leads and even a section on conducting sabotage.

The service is also explicit that he will not be engaged in strictly police work, since catching people isn't always the strategic thing to do. "Investigations, as conducted by the Naval Intelligence Service,[47] are not usually for the purpose of effecting immediate arrests and prosecutions,"

---

46. The author of this manual, an obstetrician-turned-spy named Cecil Coggins, was actually working in Hawaii at the main office of 14th District Intelligence Office at Pearl Harbor Naval Base. This quote is from the 1941 edition, but it's a core ethos of ONI.

47. The Naval Intelligence Service, under the primary direction of the chief of naval operations, was made of the combination of the ONI, a division of the Office of the Chief of Naval Operations, and agents within naval stations and ships at sea. This manual was to be used by all of them, but Wada worked within the ONI structure.

the manual reads. "Our purpose is to discover, step by step, the identity, location, purpose, and activities of entire espionage, sabotage, and propaganda groups—not with a view to routine arrest, but with the purpose of maintaining a close and constant surveillance of the members and their activities. In this way we shall be able, upon the outbreak of open or declared hostilities, to seize the entire organization and thus to paralyze the enemy."[48]

The *Nippu Jiji* had the virtue of a job opening—and the owner is a baseball fan—but it's also a good place for an intelligence agent to gauge the mood of the local population. There are a dozen Japanese newspapers in Hawaii, but this is one of the two major ones, the other being *Hawaii Hōchi*. This newspaper is popular among Japanese migrant workers and previously rallied support for social movements in Hawaii, a predilection for organization that could prove a wartime liability.

As the newspaper staff files out after the bulldog edition is put to bed in the afternoon, Wada surreptitiously collects the next day's edition of *Nippu Jiji*, delivers it to the 14th DIO, and there types out a quick report on the paper's contents and the baseball player's off-the-record comments. His duties to both employers fulfilled, he finally heads home.

Now that Douglas Wada has a window into the world of counterespionage, he realizes the military sees some of the institutions at the center of his life in an entirely new, suspicious light. And that light is creating dark shadows on Kama Lane.

Shrines, including Wada's neighborhood mainstay, are considered suspect institutions that worship the emperor. Buddhist and Shinto priests often serve as principals and teachers at Japanese language schools and many double as Japanese consular agents. With strict supervision of religion, a characteristic of Japanese governmental policy, the military intelligence apparatus regards both priests and teachers to be as good as

---

48. ONI Training Manual for personnel assigned to investigations sections of Naval Intelligence Service, Office of Naval Intelligence, US Navy, 1941.

"under orders from Tokyo."[49] The shrines of Honolulu also resemble the state Shinto buildings in Japan, and this also seems to make them suspect.[50]

The ONI finds itself stymied when it tries to act against suspect Shinto shrines of Hawaii. Kilpatrick searches for connections between some shrine leaders and the Japanese military, and finds several are former Army officers. He asks for one to be deported, but diplomatic agreements between the nations prevent any action.[51]

Wada has another, very different view of the Shinto shrines of Honolulu, especially the one he's been neighbor to since boyhood. He sees Kotohira's three multi-building facilities as a rally point where his family's religion and culture can be celebrated. Aside from religious services, Rev. Misao Isobe uses the land to host meetings, sumo and archery bouts, fundraiser movie nights and annual public festivals.

Isobe is the head of three linked shrines, and the group is flush with donations. However, since the Japanese government has militarized Shinto, the Kotohira Jinsha's 1,500-strong membership is seen by some as a political declaration or even a mobilization.[52]

Wada's first purchase with his salary is a Chevrolet, paying forty-five dollars a month for its auto loan. He takes it along King Street, leaving the downtown government buildings for the Japanese heart of Kapalama, Kama Lane. It's a ride between worlds.

---

49. This view will only harden over time. "Inasmuch as, it follows that both are to a considerable extent subject to orders from Tokyo or what amounts to the same thing from their religious superiors in Japan." Office of Naval Intelligence, memo, "Subject: JAPANESE INTELLIGENCE AND PROPAGANDA IN THE UNITED STATES DURING 1941," December 4, 1941.

50. A judge will one day note that, "Due to the presence of a torii in front of the shrine and to its general appearance as well, it can be said that plaintiff's shrine looked like a state Shinto shrine in Japan" as a way to explain why it aroused government suspicion. Kotohira Jinsha v. McGrath, 90 F. Supp. 892 (D. Haw. 1950).

51. "It had been developed years before that some of the priests were ex-Army officers," Admiral William Smith, US Pacific Fleet commander, will later tell Congress. "I was informed by Captain Kilpatrick, who had been a previous intelligence officer, that an effort was made to deport one of these priests, but it was found nothing could be done because of an old agreement between the United States and Japan." Hearings Before the Joint Committee on the Pearl Harbor Attack, S. Doc. No.79–27 (1946).

52. Buddhism is well-established and growing; by 1941 Shinto shrines across Hawaii will have about fifty thousand members and the Buddhist temples about twice that number.

Wada wonders what the authorities would think if they watched his father laboriously carving panels of wood, perfecting woodworking skills needed for some future shrine. Would they see a man expressing his faith, or a potential threat who'd choose his religion over the United States?

The longer he works in counterintelligence, the more Wada thinks like an agent. And the less he likes the answer to that question.

# PART 2

# POSITION PLAYERS

# DILLINGHAM TRANSPORTATION BUILDING

## HONOLULU
## AUGUST 23, 1939

FBI Special Agent in Charge Robert Shivers arrives in Honolulu with a full plate and a small staff. His job is enormous: to stand up the first Honolulu FBI office and use it to assess the loyalty of 160,000 people: 125,000 American citizens of Japanese origin and 35,000 Japanese citizens. Yet his office at the Dillingham is staffed with just two agents and a stenographer.

SAC Shivers is a serious man with a solid pedigree. He served as an Army sergeant in the ordnance supply of artillery during the Great War. He only graduated high school, but the FBI accepted him in 1923, after which he rose through the ranks. During the 1930s, Shivers served as a special agent in charge of various stations around the country, gaining the ear of director J. Edgar Hoover along the way by targeting bootlegger gangs and the Ku Klux Klan.

At age forty-four, his future is hindered only by his health. He suffers from high blood pressure and heart problems, ailments that make his doctors recommend light duty and warm weather. Shivers's wife, Connie, wholeheartedly endorses these measures if it means being stationed in Hawaii. She doesn't know that this so-called "light duty" is fraught with stress; at least they'll find warm weather in Oahu.

Shivers needs to work closely with military intelligence—everyone in Hawaii realizes the job is too vast not to—but there's no designated lead agency. Information is being collected and shared, but actual coordination among the counterintelligence operatives is lacking. This ambiguity comes from the White House. In June President Franklin Roosevelt signed a confidential directive establishing the lines of responsibility for domestic counterintelligence, but it left unresolved the question of who controls the counterintelligence operations aimed at foreign agents on US soil. The military sees a pressing need to protect its facilities, as well as its personnel, and has its own priorities and methods in doing so.

So now the Army, Navy, FBI and local police in Hawaii all have counterintelligence operations underway. Yet there's no singular plan for the agencies to follow when it comes to a reaction to any future war with Japan. The formation of this integrated plan is a primary focus of Shivers's, a job that'll take diplomatic, organizational and law enforcement skills in equal measure.

The G-man's mission starts with cleaning up the "pickup lists" of those to be arrested in the event of war. The idea of mass detentions inside the United States has been part of military planning for decades; establishing "concentration camps" for those arrested has been specifically mentioned in Roosevelt administration documents since at least 1937.

The FBI has a list of 125 suspects on their list. The Army has given the names of more than two hundred, and there's nearly as many on the list generated by the Office of Naval Intelligence, curated by naval reservists Lieutenant William Stephenson and Lieutenant Commander Cecil Coggins, an obstetrician with a budding talent for spycraft.

Shivers does the hard but fair thing by assigning his men to investigate these names on a case-by-case basis, despite his short staffing. It's a sign of the lack of trust any true-blue FBI man feels for any another agency, but also a moral responsibility to get it right.

One group that Shivers sees rife for investigation is Japan's network of "consular agents." This is a catchall term for the more than two hundred hired assistants across Hawaii who the Japanese Consulate engages to assist visiting Japanese citizens and local Issei who need help with official paperwork. They also spearhead the local efforts to collect funds for Japanese soldiers and collect "comfort kits" for those deployed in China.[1] Since the consulate tends to hire Japanese language school teachers, he's under the same widespread assumption among law enforcement officials that all such instructors are puppets of the imperial government.

Shivers is ready to launch an investigation but doesn't have the manpower to monitor all the consular agents. He selects twenty for scrutiny, most of them prominent professors with a penchant for public, nationalistic sentiment in support of Japan.

Finding sedition in Honolulu isn't easy. Japanese ultranationalists are even more rare in Hawaii than the mainland, favored only by a slender percentage of Issei immigrants. But it doesn't take actual disloyal behavior to land on the official Navy suspect list.

The FBI has developed a tool for its agents to classify local intelligence threats. They call it an "evaluative matrix," and it ranks suspect organizations into three categories: A, B and "Semi–Official and Subversive Japanese firms in the United States." According to the Navy, A-designated organizations "constitute an actual threat to the internal security of the United States. All officers and members, whether full or associate, of these organizations should be given serious consideration before employment in any position of confidence or trust in this country." Class A threats are to be detained immediately upon the outbreak of war. Class B threats are judged by their potential to do harm. They haven't crossed any lines, but if they did, their community influence could cause major havoc. The final C designation is reserved for Japanese commercial interests with possible ties to the Japanese government, like steamship companies, banks and newspapers.

---

1. "Gifts, Money from Hawaii Go to Japan by 'Warship,'" *Honolulu Star-Bulletin*, June 7, 1939. Public reports of donations like this one begin with coverage from Domei, the Japanese government news service, and they are reprinted in English language media. In another example, Domei reports in December 1938 that Hawaiian donations resulted in the purchase of eight heavy trucks for use in China. Domei says the donors wanted to "demonstrate their attachment to their homeland" and the English-speaking press use the comment in their reprint of the story, "Japanese Here Send 8 Trucks to China Front," *The Honolulu Advertiser*, December 22, 1938.

The painful truth is that Shivers has no experience with Japan or its culture. He feels this gap every day on the job, but he's committed to changing it. The new SAC sees a reflection of his failings in the overall counterintelligence effort in Honolulu. Although never shy about using more aggressive tactics, he's seeing a lack of what later would be dubbed "community engagement." Military agents here acknowledge a latent patriotism in the Japanese American community of Hawaii, one that could be tapped to counter foreign influences. The problem is, it's never been tried.

There's already a reservoir of Japanese American knowledge in Honolulu—the University of Hawaii. Shivers makes a point to meet the university's founding chairman, local businessman Charles Hemenway, and puts the problem before him. Shivers is ready to listen to the community's ideas, but he needs someone to talk to.

The well-connected school regent quickly comes back with a name: Shigeo Yoshida.[2] The thirty-two-year-old professor and writer was born in Hilo, a town on the Big Island, and excelled as a university debater. He even lived with Hemenway as a student and is considered a big influence on a worldview that allowed a generation of students, including Wada, to find a comfortable home at UH. Yoshida is well-regarded across Hawaii: in 1937, he and local attorney Masaji Marumoto even testified before a visiting congressional committee on behalf of statehood for Hawaii, the first Japanese Americans to address Congress.

The meeting between Shivers and Yoshida is set up before the end of the month. Shivers meets an academic, wary of the future and eager to collaborate to steer that future in a better direction. Yoshida doesn't obsess over the injustice of having to prove his community's loyalty—it's a fact of life that must be dealt with proactively and head-on.

Shivers now sees signs of hope. The pair may be able to form a larger cabal to promote the patriotism of Japanese residents in Hawaii. If he and Yoshida can muster support from the community, they could inoculate

2. Dennis M. Ogawa, *First Among Nisei: The Life and Writings of Masaji Marumoto* (Honolulu: University of Hawaii Press, 2007).

the population from foreign meddling—and protect innocent citizens from unwarranted government reprisal.

Shivers is committed to his effort to understand the Japanese community in Hawaii. With the University of Hawaii, he and Connie arrange for an exchange student from Japan, Shizue Kobatake, to live with them. She becomes his tutor on Japanese culture, as well as the Filipino, Korean and Chinese communities. The student also fills a void at home—Connie soon dubs her "Sue" and the pair become constant companions, so much so that people think the couple adopted her.

# JAVORINA

## POLAND-SLOVAKIA BORDER
## SEPTEMBER 1, 1939

The tanks of the German Army's 1st Division move at five in the morning, rumbling less than an hour later into the Polish village of Javorina. It's the first maneuver of the invasion, but not the only one. Across the front, nearly nine hundred Nazi bombers and over four hundred fighter planes are bombing cities and attacking airfields. More than two thousand tanks are pushing into Poland, one spearhead in the north from Germany and East Prussia and another here in the south from the German client state of Slovakia. Both armored columns of the invasion are converging on Poland's capital, Warsaw.

Javorina's occupation is just one small step on the way to the equally obscure Polish town of Zakopane, part of a push to protect the right flank of the quickly advancing German 2nd Mountain Division. But it's also, for the moment, one of the most significant places on the planet. Javorina is the first place to fall in what will soon blossom into World War II. In response to the Polish invasion, two days later the United Kingdom and France declare war on Germany.

The ramifications are immediately felt by the Japanese Empire.

35

Their war with China, engaged since 1937, has entered a new, grinding phase. Japan can win battles and massacre civilians, but the land forces are overextended and easy prey for guerillas. Half of the Japanese Army is tied down in China the day the German tanks roll into Poland.

But the war in Europe changes the balance in the Pacific in their favor. The existential threat to Japan's hegemony is the lack of indigenous oil and rubber production, making energy production centers in Southeast Asia tempting targets for Japanese aggression. These are colonial possessions of Great Britain and France, currently fighting for their respective lives at home.

The conflict in Europe is bound to bleed the Europeans' resources and attention. With the two great powers distracted, there may be no better time to expand Japan's control over Southeast Asia and the Pacific, making the island nation self-sufficient. But there's one key player still on the board. The remaining obstacle to Japan's future is the United States, backed by the power of its Navy.

# PIER 7

## HONOLULU HARBOR
## OCTOBER 16, 1939

Douglas Wada studies the profile of Japanese armored cruiser *Yakumo* as he stands at the rail from the ship's lower deck. She's moored at the civilian piers in downtown Honolulu, and after three decades of service, she's outdated and outmoded, good only for training cruises like this one.

*Yakumo* is one of six armored cruisers built in overseas shipyards after the First Sino-Japanese War and is the only one built in Germany. However, the guns are English, to keep the ammunition the same as the rest of the fleet. But an old warship is still a warship, and Japanese military training boats all land at Pier 7, outside of Pearl Harbor.

Wada himself is onboard *Yakumo* under the guise of a uniformed Shore Patrol officer. He's actually in the field as a naval intelligence agent.

In 1938, Douglas Wada became the first American of Japanese ancestry (or "AJA," as they came to be known in Hawaii) to serve as an ONI agent. He was commissioned by the Navy at the same time, commissioned (to his happy surprise) as a lieutenant.[3] That also makes him the first AJA to be commissioned as a US naval officer. His achievements are known by nearly no one, but the pressure of it is a daily reality.

The 14th DIO is changing, getting more serious as diplomatic relations with Japan steadily deteriorate. Some of the faces are different too: Walter Kilpatrick left the 14th District Intelligence Office in 1938, replaced by Capt. W. H. Hart Jr. But Ringle is still here, and that means Wada has a steadfast champion.[4]

Wada hoped that the small-time work would ease when he became an agent, but he's quickly tasked with working with the military policemen of the Shore Patrol. The pressing need is for someone, anyone, in the Navy to help collect statements from Japanese-speaking storeowners who have run afoul of drunken sailors.[5]

However, he's also afforded an opportunity to conduct fieldwork. He has a cover established as a customs inspector, tasked with scouring passenger luggage for incriminating documents about the US Navy. He's happy to see a fellow Nisei in the office, Noboru "Hunchy" Murakami. The pair board passenger ships from the Nippon Yusen Kaisha and comb through the suitcases and parcels when the passengers can't watch. They use passenger lists to target some luggage for special scrutiny, including those who have lived in Japan for extended periods of time. People like

---

3. What appears to have happened was that Wada was given what is known as a direct commission to the rank of lieutenant. Direct commissions are rare because you don't have to go to an academy or ROTC or be an OCS grad to receive the commission.

4. Six decades later, Wada will credit Kenneth Ringle above all others for making this possible. "Wada told me that if it hadn't been for my father, he never would've become a naval officer. He was extremely proud of that, and tremendously gratified that he had that chance." Kenneth Ringle Jr., interview with authors.

5. MIS Veterans Club of Hawaii interview.

Douglas Wada. Murakami and Wada quickly become friends and confidants. Besides Murakami, the other inspectors think Wada reports to the local police, not the Navy.[6]

In September 1939, news comes to the Shore Patrol of an impending visit to Honolulu by the Japanese Navy, a stopover on the way to California and the first one in two years. It's to be stocked with top-tier officials, part of a diplomatic effort to ease tensions between the nations even as war rages in Europe and China. The city's United Japanese Society is taking the lead on demonstrating some local hospitable goodwill, holding planning meetings months in advance at the city's chamber of commerce.[7]

This trip also seems to be a good way for the Imperial Navy to look at the most westward parts of America, including its military facilities in Hawaii. Feeling that turnabout is fair play, Wada has been tasked with taking a look at the Japanese fleet on the quiet behalf of Naval Intelligence, using his established Shore Patrol cover.

"Wada!" calls Shore Patrol Capt. George Dickey. Wada's here to serve as translator when he speaks with the officers in command of the Japanese ships, who even now are approaching like walking statues. This is the Shore Patrol's first courtesy call with the head of this flotilla, Vice Admiral Yurio Samamoto, who arrives with the *Yakumo*'s captain, Shigeaki Yamasaki.

Wada fixes his face with respectful seriousness before he turns away from the railing. The Japanese officers and Shore Patrol exchange polite bows before Dickey delivers his greeting, which Wada dutifully translates. "Welcome to Honolulu, sir. I understand you have a full itinerary, but should anything unexpected come up, please do not hesitate to contact us. In the meantime, we can help orient you to the island's landmarks, several of which we can see from here . . ."

The Japanese ships stay in Oahu for six days, filling Wada's schedule

---

6. His trusted relationship with Murakami is mentioned in the MIS Veterans Club of Hawaii interview and *Douglas Wada Remembered*, 2007.
7. *Honolulu Star-Bulletin*, September 5, 1939.

with receptions, tours, speeches and meetings. At least once, Wada comes back to the Shore Patrol office drunk enough for officers there to notice.

"I just had a few," he explains lamely.[8]

After the six days are over and the ships are headed for Hilo, Wada reads a positive editorial about the Japanese military visit in *Nippu Jiji*. "Training cruises are important in many ways. They afford an opportunity for the Japanese navy men to extend consolation to Japanese abroad. They enable the cadets to gain knowledge of the places they visit and make friends, all of which gives them better understanding of the countries visited when they become officers of the navy.

"Such fleet diplomacy will go a long way toward promoting better relations between Japan the United States."[9]

# FEDERAL BUILDING

## HONOLULU
### FEBRUARY 12, 1940

A shadow crosses over the copy of a local Japanese newspaper, *Nippon Shuho*, that Douglas Wada is reading. It's Lieutenant Commander Ringle, who only has two words to say: "Black Room."

Wada stands from the long desk, a shared space used by the agents in the office. He doesn't have his own desk, or a phone. It's nothing personal—even as the number of staff increase, the number of desks in the Bureau of Information office isn't keeping up. The worst part is, the desks and chairs they do have are cheap, uncomfortable rentals.

With only thirteen naval intelligence agents assigned to the 14th

---

8. MIS Veterans Club of Hawaii interview.
9. Japanese officers filed intelligence reports about what they saw from these trips to Hawaii, according to postwar analysis, and would take on supplies and water at Hilo specifically so they could see the coastal defenses there. See: Lt. Cmdr. Wade Coleman Jr., USNR, "Japanese Activities Directed Against the US Indicative of Preparation for World War II," Memorandum for Op-23C242, June 18, 1946.

DIO, his presence is felt and increasingly appreciated. Wada's linguistic talents are rare and in demand. In a survey of 3,700 Nisei, military officials assess only three percent as being accomplished linguists. They consider another four percent proficient, barely good enough for training. The fact that Wada excels is a testament to his travel experience and work ethic, combined with an aptitude for language. Translation is about more than just fluency; there's context. With his experience in Japan and his lifetime in Hawaii, Wada has unmatched experience.

The daily grind is straight translation work. He translates Domei, the Japanese government's news service, for a daily report on its contents. Domei maintains a network of offices outside Japan, staffed with reporters across the world. These journalists also unwittingly produce a steady influx of open-source intelligence for the Empire of Japan. The service also exports news as an outlet for government-produced film and radio propaganda. Added to Wada's translation list are a dozen local Japanese newspapers. The flow of local open-source information is a firehose he must constantly drink from.

His language skills also make him a fixture as an interpreter during interviews, and he's increasingly conducting his own. Among those he speaks to are returnees from Japan, and his style is far from an interrogation. He employs a simple trick—he's unfailingly polite, attuned to Japanese sensitivities like no *haole* can be. Even innocent travelers can unwittingly provide helpful information about attitudes in Japan that can put an edge to his reports and provide data for military cartographers.

But the most rewarding times come when he's summoned to the Black Room. This is where he can translate materials that come from sensitive sources. This can include radio intercepts, personal correspondences and purloined documents. No one is allowed inside the Black Room except Ringle, Hart and Wada.[10]

---

10. Capt. Dick MacDonald USN (Ret.) and Lt. Dick Parsons USNR (Ret.), "Doug Wada Remembers," *Naval Intelligence Professionals Journal*, 2007. Colleagues of Wada's, they include quotes and information about the Black Room directly from him.

But the more he handles these materials, the less risk his Navy handlers are willing to consider and the more they want him to keep his job a secret. Wada finds himself growing in stature but sidelined from undercover duty.

As trust in the young translator grows inside the Federal Building, the gulf Wada feels between himself and the Japanese community seems to widen.[11] When he leaves the crowded office at the Federal Building for the familiar surroundings of Kapalama, he's surrounded by people under suspicion, largely oblivious to the clandestine world swirling around them. And he must lie about his work, telling his neighbors he works as a translator and telling strangers he works selling insurance, a cover identity the DIO established for him to use as needed.

There is one member of Honolulu's Nisei community he's especially interested in: Helen Fusayo Ota, who lives with her mother, sister and stepfather on nearby Webb Lane, off King Street. Helen is a year younger than Wada, born in Kauai in 1912. Her widowed mother, Kiku, moved to Oahu, and by 1940 she and two daughters are living in downtown Honolulu with a man ten years Kiku's senior, Yohichiro Kawasoe. Two other of Helen's sisters and a brother stayed in Kauai. Like Wada, she travelled to Japan as a teenager, returning from a trip to her parents' homeland in Yokohama in 1926, when she was fourteen.[12]

He's building a life in Honolulu, but it's hard to turn off his developing professional instincts. As the ONI training manual says, "Members of the Investigating Service are, in a sense, always on duty." Maybe so, but it doesn't make daily life on Kama Lane any easier.

---

11. Wada later says he "was looked upon with a jaundiced eye by the Japanese community" during this time. Douglas Wada, "Letter to Commander, US Army Intelligence Center Re: Gero Iwai," May 20, 1994. The letter was discovered and shared by Lori Stewart, historian at the Army Intelligence Museum at Fort Huachuca, AZ.

12. Helen Ota's biography can be traced through census records, ship manifests and the *Honolulu Star-Bulletin* of September 22, 1967. The 1940 census records the name of her mother as "Kiku Kawasoe" but there is also a marriage announcement for Helen's mom in the July 16, 1943, edition of *The Honolulu Advertiser*, so maybe the arrangement was unofficial in America for a while. It's the same couple, since the witness for this wedding is the same person who witnesses Helen's coming nuptials.

# NUUANU YMCA

## HONOLULU
## MAY 22, 1940

Masaji Marumoto watches the guest of honor take the podium at the downtown YMCA gymnasium, tonight turned into a banquet hall.

The evening's dinner is celebrating the announcement of a new board of directors of the Prince Fushimi Memorial Scholarship Society, of which Marumoto is a newly named director. The guest speaker for the dinner is Kiichi Gunji, the Japanese Consul for Hawaii. Gunji is an experienced diplomat, able to push his nation's increasingly bellicose agenda and simultaneously engage in local glad-handing.

The topic of his speech tonight is calibrated to be polite: conditions in British-run Singapore, where he served as consul in 1937. In the 1930s, the United States, Britain and Japan had a shared interest in suppressing anti-Japanese sentiment there, since those demonstrating were affiliated with Chinese Communists. It's a suitable speech for the crowd, here to celebrate decades of cultural cooperation between the two nations in Hawaii.

For more than thirty years, the Society has funded language lessons for Japanese American students, an effort that began with a two-hundred-dollar donation from a visiting prince in 1907. The Society was also instrumental in establishing an "Oriental Department" in the Library of Hawaii.

The Fushimi Memorial Scholarship is run by leaders of the Japanese community, and several are here tonight. Dr. Iga Mori, one of Hawaii's key Issei figures, is a Japanese physician who has practiced medicine in Hawaii since 1891. He's also an active community leader, considered an elder statesman with ties to the Japanese Benevolent Society, the United Japanese Society and the Higher Wage Association. Mori also serves as an advisor to the Japanese Consulate.

But the new directors of the Society represent new blood, powerful Nisei who are enjoying a growing influence. Marumoto is a leading light among them, an archetypical success story who attended McKinley High School in Honolulu and received a Fushimi grant while a student. After graduating from Harvard Law, he returned home to Honolulu to hang a shingle. In October 1939, he was admitted to practice law before the US Supreme Court. His celebration ended tragically when his father, Tamajiro, was struck and killed by a DC trolley three days after the accomplishment.[13]

Marumoto is more than a local boy turned influential attorney; he's a rising public figure who helps run some of the biggest charities and civil groups in Honolulu. One of these is the Japanese Benevolent Society, established in 1892, of which he serves as secretary. He's the only executive who was born in the United States. The group's chief asset is the Japanese Hospital, founded as a charity in 1900 after a massive fire swept through Chinese and Japanese neighborhoods. In 1918 the Society used its funds, augmented by a sizable donation from Japanese Emperor Taisho, to build a medical compound on Kuakini Street. With more than 120 beds in a dozen buildings, spread over four acres, it's the second-largest civilian hospital in Hawaii.

Marumoto is also the chairman of the Young Men's Buddhist Association. A priest at the Honpa Hongwanji Temple named Yemyo Imamura formed the group as the Japanese community's answer to the YMCA. The founder died in 1932, leaving the YMBA in the hands of emerging Nisei leaders like Marumoto.

When it comes to candidates for a pickup list of those in positions to organize resistance during a war, Marumoto would seem to amply qualify.[14] But the attorney's true colors will soon reveal themselves to the US counterintelligence community.

One quiet aspect of Marumoto's work with Japanese societies is

---

13. Ogawa, *First Among Nisei: The Life and Writings of Masaji Marumoto.*
14. Gen. George Patton placed him on an early version of a pickup list in the mid-1930s, according to historian Michael Slackman, citing records from the National Archives. UPI Archives, February 27, 1984.

defending them from overzealous investigations of local and federal authorities. Part of his strategy to put the intelligence agencies on notice is by calling them to testify, presumably to say members have been examined for subversion and cleared.

When he calls on the 14th District Intelligence Office to testify, one of the men he names is Douglas Wada. It's not clear how Wada became ensnared in this litigation—Marumoto is involved in so many organizations, and represents even more, that it's hard to know which one he was representing. Presumably, Wada either evaluated or generated information about the group—exactly the kind of exposure his superiors try to avoid these days by keeping him in the office and away from street-level counterintelligence operations.[15]

When Wada supplies testimony, he also reveals his job as an agent to Marumoto. The attorney surprises many by agreeing to keep the young Nisei's position a secret; Wada's gratitude for this discretion is deep and lasting.[16] Word spreads among the counterintelligence community that the attorney is sympathetic.

In late May, Marumoto attends a party aboard a Japanese luxury liner on its maiden voyage and is seated next to SAC Robert Shivers. The meeting is likely no coincidence—covering for Wada is a sign of the man's loyalty, and Shigeo Yoshida, his fellow speaker before the congressional delegation, can also vouch for Marumoto. If this influential man can be brought into the loyalty cabal, it could bring new life into the movement.

The cruise is taken with small talk of well-educated men—and Marumoto gets drunk enough to not remember the conversation the next day. But apparently he's agreed to meet with the FBI man, because

---

15. This is mostly inference from a biography of Wada written by his colleagues Dick MacDonald and Dick Parsons, with his direct input. It says, "Marumoto encountered Wada as a witness for the Office of Naval Intelligence in a litigation against a Japanese society that Marumoto represented." The attorney was involved in so many organizations, it's hard to narrow it down, and corroborating records are not extant. Quote and detail about his bosses' fear of "blowing my cover" are found in: Capt. Dick MacDonald USN (Ret.) and Lt. Dick Parsons USNR (Ret.), "Doug Wada Remembers," *Naval Intelligence Professionals Journal*, 2007.
16. MacDonald and Parsons, "Doug Wada Remembers."

he calls his office. When Marumoto arrives at Shivers's office that afternoon, the SAC admits he's being bombarded with anti-Japanese information from Washington, DC.

"I want to find out the Japanese side of the story," Shivers says. "Can you help me?"[17]

# KAMA LANE

## HONOLULU
## JULY 28, 1940

Summer in Hawaii is particularly lovely. It's a perfect time for a wedding.

Douglas Wada stands in the center of the ceremonial hall of the Kotohira Jinsha, nervously staring at his bride, Helen Fusayo Ota. Rev. Misao Isobe stands to the right of an altar, a Shinto shrine maiden (or *miko*) standing on the left. The altar has salt and fruits for the local *kami* and three cups of sake of varying sizes for the celebrants. Helen is wearing a bright kimono; Douglas, a dark suit with a flower pinned to his lapel.

The couple each make three oaths, one for each sake cup. Isobe fills the smallest cup, which Helen and Douglas each drink from. The second goes to Helen first, and the last cup repeats the first. There's no clear historic origin to this *san-san-kudo* ceremony, but the most common interpretation is that it's an invocation to stay together in good times or bad.

Missing from the ceremony are Kenneth and Margaret Ringle. The 14th Naval District stalwart was reassigned in June, tasked with evaluating the "Japanese problem" in California. He's now the Assistant District Intelligence Officer for the 11th Naval District in Los Angeles, the front line of the counterespionage effort in the state.

---

17. Ogawa, *First Among Nisei: The Life and Writings of Masaji Marumoto*. "I had taken too much liquor to notice or remember who was at my table," Marumoto is quoted as saying of the fateful meeting.

Wada is but one of many superiors and subordinates who lament the loss of Ringle's insight. His classmate and unlikely friend set him on this strange path, and now he's gone. Luckily, Lt. Commander Denzel Carr has been brought into the DIO to replace him. He's a University of Hawaii professor and naval reservist who taught at schools in Kyoto. Above all, Carr appreciates Wada's skills and the uniqueness of his position.

Others do as well. Assignments for him now come in from places other than the DIO, such as Station Hypo, a unit formed in 1939 with a mandate to break codes used by Japanese diplomats and key naval officers. It's ingloriously located in the basement of the Administrative Building at Pearl Harbor, a place so dank the staff call it "the Dungeon." The key aim is to be able to both track the Japanese fleet and divine its intentions. Station Hypo has a massive job and too few people to do it, leaving its officers seeking help elsewhere in the Navy. Its head since 1940 is Joseph Rochefort, and he and Lt. Cmdr. Yale Maxon (the 14th District Intelligence Office's chief translator) are on good terms.

Wada and Carr's Black Room skills are occasionally loaned to Station Hypo to translate radio traffic from the Japanese military. From Hawaii, the Navy can spy on their communication from Buenos Aires to Japan, often relaying messages from Germany. Even better, Wada sometimes receives messages between Japanese warplanes and their carriers to transcribe, seeking nuggets of information that can be used to locate the ships.[18] Even though he doesn't work at Station Hypo—which is just as well, given its grim Dungeon nickname—these highly classified hide-and-seek games make him feel closer to the front lines of intelligence operations rather than the back office.

---

18. In the MIS Veterans Club of Hawaii interview, Wada notes they "were able to locate lot of aircraft carriers with the planes talking too, you see." This work, out of the scope of his acknowledged duties, would fall under MAGIC classification and therefore would be highly secretive. Wada also said he was involved in MAGIC-level duties in a late-life conversation (authors' interview with Kenneth Ringle Jr.). Ship tracking isn't destined to be a primary role for Wada, as he also says in his MIS Veterans Club of Hawaii interview that Combat Intelligence Officer Cmdr. Edwin Layton (who arrived in December 1940) never gave him an assignment. The influx of naval reservists filled gaps in manpower needs, and Wada had other things to do.

Wada is getting better at balancing his heritage, community and national security job. As usual, one outlet is baseball: he manages a private league of Japanese ballplayers. He's also joined the Lions Club, a distinctly American but mixed-race organization.[19]

There may be no more dramatic example of the disparate directions of the Issei and Nisei in Hawaii than a budding naval counterintelligence agent building his career in 1940 and his traditional father devoting his time to building Shinto shrines that the authorities consider to be outposts of the Imperial Japanese government.

As a newlywed, Wada has the opportunity to get some distance from his culture and community—to become more like the men he works with. But he and Helen start their new life together in familiar territory. The couple move into a home on 1304 Kama Lane, a few doors away from his sisters and parents. Itoyo's family, with an additional child, are also on the block at 1110 Kama Lane. Hanako has moved out to work as a waitress and lives on Hall Street, in Hell's Half Acre.[20] It's not as bad as the name sounds, instead being a lively, multiracial neighborhood filled with lower-income housing, bars, shops, eateries and theaters.

Wada feels an unwelcome chasm between his family and his country, but he's not resigned to choosing between the two sides. His traditional wedding and Kama Lane address are proof that he's not distancing himself from his parents, religion or community.

This feeling of balance evaporates on July 29 as he settles into his usual regimen of newspapers, among them *Nippu Jiji*, its front page featuring FDR's recent call for National Guard mobilization. Wada soon scans the local news: the Japanese Hospital needs nurses and is offering a three-month training program; a Navy man from the USS *Yorktown* fell to his death from a hotel balcony; the newly arrived Japanese Vice-Consul Otojiro Okuda appeared with Honolulu Mayor Charles Crane at a dinner at the Ishii Garden hosted by the Japanese Contractors' Association.[21]

---

19. MacDonald and Parsons, "Doug Wada Remembers."
20. US Census Records, 1940.
21. *Nippu Jiji*, July 29, 1940.

Wada is flipping past the funnies on his way to the sports section when a headline hooks his eye. "Douglas Wada Weds Miss Helen Ota." He smiles as he reads the announcement, but his face soon falls as the brief notes that "the erstwhile baseball star . . . works with the local naval intelligence office."

The newspaper where he worked undercover clearly hadn't been as clueless as he supposed. People there know Wada's current job—and perhaps his surreptitious role on the staff to begin with. Or perhaps some family member sent the information and inadvertently disclosed his professional identity.

This disclosure is bad but not catastrophic. The article never says he's an actual agent. And as guarded as the Navy has been about his position, Wada's not primarily an undercover operative. There's nothing about the subtle disclosure that precludes his work as a Navy translator; his value in the office is simply too high. But it still stings.

# FORT SHAFTER

## HONOLULU
## AUGUST 24, 1940

US Army Colonel Thomas Green takes in the view from his new post at Fort Shafter, gazing at the Kalihi and Moanalua valleys. The Army base is still in Honolulu, but it's located away from downtown, perched on a ridgeline rising from the coastal plain. The peaks of mountains loom on the horizon, and every inch of unmaintained space seems overrun with lush growth. The landscape here is nearly alien—and so are many of the people.

Green freely admits to having no knowledge of, or experience with, Japanese culture, not to mention the subtleties of the Nisei and Issei. Yet he's a key architect of their futures in Hawaii if there is war in the Pacific. He now works among the senior Army leaders in Hawaii;

the headquarters of the Hawaiian Department moved here from the Alexander Young Hotel in June 1921.

Green is a freshly arrived lawyer, serving as a judge advocate. He graduated from Boston University in 1915; the next year he joined a cavalry unit of the Massachusetts National Guard and deployed to the Mexican border. Military life suited him, and he joined the regular Army. During the Great War he served overseas as a second lieutenant with the 15th Cavalry and returned in command of the regiment.

In 1921, Green married Ruth Tuthill and was assigned to Washington, DC, where he worked in the office of the assistant secretary of war while earning a master's degree from George Washington University Law School. After duties in New York City, he transferred to the judge advocate general's department in 1925 and helped adjudicate claims from German detainees during the Great War.

Green arrived in Hawaii on a lawyer's mission: the search for a definition of "martial law." It's a hazy term that's barely protected by US Supreme Court precedent. In 1849, the Court upheld the legality of a military seizure of control in *Luther v. Borden*, but that case centered on a state's declaration (Rhode Island) and managed to never explicitly enshrine "martial law" as a legal term. After the Civil War, the federal government used martial law quite a bit less than individual states. Military generals also invoke it more than presidents to handle imminent crises; for example, in 1920, General Francis Marshall imposed martial law in Lexington, Kentucky, to protect a courthouse from a riotous lynch mob.

Green is finding that the precedential gray area can be exploited. "Martial law is not a law nor are the limitations or the responsibilities well defined anywhere," he writes.[22] He'll pass this understanding to General Charles Herron, one of four district Army commanders. The idea that martial law is whatever the Army wants it to be informs the service's wartime plans for the Hawaiian population.

---

22. Quoted in Tom Hoffman, *Inclusion*.

That includes Green's other assignment: drafting a set of General Orders to be implemented if shooting starts with Japan. The framework Green envisions will consolidate all the functions of government under the sole authority of the commander of the Army in Honolulu. When fully written, they'll become the plan for a military governor to usurp the civilian government in Hawaii.

# DILLINGHAM TRANSPORTATION BUILDING

### HONOLULU
### SEPTEMBER 1940

SAC Robert Shivers knows his new request will shake up the Justice Department and Roosevelt administration. He doesn't care—he's recommending to his FBI superiors that the 234 consular agents working in Hawaii all be arrested.

Two years ago, Congress enacted the Foreign Agents Registration Act, requiring virtually anyone working for another government to notify the United States. The law was created to combat propaganda and collaboration, in that order, and Shivers wants to employ it to dismantle the Japanese Consulate's support network. Surely not all of the hundreds of agents are guilty, but a mass arrest would drain the swamp of bad actors.

Lt. Col. George Bicknell, the local head of Army counterintelligence, is all for charging the cadre-hired diplomatic helpers for not registering as foreign agents. But Gen. Walter Short, head of the Army's Hawaii Department, doesn't agree, and his words carry a lot more weight.

Short has his eye on the Nisei now immersed in basic training at the local Schofield Barracks, who are already proving themselves to be dedicated, quick learners. Short is even now reforming the 298th and 299th Regiments as integrated National Guard units, and he sees the possibility of including Nisei in a future draft. Arresting Japanese diplomats and any local collaborators could ignite a backlash that would interfere with these efforts.

That's the argument, and not the military intelligence experts' warning of spy rings, that Secretary of War Henry Stimson takes to the US Justice Department. "We are at present engaged in a counterpropaganda campaign whose object is to encourage loyalty of the Japanese population in Hawaii on promise of fair treatment," Stimson says.

The Justice Department tells Shivers there will be no arrests or prosecutions. Unless the FBI and military intelligence can prove the threat is somehow more pressing, the diplomats and their local assistants are to be kept under watch, but free, on US soil.

# PART 3

# SETTING THE BOARD

# IMPERIAL NAVAL HEADQUARTERS

## TOKYO
## OCTOBER 1940

Takeo Yoshikawa tries to maintain his composure as he stands before his section head, awaiting his fate. The twenty-eight-year-old considers himself well-groomed for undercover work, with the language and subject matter knowledge to be the admiralty's trusted eyes and ears in what may soon become enemy territory. Representatives of Germany, Italy and Japan just five days ago signed a defensive alliance called the Tripartite Pact. When war comes, it will again be global.

Yoshikawa spent the last three years learning English and studying every available resource about the US Navy. His copy of *Jane's Fighting Ships* is well worn when it comes to the sections on American warships. He's also, by now, fluent enough in English to be a linguist. One of his duty assignments is to monitor and translate intercepted shortwave transmissions, seeking nuggets of intelligence. He claims that his work identifying English ships leaving Sierra Leone for Liverpool helped German U-boats cause numerous sinkings and earned him a letter of thanks from Adolf Hitler.[1]

Yoshikawa stands stiffly as the captain, the chief of his naval intelligence section, bluntly spells out the assignment. "You are going to Honolulu as vice-consul," he says. "Shortwave transmitters can be too easily spotted by radio direction finders. So you will go as a diplomat and report on the daily readiness of the American Fleet and bases using our

---

1. Takeo Yoshikawa, *Japan's Spy at Pearl Harbor* (Jefferson, NC: McFarland, 2020). In his published memoirs, Yoshikawa cites seventeen troop transports sunk while leaving Sierra Leone. Finding a U-boat attack that matches this description has yielded no results.

encoded diplomatic dispatches. This is the only truly secure channel of communication." An assignment using diplomatic cover isn't as shocking now as it would have been even two months ago. On August 22, the Japanese government announced an overhaul of its diplomatic corps and recalled forty Japanese diplomats stationed abroad, including Kiichi Gunji from Hawaii. It's part of an overall hardening of its foreign policy, announced by Overseas Minister Yosuke Matsuoka.

The captain pauses for effect. "I do not have to tell you the importance of the mission."

"*Hai*," Yoshikawa replies, an affirmative *yes*. Per Imperial Navy etiquette, this is the only acceptable reply.

"We have arranged for a new consul general to be your chief for this operation," the captain continues briskly. "Nagao Kita, a diplomat now at Canton, has been dealing closely with the Imperial Navy on intelligence and other matters there. He can be trusted to cooperate with you fully. Kita goes to Honolulu first, and you follow."

The superior officer softens his tone and offers the agent, on the eve of his first undercover assignment, some hard-won advice. "If you want to deceive your enemy," he says, "you must first dupe yourself."[2]

# ALEXANDER YOUNG HOTEL

### HONOLULU
### JANUARY 15, 1941

Douglas Wada stands at the loading dock of the Alexander Young Hotel, watching the shipping crews heft equipment from Navy trucks parked there. It's moving day for the 14th Naval District Intelligence Office.

He won't miss the Federal Building, with its cramped desks and stifling atmosphere. It wouldn't take much to trade up, but the Navy has

---

2. Ibid. Yoshikawa recalls the conversation in detail.

outdone itself by choosing to house a counterintelligence operation in the swankiest building in Honolulu.

There are desks being unloaded, new and regulation Navy. Gone is the dismal, rented equipment at the Federal Building. Wada leaves the dock, turns the corner of the building and walks along the hotel's intimidating façade. The two-hundred-room hotel extends along an entire city block in downtown Honolulu, along the swanky "Avenue of Pioneers."

Its face is adorned by round arches, each a story-and-a-half high, and a pair of towering, fluted Corinthian columns. There are two wings, standing like stubby turrets on each side. Wada's new office is now on the sixth floor, on the *mauka* side (literally "mountainside," as it doesn't face the water).

The building has shops on the first floor, a bar on the roof, and in between are ballrooms and hotel suites. There are also dozens of offices, many of which are rented by government agencies. Some of these are military—the hotel has its own electric plant and water well, making it self-sustaining as well as strategically located, just a few miles from the Navy base at Pearl Harbor.

Inside, Wada can only admire the commitment to adornment. Alexander Young built the hotel in 1902 to anchor the central commercial, government and social district of Honolulu, and it does. He spared no expense scouting the world for the best supplies to build it—there's iron and steel brought from New York holding slabs of Colusa sandstone from California, ornate embellishments carved from Scottish granite and a grand staircase in the lobby made from Vermont marble. When it opened, the hotel was the biggest in all Hawaii, and more than three decades later it's still regarded as one of the finest hotels in America.

The wing of the sixth floor occupied by the Navy is the former home of the hotel's Gold Room, a banquet hall with an attached kitchen. It's now busy with workmen, kicking up dust. There's telltale metal scraping of partitions being moved, the sound of new rooms being created inside the space.[3]

3. "Naval Agents Get New Office," *The Honolulu Advertiser*, January 16, 1941.

Captain Hart has come through with new digs. Part of the sixth floor is already occupied, but the extra space will be welcome. There are more than a dozen new staffers expected, and now they'll have a place to work. For Wada the increase in manpower is welcome, but it's yet another sign that the odds of war with Japan are going up—and with them, the chance of a crackdown against Japanese in Hawaii.

The Navy intelligence agents now regard all Japanese civil societies in Hawaii as part of a network run by the consulate. "The center of the consular organization, as well as of alien Japanese activity, is the Japanese Consul General at Honolulu under the direction of Consul-General Nagao Kita," one 1941 ONI report reads. "For purposes of disseminating instructions of news, it is said to utilize the services of prominent organizations as the United Japanese Society of Honolulu, the Honolulu Japanese Chamber of Commerce, the Hilo Japanese Chamber of Commerce as well as the Hilo Japanese Society and the Japanese Language Press."[4] These are some of the most mainstream groups in the territory.

The ONI's list of suspected organizations in Hawaii includes eighty-eight Japanese groups. In the eyes of military intelligence, the bigger the group is, the more trouble it could cause. "It is believed that every Japanese resident in Hawaii belongs to one or more purely Japanese organizations," one ONI report puts it. "However, only the more important groups are of interest, since they are in a position to engage in espionage, sabotage and other acts inimical to the best interests of the US."[5]

Despite all these plans and damning classifications, intelligence professionals in Hawaii—even those who work on these pickup lists—regard the vast majority of the Japanese population here as loyal. But that doesn't always mean patriotic. Military intelligence assessments show that ambivalence is common among many Japanese residents, who understandably wouldn't do anything to harm either side.

Despite their generational differences, neither the Issei nor the

---

4. Office of Naval Intelligence, memo to Washington, DC, "JAPANESE INTELLIGENCE AND PROPAGANDA IN THE UNITED STATES DURING 1941," December 4, 1941, http://www.mansell.com/eo9066/1941/41-12/IA021.html.
5. Ibid.

Nisei of Hawaii seem to pose much of a threat to the United States. Many Issei, caught between a home nation that has become unrecognizably twisted by authoritarianism and a new nation that mistrusts them, tend to become insular, making authorities more suspicious. The Nisei have more firm American roots, and many are eager to actively distance themselves from the actions of the Japanese Empire through public service.[6]

Douglas Wada has a less charitable view of many Nisei, seeing them as spoiled. "Most of them live easy and just work when they feel like," he says to those who ask. "But their loyalty is for US, as much as mine."[7]

## NUUANU AVENUE

### HONOLULU
### JANUARY 1941

Warrant Officer Theodore "Ted" Emanuel didn't join the Navy to be an undercover operative. His job as chief ships clerk is dedicated to keeping internal records, reports and correspondence. But now that he's assigned to the 14th Naval District Intelligence Office, Emanuel is capturing *another* nation's communications in yet another undercover assignment.[8]

Today he's on the streets of Honolulu dressed as a telephone repairman, unhurriedly working on the junction box near 1742 Nuuanu Avenue—the Japanese Consulate. As SAC Shivers is working on getting

---

6. This dynamic is discussed in: Max Everest-Phillips, "The Pre-War Fear of Japanese Espionage: Its Impact and Legacy," *Journal of Contemporary History* 42, no. 2 (April 2007).

7. MIS Veterans Club of Hawaii interview.

8. In later testimony to the Army Board investigating Pearl Harbor, he says, "My functions and activities . . . included the obtaining of the telephone conversations originating in and going to the Japanese Consulate and persons therein at Honolulu. Such conversations were obtained by me during the period from January 1941 to and including 7 December 1941." *Hearings Before the Joint Committee on the Pearl Harbor Attack*, S. Doc. No.79–27 (1946), https://ia800202.us .archive.org/0/items/pearlharborattac35unit/pearlharborattac35unit_bw.pdf.

clearance from his FBI bosses to bug the consulate phones, Captain Hart goes ahead and just does it.

The hardest part of setting up a wiretap is knowing the right circuits to target, but in this case that's easy. After that, it's as simple as scraping the insulation from a segment of the two wires required to make a telephone circuit. A receiver is attached to the exposed portions with metal clips and extension wires. This is known as "cutting in" on a telephone circuit and can be done at a streetside phone junction box.

Emanuel finishes up and casually drives away. The taps he's placed cover half a dozen of the consulate's telephone lines. It's a tightly compartmentalized operation. The calls, about fifty a day, will be translated and summarized at the Young Hotel by Denzel Carr, the master linguist. When he doesn't have the time, he'll rely on Douglas Wada to handle the workload.[9]

The US Navy has some ears inside the consulate. Now it's up to the staff inside to make an indiscreet phone call.

## PIER 11

### HONOLULU HARBOR
### MARCH 14, 1941

Captain Irving Mayfield reads the report about Nagao Kita, the newly appointed Japanese consul general to Hawaii, who today arrived in Honolulu aboard the luxury liner *Tatsuta Maru*. Undercover ONI men, tasked with identifying new arrivals from Japan, were there too.

This is a well-practiced procedure, conducted since 1936 when a memorandum from President Roosevelt mandated: "Every Japanese citizen or noncitizen on the Island of Oahu who meets these Japanese ships or who has any connection with their officers and men should be secretly

---

9. Capt. Dick MacDonald USN (Ret.) and Lt. Dick Parsons USNR (Ret.), "Doug Wada Remembers," *Naval Intelligence Professionals Journal*, 2007.

but definitely identified and his or her name placed on a special list of those who would be the first to be placed in a concentration camp in the event of trouble."

His men, Lt. Commander Denzel Carr and Warrant Officer Ted Emanuel, connived to photograph Kita on arrival, but it's more of a formality. By the nature of his position, Kita automatically rates inclusion on the list of suspicious people in Honolulu.[10]

Mayfield is also a new arrival to Hawaii. Tomorrow, he'll start his new job, replacing Hart as the head of the 14th District Intelligence Office. The Office of Naval Intelligence's Hawaii office consists of three divisions: Combat Intelligence under Lt. Commander Joseph Rochefort, Fleet Intelligence under Lt. Commander Edwin Layton, and Counterespionage under Captain Mayfield.

Among Mayfield's duties is to take up the watch on Kita and his consulate; today's reading is in preparation for his own first day.[11] Hart is moving up, becoming the head of Mine Division 4, a flotilla of minesweepers stationed at Pearl Harbor. Good for him—it's easier to be promoted from a ship deck than an intelligence position.

The departing chief warned Mayfield that the Navy, the Army, local police and the FBI were each working the "Japanese problem" at the same time, but often in discord. Apparently, Shivers still doesn't trust the competence of the other agencies, leading to his FBI agents continually double-checking everyone else's investigative findings. His Army counterespionage counterpart, Lt. Col. Bicknell, is willing to collaborate, but his superiors rarely favor aggressive tactics.

Mayfield hears that the hardest thing for any intelligence agency in Honolulu to find is a local collaborator to turn into an informant. It's next to impossible to get someone who is sufficiently close enough to the Japanese Consulate to be in a position to know what's going

---

10. Kiichi Gunji's been replaced; he'll soon make an impassioned speech in Tokyo describing the loyalty of the Japanese population in Hawaii to the emperor. Kita's arrival covered in local newspapers, including the *Nippu Jiji*.

11. Mayfield will report directly to Admiral Claude Bloch, the commandant of the 14th Naval District.

on. And even when one is recruited, it seems nothing is done with the information.

The June prior to Mayfield's arrival, the Navy's intelligence office in Honolulu developed "a most reliable informant" with access to a Japanese consular agent whose Maui home overlooked Lahaina Roads, which the US Navy uses as an alternative anchorage to Pearl Harbor. The agent made two reports about the fleet's movement in and out of Lahaina, according to the informant. The Navy and local police asked for permission from Washington, DC, to prosecute consulate workers in Hawaii—they were still waiting for a reply but remained skeptical of approval after the FBI's effort against consular agents failed.

Mayfield frowns at the report of Kita's arrival. He can't see anything good about this change in consular staff, given the crumbling nature of the US relationship with Japan. Besides, Kita is a young bachelor with bare-knuckle diplomatic experience in China. *This man could make my life difficult*, he thinks. Then it occurs to him: Kita could be reading a report about Mayfield's arrival and thinking the same thing.

# HONOLULU HARBOR

### HONOLULU
### MARCH 27, 1941

Takeo Yoshikawa walks off the gangplank of the Japanese liner *Nitta Maru*, berthed in Honolulu's Pier 8. His paperwork gives his name as Tadashi Morimura. If anyone doubts his diplomatic role here, it'll be dispelled by the appearance of Vice-Consul Otojiro Okuda.

Nearby, Denzell Carr signals to Ted Emanuel, who is waiting with a hidden camera inside his Aloha shirt to get Morimura's photograph. Carr is dressed as a health inspector, gaining him access to the vessel and putting him in place as a spotter. Emanuel maneuvers into position, the shutter clicks and with that, Morimura is on his way to the

Navy's official list of suspect Honolulu residents.[12] It means the FBI and Army will also know about him, since the local agents share that information.

Unaware of the lurking ONI men, Okuda and Yoshikawa shake hands, navigate customs and climb into a car. The conversation en route to the consulate is polite and discreet, but it leaves Yoshikawa feeling the diplomat wants him to know he's aware of the mission. After all, he is the one who directed operations observing the US Fleet before the new consul general arrived.

Yoshikawa is unimpressed by the man and doesn't offer details, just watches Honolulu pass by as the car wends its way from the airport. Seeing this multicultural city, built among shattered volcanic cones in the middle of the Pacific, makes its existence seem even more improbable. He passes Buddhist temples and Shinto shrines, scores of uniformed Caucasian sailors and Army personnel and streets lined with brick buildings run by Chinese merchants. The horizon is dominated by mountains, and Yoshikawa silently names each peak he recognizes from maps.

The car halts at 1742 Nuuanu Avenue, the Japanese Consulate. This will be his home and office in Hawaii—all of the foreign staff live here. The first person he's introduced to is Consul General Kita, seated in his office. Yoshikawa bows and gives his name as Tadashi Morimura. There's no reason for anyone to know his real identity.

Kita and the spy sit alone to get acquainted. Yoshikawa finds his handler to be surprisingly amiable and quick to laugh. The pair quickly finds a common bond as fellow drinkers and bachelors. Kita seems nervous to have Yoshikawa start surveillance, but when the discussions about operation begin, the diplomat proves to be entirely cooperative.

---

12. Denzel Carr describes this tradecraft to *Day of Deceit* author Robert Stinnett, whose conclusions about a conspiracy to provoke war by ignoring the attack have largely been debunked. Still, he interviewed primary sources for details, and there's been no refutation of this interview. That "Morimura" was known to the intelligence community since his arrival should be no surprise, since the Army, Navy and FBI took care to identify all the consulate officials working in Honolulu; recall that the White House ordered the Navy to chronicle the arrival of *all* Japanese residents and aliens since 1936. No other source from *Day of Deceit* is included in this book.

Kita tells him the city is friendly, but also confirms the warnings that Yoshikawa heard from his Navy superiors. Polite residents are easy to find, but nearly none can be counted on to be actively supportive. The United Japanese Society in Honolulu might invite them to banquets at the Shunchoro Tea House, but the mainstream group is hardly a reservoir of eager collaborators.

The guidance for the spy is not to trust the Japanese who live in Hawaii. But that doesn't mean he'll have no support in the field. Within days he's taking a harborside tour with Third Secretary Kokichi Seki, the consulate's acknowledged treasurer and Okuda's secret organizer of intelligence information on the US Fleet.

Seki has no formal training as a spy, but like Yoshikawa, he's a graduate of the Imperial Japanese Naval Academy at Etajima. The thirty-nine-year-old is ordered to be helpful, and a subservient pose masks the humiliation of being usurped. He had sporadically charted the military vessels at the harbor, information funneled via diplomatic communiqué to the Ministry of War in Tokyo. Now he's been reduced to the role of the enabler of a young spy he's finding to be both needy and arrogant.

The pair stroll the Pearl City shoreline, on the northern edge of Pearl Harbor. Their pace is casual but there's something exciting about Yoshikawa's first foray. Before the consulate employees, like a movie reel but in color, is the airstrip on Ford Island and the silhouettes of warships. There are aged training ships, combat support ships and seaplane tenders parked on the side of Ford Island facing Pearl City; Battleship Row is located on the other side.

"There's a drink stand here," says Seki, motioning at a Japanese man selling shave ice and lemonade. "Oto, the vendor, watches the ships come in, which is sometimes useful."

Yoshikawa silently scrutinizes the harbor and airfield, trying to take in all the details of the work being done on the water and shore. The sooner he understands the rhythm of the military installations here, the sooner he'll be able to distinguish when something noteworthy is happening.

"I have a driver for you, one of our consular secretaries," Seki continues. "He was born here and even has dual citizenship. He owns his car and can take you to wherever you need to go. Even more importantly, he can be discreet."

"I have been told those born here are to be considered unreliable," Yoshikawa says.

"Which is true. He is reliable, but I did not say entirely trustworthy. Exercise all due caution, but you'll find no better guide here. His name is Masayuki Kotoshirodo. He calls himself 'Richard.' He's immune from Foreign Agent Act arrest because he's registered with the federal government."

In April, Yoshikawa and Seki make an excursion together across the island in Kotoshirodo's 1937 Ford sedan. The spy likes the look of the driver, from his casual Aloha shirt to his knowledge of the best places to find drinks and women. There's a sly appeal behind his thick, swept-back hairdo and stylish mustache.

The trio climb higher into the hills as they leave the city behind. From the passenger's seat, Yoshikawa can take in the view of the glorious coastline behind them, broken only by the concrete patch of Honolulu and the jagged masts of warships at the naval base.

Kotoshirodo is not an idiot. He sees the binoculars around the neck of "Morimura" and hears the itinerary, dutifully driving without asking questions. But he is sure to impress the new man with what he's noticed, spoken as casually as the presence of any landmark. "The US Fleet has a rotating pattern," the consular secretary notes. "Half of the ships are in port for a week while the others go out at sea. Then the next week, they switch."

The car crosses through the Nuuanu Valley across the Pali Highway, an ancient trail cut through the lush peaks by the first humans to inhabit the island. Now it's a paved road used by thousands of cars and trucks.

There are also nearly two dozen hairpin turns winding around steep, wind-whipped gorges—curves that make Yoshikawa happy an experienced driver is behind the wheel.

"This road needs tunnels," Yoshikawa remarks.

"So says everyone who's traveled across it," says the driver amicably. "The government was set to build a big one in '37 but got scared by the cost."

Reaching the northern side of the island, they turn onto the Kokokahi Road, just before the town of Kaneohe. Yoshikawa orders Kotoshirodo to slow down. Across the bay is Kaneohe Naval Air Station, under construction. The hangars at the air station appear close to completion. Then the car moves on, but the driver suggests a new spot where they can stop. He heads through the beach town of Kailua and stops at a beach pavilion. The trio watch the activity at the unfinished base from their seats for five minutes before moving on.

Kotoshirodo guides the car to the highway, heading back to Honolulu. But he tells them there's another opportunity to scout the US Army Air Corps base at Bellows Field. It's been a military facility since 1917, renamed in 1933 for Great War hero Lt. Franklin Bellows, but the Army is now converting it into a permanent post. More signs of the impending war.

They stop at Waimanalo Beach, near an aged pier. The driver parks and the three men walk its length, eyes fixed to the north. But the airbase is set back too far for direct observation. Yoshikawa is disappointed but not discouraged: the day's excursion confirms that it's remarkably easy to observe the US military installations on Oahu from public places. This makes possible many novel, low-risk schemes to get even closer to the military bases here, and he plans on employing them soon.

And now, he has an accomplice. It's time to start operations, and without the stodgy Seki mooning over him. Kotoshirodo, on the other hand, is the kind of man he's looking for: someone who can be helpful and exercise discretion in social matters as well as espionage.

The three men turn their backs on the water and return to the car. They should be back in Honolulu in time for a late lunch.

# FEDERAL BUILDING

## HONOLULU
## APRIL 8, 1941

Gero Iwai steps out of the elevator at the second floor of the Federal Building. The US Army occupies the whole second floor, home to its local counterintelligence operations.

When Iwai enlisted in the Army's Corps of Intelligence Police in 1931, he became its first Japanese American member. The CIP formed in the Great War to comb German recruits for signs of disloyalty. Iwai's enlistment into the organization is an early example of the Army's focus on Japan as a threat, and it makes him a hidden trailblazer in military intelligence.

Today, Lieutenant Iwai's been honorably discharged. Leaving the CIP actually cements his position as an undercover military agent in Honolulu. Iwai is immediately appointed as a reserve officer and tapped to be assistant to the associate chief of staff of intelligence in Hawaii. There, Iwai can remain immersed in his counterintelligence assignment—monitoring Hawaii's population for foreign spies and sympathizers. He doesn't even have to change offices.

Iwai's main job these days is to create pickup lists. He scours temples and civic society meetings for signs of subversion. He doesn't always see the inherent risk in some of the telltales he's ordered to report, but seen through the military intelligence filter of possible threats, they make a certain, paranoid sense.

One seemingly innocuous group that draws scrutiny are martial arts groups. Teaching or learning kendo is considered suspect, largely a legacy fear stemming from the 1930s, when the nationalist Black Dragon Society operatives opened secret dojos for members of nationalist groups to join.[13] These days, martial arts are becoming more inclusive to other races and are growing in mainstream popularity.

---

13. The Japanese society's outreach included direct ties to the just-forming Nation of Islam organization. Since 1937, when the Black Dragon Society's founder died, its influence in Japan and abroad has been waning.

Iwai regards the Japanese diplomats and their staff as the real spies in Hawaii; uncovering them will hopefully protect the innocent Hawaiians. So on top of his other duties, Iwai runs a small string of informants who work at the consulate. They are low-level types who can read the mood of the staff but have no real access to sensitive intelligence. Even the consular secretaries are hardly a vanguard for an invasion or a lurking cadre of saboteurs. Many of these are volunteers who simply help less-literate Japanese with legal and government paperwork. The loyalty of the Issei and Nisei communities makes counterintelligence harder, since there aren't many collaborators to ensnare.

Iwai walks the streets imagining the city at war. He passes neighbors who he knows would be arrested during a war, businesses to be closed and shrines designated to be shuttered. He speaks to people knowing their words will damn them in the eyes of the authorities. This dark knowledge isolates Iwai from his neighborhood, his friends and even his loved ones. His dedication is so complete that he doesn't even tell his family what he does for a living.

He does have a friend who can empathize: Douglas Wada.

The ad-hoc ties between Army and Navy counterintelligence have existed in Hawaii for years, which is now helped by the proximity of their headquarters; the Dillingham building and Alexander Young Hotel are just blocks apart. Given the linguistic help Iwai delivered to the short-staffed Navy over the years, he's a well-known figure to the ONI.

It was only a matter of time until these two trailblazing counterintelligence agents would meet, and when it happens in spring 1938, the pair take a genuine liking to each other. Iwai has someone to take up the slack for the Navy, who bother him for linguistic help, and to use as a sounding board when something, or someone, interesting comes to his attention. Wada has more than just a peer—he has an experienced intelligence professional who's worked the job in Honolulu while Wada was still playing second base.

"Iwai and I more or less isolated ourselves from the rest of the Japanese community in Hawaii and developed a close personal relationship,"

Wada will later say, "mutually enduring mental anguish and suffering inherent in the unique and sensitive military intelligence role we were performing."[14]

But there are limits to how open they can be, on or off the clock. "The motto that they use in intelligence is, keep your ears and eyes open and your yap shut," Wada will say. "So, what you know, you don't discuss with anybody."[15]

---

14. "Letter from Douglas T. Wada to Commander, US Army Intelligence Center," May 20, 1994, endorsing (for a second time) Iwai's inclusion into the Military Intelligence Hall of Fame.
15. MIS Veterans Club of Hawaii interview. He also remarks of Iwai, "I did not know the details of what kinds of intelligence work he was engaged in because these matters were never discussed."

# PART 4

# IDENTITY CRISES

# OLYMPIC HOTEL

## LOS ANGELES
## JUNE 8, 1941

Al Blake, proprietor of a dancing girl show at the San Francisco Fair, walks outside the Olympic Hotel and brushes some lint off his shoulder. For the FBI and naval intelligence agents gathered outside, it's the signal to move in.

Their target is the apartment of thirty-eight-year-old Itaru Tachibana. He came to the United States posing as a language student in 1939, but he was actually an Imperial Japanese navy commander being groomed as an intelligence agent. He stayed in Los Angeles after graduation, landing a job with the Japanese Consulate in Los Angeles.

The Tachibana spy ring has some unlikely members, but then again, this is LA. The key players are Tachibana; a British war hero named Frederick Rutland; Charlie Chaplin's former personal assistant, Toraichi Kono; along with Al Blake, silent film star turned double agent.

Blake is a former Navy man who placed himself undercover when he ran into Kono in Los Angeles. The pair knew each other from Blake's glory years—he costarred with Chaplin in a film—and one of Blake's dancers happened to be on a softball team that Kono managed.

The intrigue began when Kono mentioned, "It's too bad you're not still in the Navy. You could make a lot of money." The silent film star followed up and only contacted the ONI after he was offered cash for photos and information on US Navy ships.

What followed was a subterfuge that sent Blake to Honolulu to meet with a fictitious US Navy captain, supposedly collecting information for

Blake to sell. The ONI in California kept the FBI out of it until they learned the G-men were working the ring through Rutland, tipped off by the MI5. After that awkward discovery, a joint operation was crafted.

The ONI-FBI raid at the Olympic Hotel will come after Blake collects nearly five thousand dollars for his information, the fruits of a second whirlwind trip to Honolulu. During both trips, Blake says he's spotted Japanese and German agents tailing him, and the actor only met ONI agents in Hawaii while sneaking out of a movie theater to do it, with time to slip back in before it ended.

With the payoff complete, evidence of Tachibana's guilt is secured and the agents move in to arrest him that night. Inside his room are 107 pages of evidence implicating Tachibana and Kono for being Japanese agents and Rutland for plotting with them at his house.

Kono is arrested the same night. The Japanese Consulate pays Tachibana's $50,000 bail, but no one steps up for Kono's $25,000.

Blake's arrested, too, and taken to the LA County jail. He figures this is just a precaution—until he's relieved of his suspicious five thousand dollars and booked. The operation is so secret, the local cops and district attorney's office aren't informed ahead of time. It takes a few days for the ONI and federal authorities to intervene and reveal his status as a double agent.

"We are convinced that Blake had no criminal intent and that he was working hand in glove with naval authorities and helped expose the entire plot," Assistant US Attorney Russell Lambeau tells reporters on June 11.[1] By then, Blake's reputation, such as it is, has taken a hit when a newspaper cartoon lambasts him as a traitor; he'll soon sue the Hearst Corporation for publishing it.

Rutland's name never appears in the press coverage. He's a British national working for the Japanese Navy; it's not clear that he was breaking any British laws by collaborating with them. Even worse, the crafty man has developed connections within the Office of Naval Intelligence

---

1. "Former Sailor Praised for Exposing Jap Spies," *Associated Press*, June 11, 1941.

in Mexico and is claiming to be working undercover for *them*. After his lies are dissembled, Rutland is quietly deported to England, where MI5 can again watch him.

What the American public hears is a perfect scandal. There are spies, double agents, lurking subversives, and behind it all are the drumbeats of a possible war. But it also involves the world's largest movie star. Chaplin loves Japan, as a market and as a culture, and has toured the nation many times during his life. In 1932 he was even marked for assassination by naval officers involved in a *coup d'état* that killed Prime Minister Inukai Tsuyoshi. Chaplin wasn't with the prime minister at the time, instead taking in a sumo wrestling match with Tsuyoshi's son when the killers struck.

The Japanese government has been caught red-handed, but the wheels of justice turn differently for spies. With Japanese complaints filed to the US State Department and an international incident looming, Tachibana is released and deported. Without him, there's no case to be made against Kono.

The real loser, then, is the Japanese American community. The press coverage of the case runs worldwide, giving credence to the idea that there are fifth columnists, a group within a country at war who are sympathetic to or working for its enemies, operating in California and Hawaii. With an actual spy ring busted up, many take it as a given that most Japanese in the United States are inherently disloyal.

At his new post with the 11th District Intelligence Office in California, Cmdr. Kenneth Ringle sees a larger lesson being lost among the hysteria. The real espionage threat doesn't come from the Japanese population but the Japanese Consulate.

Ringle comes to this conclusion after intense study. He spends his time away from the ONI's 11th District headquarters, instead working by himself out of a small office in the San Pedro YMCA. His self-separation is telling. Instead of chasing spies, he's spent his time in California gauging the actual threat posed by the Japanese population.

He's focused his loyalty study among the vegetable farmers and tuna fishermen before moving on to businessmen. Over the course of his investigation, Ringle's built a network of informants within the targeted community, particularly among members of the Japanese American Citizens League (JACL). He finds that Japanese militarists had tried to send over visitors and fake immigrants to rile the Japanese American community. He knows this because those loyal to the JACL report them.[2]

Ringle's time in California has validated what he found in Hawaii. He reports officially in 1941 that "better than 90 percent of the Nisei and 75 percent of the original immigrants are completely loyal to the United States."[3]

Yet, this summer, the public sentiment against Japanese in America seems to be building. Ringle ends his population surveys and focuses on the Japanese diplomats in California. If he can get evidence that identifies specific spies here, the ONI can target the actual espionage threats instead of implicating an entire population.

So, he decides to break into Japan's consulate office in Los Angeles.

Ringle will need a safecracker, so he turns to prison to find one. The name of the criminal isn't known, but it must have been an interesting turn of events. One moment he's sitting in prison as a convicted felon, the next minute he's sprung for an operation that is clearly illegal—albeit one run by federal agents.

It's done in the dead of night, with the building empty. The safecracker sees police officers on the street and plainclothesmen wandering about in pairs, the latter being FBI agents patrolling the perimeter. The car doors open and the men silently deploy.

The door locks are easily picked with skeleton keys, the interior

---

2. Kenneth Ringle Jr., interview with authors. He adds, "It turned out that the Japanese Americans really resented these people, and they would later tell my father who they were. Those are the people that my father and the FBI rounded up right after Pearl Harbor. That was all on the West Coast."

3. Ringle later discusses the situation in a letter to his son: "The West Coast Japanese were vastly different from the Japanese he had known a decade earlier in Japan. While retaining much of their culture, they were increasingly Americanized and, like most immigrant groups, believed intensely in the United States and its vision of a better life." Kenneth Ringle Jr., *Washington Post*, "What Did You Do Before the War, Dad?" December 6, 1981.

memorized to keep light to a minimum, with each careful step taken toward the consul general's office. The safecracker uses his criminal skill to quickly access the safe holding classified communications and is already being escorted back to prison as Ringle's agents unload the contents.

They photograph each item, page by page, before putting everything back in place. Then they step back into the night, a treasure trove of raw intel in a bag.[4]

# ALEXANDER YOUNG HOTEL

## HONOLULU
## JUNE 11, 1941

Captain Irving Mayfield unlocks the door to the Black Room and steps inside, seeing Douglas Wada turn to greet him. "Anything good?"

The translator motions at the transcripts from the intercepted telephone conversations. "No, sir. Lots of routine stuff, some secretaries ordering taxis to the usual places. I have to say, they seemed most interested in where to find prostitutes in town."

"They can't go upstairs in Chinatown like everyone else?"[5]

"They want to know which geisha houses here are actually whorehouses," Wada says awkwardly. "In Japan, the difference is clear. Here . . ."

Mayfield nods. "Not as clear. Anything about the higher-ups? Kita or the vice-consul, Okuda?"

---

4. Kenneth Ringle Jr., interview with authors, and writing for the *Washington Post*, "What Did You Do Before the War, Dad?" December 6, 1981. https://www.washingtonpost.com/archive/lifestyle/magazine/1981/12/06/what-did-you-do-before-the-war-dad/a80178d5–82e6–4145-be4c-4e14691bdb6b/.

5. Chinatown had become Honolulu's red-light district well before 1941. Sex workers registered with the city as "entertainers," and most worked in second-floor brothels, hence the slang "go upstairs" for finding one for the evening.

"Just more gossip about Kita and the maid. The pair are still meeting in secret, except everyone at the consulate seems to know it."

Mayfield sighs. The tryst between the consul general and the maid is, so far, the biggest discovery from the risky phone surveillance operation that he inherited. "Write up whatever you've got, and I'll send it to the FBI; maybe Shivers will do the same if their taps are ever approved," he says, then leans on a desk. "I could have used some good news today. We heard from General Short. He and the secretary of war agree: no prosecution of Japanese consular agents."

Wada groans. "But they're spying on the fleet. There's a guy taking pictures of the damned fleet from a tea house in Alewa Heights."[6]

"Short thinks it'll hurt Nisei recruitment in the Army," Mayfield says sourly. This is something he and Wada both support, but neither feel the arrests are likely to prevent a patriotic young man from donning a uniform. "And word from the State Department is that there are too many American diplomats around the world in harm's way to risk retaliation. Arresting or deporting Japanese citizens working at the consulate has been deemed too provocative. Especially if all we have them doing is going to public places to take pictures at scenic overlooks."

"So it's okay because it's *legal* espionage."

The captain spreads his hands in hopeless agreement and straightens. "What can I say, they're being smart. We'll do what we're supposed to: keep an eye on the consulate staff until the shooting starts. After that, we'll be free to round them up before they can make any trouble." Then he grins. "Besides, I may have a hand to play before then," he says before walking out.

Mayfield is pursuing an angle to read the cable communications to and from the consulate. (He's largely out of the loop on higher-classified intercepts, which largely stay in DC.) But tapping these poses a tricky

---

6. Wada told the MIS Veterans Club of Hawaii interviewers that Yoshikawa was known to intelligence agencies. "We knew every time he went to Alewa Heights. He went to Natsunoya [Japanese Tea House] and took pictures. We couldn't stop him." The Army and FBI reportedly surveilled Yoshikawa, as per an article in the *Intelligencer: Journal of US Intelligence Studies*, Winter-Spring 2020.

challenge, chiefly because it's illegal. The Japanese Consulate rotates its business among the several cable companies in Honolulu, and every company has refused to violate any legal statutes.

Only one of them, Radio Corporation of America, has agreed to help—after Mayfield cornered RCA president David Sarnoff in person while he was on vacation here and pressured him into granting permission.[7]

But he'll have to be patient. RCA's turn handling the consular cables doesn't start for another five months, on December 1.

# MCKINLEY HIGH SCHOOL

## HONOLULU
## JUNE 13, 1941

Swelling patriotic music fills the auditorium, the Royal Hawaiian Band filling the space with a rendition of "America the Beautiful." There are two thousand voices singing as a chorus, a crowd of young Japanese Americans jammed into McKinley High School.

People in Honolulu have called McKinley "Tokyo High" since the 1920s. The majority of Nisei in Hawaii attend the public school here; it's more responsible for the Americanization of Japanese Hawaiians than any other institution besides the city's movie theaters.

Today's rally is the work of the Oahu Citizens Committee for Home Defense, a new group formed to promote patriotism on the island. The committee is led by Dr. Shunzo Sakamaki, a University of Hawaii teacher. He's been at the forefront of the Japanese loyalty movement in Oahu, forming aid groups to assist dual citizens to renounce their Japanese citizenship and promoting student military service.

---

7. Described in the eight-hundred-page Clausen Report. *Report of Investigation by Lt. Colonel, Henry C. Clausen, JAGD, for the Secretary of War, Supplementary to Proceedings of the Army Pearl Harbor Board* (Washington, DC: United States Government Printing Office, 1946).

Behind the scenes, Sakamaki is one of six Nisei leaders who meets Shivers to advise the FBI on domestic security. He endorses incarceration of Shinto and Buddhist priests in the event of war, citing elements of emperor worship in their rituals. He himself is Christian, rare even among the Nisei in Hawaii.

"This meeting is not an end in itself," Sakamaki tells the crowd. "It's a step toward the goal of complete national unity, preparedness and security." If war comes, he adds, "we will do everything we possibly can, giving our lives if necessary, in defense of those democratic principles for which other Americans have lived and fought and died."

The outreach that produced this display at McKinley would not have been possible if not for Masaji Marumoto, whose relationship with Shivers has developed into a close personal one. Their families vacation together, and Shivers makes sure to invite other government officials to meet the charming attorney. Marumoto makes connections with the military intelligence apparatus amid dinners in Hawaii and bouts of bridge. One of the people he meets through Shivers is Col. Morrill Marston, the new assistant chief of staff for military intelligence for the Hawaiian Department.[8]

The FBI man also gains connections. Marumoto has introduced him to a wide swath of his community, and it's borne fruit in the form of patriotic citizen groups like the Oahu Citizens Committee for Home Defense, formed earlier this year. The committee's seventy-five directors, men and women, meet with Shivers or other FBI agents once a week. One goal of the group, Shivers says, is "to prepare the Japanese community psychologically for their responsibilities toward this country in the event of war, and for the difficult position in which the war would place them."

The group's publicly stated purpose is to "promote racial cooperation, unity and unswerving loyalty to the United States." That message is certainly on display at the McKinley rally, with each speech and song.

---

8. Dennis M. Ogawa, *First Among Nisei: The Life and Writings of Masaji Marumoto* (Honolulu: University of Hawaii Press, 2007).

To speak for the US government, Colonel Marston takes the stage. He praises the Japanese community, especially those who have joined the military, and promises that the Army will "back fair treatment of all the population in Hawaii" even in the event of conflict with Japan. "Trust breeds trust. If we in authority are to expect loyalty from our citizens of Japanese ancestry, we must give them our trust in turn," he says. "In return for support, you citizens have the right to expect that your government and its armed services will do all in their power to give you the security of your liberties. Together, we cannot fail."

News of the rally is carried across the islands and the nation. It's a high point of Nisei patriotism in Hawaii, and those in the crowd act on the emotion it inspires. As a direct offshoot of the rally at McKinley, multiple small community advisory groups form to promote unity. A "Speak English" campaign begins, aimed at replacing Japanese characters on public signs and businesses.

Most interestingly, more than a hundred Nisei youth volunteer to serve in the reserve force of the Honolulu Police Department. Shivers and his brain trust, Sakamaki and Marumoto among them, huddle to decide what to do with this opportunity.

Their best point of contact within the Honolulu Police Department is John Burns. He was a patrol and vice veteran when Chief William Gabrielson picked him to establish the department's first Espionage Bureau in December 1940. He found the rumors of sabotage and subversion blown out of proportion, a vantage he shares with anyone who'll listen. Now he can help demonstrate the loyalty of the population in an undeniable way.

Behind closed doors, the group of Nisei and lawmen decide to organize the volunteers under the umbrella of something called the Police Contact Group. The reserves can be trained and readied for wartime duties, like traffic control and disaster response. Burns even has the perfect go-between to help run the program: Yoshio Hasegawa. One of the few police officers of Japanese ancestry on the entire force, he's worked his way up to lieutenant.

The committee is also a surveillance apparatus. By the time of the rally, the Honolulu Field Office has developed 172 confidential informers, seventy-three of whom are reporting on the activities of fellow Japanese residents. The Contact Group is to expand that network by reporting information on "Japan and her agents" via established contacts with beat cops in Japanese neighborhoods.

The third aspect of the Contact Group is a way to disseminate propaganda, or as Shivers puts it, information for "the protection of persons of their race from those who would prey on them due to their ignorance." Having Nisei self-police their own community is effective for the FBI, but it also subjects the earlier generation of traditional Japanese Hawaiians to extreme pressure to conform. Socially, the Issei are being sacrificed to stave off something worse.

For the Contact Group and its supporters, there is a greater good being served. With each informant, public rally, closed-door meeting and newspaper article, Shivers is doing more than inoculating the populace from foreign influence. He's building a case for Japanese loyalty to argue before the authorities in Washington, DC, including his boss and confidant, J. Edgar Hoover.

# FORT SHAFTER

## HONOLULU
## JULY 9, 1941

Gen. Walter Short reads the report on his desk with gritted teeth. It's the nature of the military to evaluate its own, but his steady rise has no black marks on it. But now there's this special inspector's report, detailing his deficiencies.

Such an official drubbing is unfamiliar to the Illinois native. Short earned his commission in the US Army in 1902 and fought in the Great War on the general staff of the 1st Division, as well as an assistant chief of staff for the Third Army. After the war ended, Short spent years stationed at Fort Hamilton in New York City before General George Marshall promoted him to head of the Army's Hawaiian command. He and his wife, Isabel, packed up and moved to paradise in February 1941.

Since then, things have gone downhill with Japan, and war is the most likely outcome. Yet the report charges that his command is not ready for "the possibility at any time . . . [of] an abrupt conflict with Japan." It also cites "the immediate need for positive preparations to prevent the success of predictable acts of planned and ordered sabotage." The report even takes a shot at Hawaii itself and "the carefree sense of easy control born in the isolation of a tropical island garrisoned by large forces."

The charge of laxity is galling. Short's mandate here is training. Preparing draftees and unblooded Americans for combat is a steep challenge, one made more daunting by the accumulating battle experience of the more modern Japanese military. He and Admiral Husband Kimmel are both playing catch-up, and the race consumes their time and attention. To both senior leaders of the Army and Navy, radar is an afterthought, of more use to track inbound B-17s than to guard against an impossible attack from Japan.

Lt. Col. H. S. Burwell, the special inspector and author of the report, knows the Army facilities and their people well. He served as commanding officer of Wheeler Field from April 1940 until that November, when he was assigned the same position with the 14th Pursuit Wing at Fort Shafter. When he receives his orders to become special inspector of the Hawaiian Air Force in July 1941, Burwell moves his headquarters to Hickam Field. He clearly works better when close to airplanes.

Burwell's report chronicles lagging morale within the Army's counterintelligence office. There is "relative inattention accorded in peacetime to intelligence functions, as compared to that given to operations and supply functions." *Well, no kidding*, Short thinks. Combat and well-oiled logistics are the things that win wars, and these skill sets are sorely lacking in the US military.

Short sees the damning document as the handiwork of the local intelligence officers; they're even credited under the section "Appreciations," where Burwell expresses thanks "for the advice of Lieutenant Colonel Bicknell, Assistant G-2, Hawaiian Department, and of Mr. Shivers, Federal Bureau of Investigation." The gripes of the counterintelligence community have found a sympathetic ear.

Stung by Burwell's assessment, Short takes some steps to tighten his operation. His biggest effort is to order his airplanes at the Oahu airfields to line up, wingtip to wingtip, to make it harder for a saboteur on land to attack them. This positioning makes them vulnerable to aerial attack, but Short sees the bigger risk stemming from ethnic Japanese living on the island.

However, widespread fear of the Japanese population doesn't seem justified by the intelligence experts. The month after Burwell's report lands on Short's desk, Assistant Attorney General Norman Littell arrives from DC to assess the "Japanese problem" in Hawaii with his own eyes. He reports, "The head of the FBI, military authorities, lawyers, judges and others confirmed that the great mass of the Japanese would not go back to Japan if they could; are fearful of Japanese intervention; and that only a small minority of them, who are being watched and are allegedly detectable, would be Japanese fifth columnists."

Annoyed by the disparate reporting in Hawaii, President Roosevelt demands some centralization of the investigations into Japanese subversion there. The Army, Navy and FBI heads are forced to hash out a "delimitation agreement" to govern the effort. They get nowhere. By September, Roosevelt ends the stagnating debate by simply placing the FBI in charge of coordinating all their activities involved with "ascertaining the location, leadership, strength and organization" of all civilian groups suspected of possible dangerous activity.

In Hawaii, Shivers makes concrete steps to increase cooperation. Most visibly, he moves his growing FBI operation from the Dillingham Transportation Building to the less swanky Federal Building. His G-men take up rooms on the third floor, one above the US Army intelligence operations. For his part, Army Lieutenant Colonel Bicknell moves into the Navy office at the Alexander Young Hotel.

Shivers organizes weekly intelligence conferences where local representatives meet to discuss their investigations and propose joint operations. Shivers, Bicknell and Mayfield start a tradition of weekly breakfasts together. It's a slow-building trust. One later CIA analysis reads: "Despite Shivers's lack of confidence in their capabilities, the Territory's Naval intelligence officers possessed a strong feeling of self-confidence and clearly wanted an equal, if not larger, role in local counterespionage activities. On a purely local level, the sharing of evidence is precisely what had happened."[9]

In late spring Shivers receives a new list: the names of 135 more Japanese residents who are willing to serve as FBI "listening posts." It's another gift from his contacts generated by the attorney Masaji Marumoto. This is the kind of news Shivers is eager to tell Hoover: there are Japanese Americans in Hawaii actively involved in protecting the United States.

The professionals are looking for sedition among the population and finding only a handful of foreign spies. Whether the politicians of the Roosevelt administration are listening to this fact is yet to be seen.

# SPRINGWOOD, ON THE ROOSEVELT ESTATE

### HYDE PARK, NY
### JULY 25, 1941

The handful of reporters file into the study at Springwood, walking across the carpet, past the plush seats and cold fireplace where Roosevelt

---

9. "Intelligence Lessons from Pearl Harbor," CIA Document Number 0006122443, accessed via CIA's Freedom of Information Act Reading Room: https://www.cia.gov/readingroom /document/0006122443.

addresses the nation in personal, effective radio broadcasts.[10] They cluster around the desk where the president of the United States is seated, lamplight illuminating the tools of his trade—a telephone, pens, books and an ashtray.

The home here at Hyde Park is FDR's refuge from Washington, DC. He was born in the building, planned his political campaigns from here and has used it to host dignitaries, including Winston Churchill. It's also well-suited to the man's paralyzing illness of polio and is even outfitted with an elevator so he can access the upper floors.

The reporters are here for an 11:30 a.m. press conference. They're eager for word of FDR's response to Japan's seizure of French Indochina. The Vichy government in Paris handed over the territory, which will literally fuel the Empire's goal of dominating Southeast Asia.

FDR's men at Hyde Park have been floating the idea of an executive order that freezes all Japanese assets in the United States. But when pressed, the president demurs. "There will be something out of Washington tomorrow," he tells them, feeling the waves of frustration from the assemblage.

His decision has already been made, and the order to seize all Japanese assets is already prepared for his signature, but FDR has more work to do before going public. He'll spend his day coordinating with the British and Canadians so that each nation can take the provocative step at the same time.

It's a drastic action that will cost Japan access to three-fourths of its overseas trade and 88 percent of its imported oil. With reserves of only three years, FDR's move is meant to deter the Japanese from more expansion.

Navy intelligence officials see Japanese banks operating in America coordinating with Tokyo to prepare. "Through confidential sources it was learned that on July 25, 1941, cash funds amounting to $180,000 were allotted by the management of the Yokohama Specie Bank in San Francisco to its officers and employees, most of whom are Japanese

---

10. From FDR's Daily Log: "11:10am, Press Conf. PC#758, Hyde Park, NY, Study."

nationals," reads another ONI report. "This move appears to have been made in order to prevent total loss of funds through seizure by the US government in time of war."

In Hawaii, the news is cause for alarm, particularly among the Issei. Military intelligence agents (presumably including Gero Iwai) monitor the panicked reaction. One Army intelligence memo in August 1941 notes "excitement and apprehension became strikingly evident" but that "apprehension is of a financial nature more than anything else." Agents chart withdrawals of about $300,000 from the Sumitomo Bank and $40,000 each from the Pacific Bank and the Yokohama Specie Bank the day after FDR's announcement. Many Issei are also trying to transfer land titles and bank deposits to their children.[11]

The August memo describes a fatalism that is settling into the Nisei and Issei alike. "In spite of the tense America-Japan relations, the Japanese here manifested very slight excitement and apprehension and remained practically unmoved," it reads. "They have been imbued by local Japanese press with the idea that the international situation between these two powers was getting better . . . and because they have been given assurances frequently that they will be treated fairly by the constituted authorities if they act properly. However, they lost this optimistic view when the freeze order was announced and started to harbor the feeling that a clash between America and Japan is imminent."[12]

One Issei who doesn't submit to the panic is Hisakichi Wada. Whether it's hopefulness or stubbornness, he keeps his savings in the Yokohama Specie Bank's Honolulu branch, the largest Japanese bank in Hawaii.[13] And for the moment, his faith is rewarded. When FDR announces the seizures of Japanese government property, its Hawaii accounts remain untouched.

But hopes to deter Japan quickly fade. Tokyo's immediate response to Roosevelt's executive order is to occupy Saigon.

---

11. "Memorandum For Col. Bicknell, Subject: Local Japanese Situation During the Period 26–31 July 1941," US Army, August 1941.
12. Ibid.
13. *The Honolulu Advertiser*, November 10, 1949.

# CAVITE LISTENING POST

### PHILIPPINES
### SEPTEMBER 24, 1941

[Intercepted Message]
From: Teijiro Toyoda, Minister for Foreign Affairs, Tokyo
To: Japanese Consul General Kita in Honolulu

Henceforth, we would like to have you make reports concerning vessels along the following lines insofar as possible: The waters [of Pearl Harbor] are to be divided roughly into five subareas . . . With regard to warships and aircraft carriers, we would like to have you report on those at anchor (these are not so important), tied up at wharves, buoys and in docks. Designate types and classes briefly. If possible, we would like to have you make mention of the fact when there are two or more vessels alongside the same wharf.

The encrypted instructions, sent in code used for important diplomatic traffic, don't light the intelligence community on fire. Missives like this one have been sent to Japanese agents throughout the world before, to places like the Panama Canal, Philippines, and the West Coast of the United States.

The intercept heads to Washington, DC, as per protocol, but none of this information is communicated to Pearl Harbor. The Army, Navy and FBI investigators in Hawaii are never told the message was sent.[14]

Toyoda's request to the consulate in Honolulu isn't routine nor

---

14. *Proceedings of H. Kent Hewitt Inquiry on Pearl Harbor Attack, 1941*, in the Hearings Before the Joint Committee on the Pearl Harbor Attack, S. Doc. No.79–27 (1946). Via http://www.ibiblio .org/pha/pha/hewitt/hewitt-3.html. Edwin Layton's book, *And I Was There*, contains a solid summary of what happened. Officials in Washington were reading the highest-level Japanese diplomatic code, designated Purple, but almost none of it was ever made available to the field commanders (except Gen. Douglas MacArthur). This left the most incriminating information to and from the consulate in Honolulu out of the hands of the people who could have used it most.

innocuous. He's asking for a grid to plot the location of ships in the harbor, a plea to help plan an aerial attack.

# NIKKO RESTORATION SANITARIUM

### HONOLULU
### OCTOBER 4, 1941

Robert Glover bows to Tadashi Morimura, the newest member of the Dai Nippon Butoku Kai kendo club.

Glover, although born in California in 1915, is a hometown guy. He attended Punahou School and the University of Hawaii, where he developed a record of both science and martial interests. He built a homemade telescope as a high school student and was an accomplished competitive rifle marksman. Glover's also currently a naval reservist who works with the Office of the Cable and Radio Censor.[15]

Glover is still dedicated to Japanese martial arts, and the gymnasium of the Nikko Restoration Sanitarium is one of the world's best places for a Caucasian to pursue it. It was founded in 1929 by Seishiro "Henry" Okazaki, one of the first to break from tradition and teach his nation's martial arts to non-Japanese students.[16] Glover has been training under Okazaki since 1934 and has risen in stature enough to conduct classes.

Kendo, the Japanese martial art of wooden sword fencing, came to Hawaii in 1868, practiced by samurai among the immigrants recruited to work the sugar plantations. (The group is known as the *Gannenmono*.) The martial art's popularity spread and endured, both as an athletic pursuit and an expression of Japanese identity. By 1940 the Japan-based Dai Nippon Butoku Kai had opened a branch in Hawaii, with a membership of around 3,500.

---

15. *Proceedings of H. Kent Hewitt Inquiry on Pearl Harbor Attack, 1941,* via the Hearings Before the Joint Committee on the Pearl Harbor Attack, S. Doc. No.79–27 (1946).
16. As a teenager, Okazaki beat tuberculosis by practicing intense judo and dedicated his life to its practice. He's also a legendary masseur: when Franklin D. Roosevelt came to the Islands in the '30s, Okazaki massaged him.

Morimura is the newest member. He's introduced by a club member from Maui, George Hamamoto, who has been on a quest to recruit seasoned kendo practitioners. Hamamoto tells Glover the young Japanese man just arrived in Hawaii three months ago, works at the consulate and is an experienced kendo man. The prospective member stands quietly, speaking in broken English but mostly watching the conversation keenly.

When it comes time to don the armor and spar, Glover sees another side of Morimura. Glover, left-handed and experienced, is facing a confident, lifetime kendo student. The wooden swords clack together, and the naval reservist is caught off guard by the power of his opponent's chopping blows. The Hawaii school's fighting style features short, rapid thrusts, striking often but without much power. Morimura relies on heavy strokes meant to deliver force—and damage.

It's an aggressive style that the consulate employee defends as superior, saying that "it proved best during the China incident." Glover is too polite to correct him by calling it an invasion, war and massacre. As they speak, holding their *bōgu* training gear, he notices the tip of one of Morimura's fingers is missing.

Glover is the top-ranking Caucasian in the kendo club, but he's not the only one: naval reservist Ted Fielding and Harold Schnack, a junior draftsman at the Navy Yard, are fellow classmates. The pair heads over to the sparring men. "Your friends?" asks Morimura. He shows his more diplomatic side when he meets each in turn, asking earnest questions about their families, education and jobs.

Over time, despite his disdain for the local style, Morimura starts to become just another face at the kendo club. Familiarity comes with an offer for friendship: the young diplomat shares stories of fun times with the many available women he knows from the consulate. Before too long, Morimura invites Glover and Fielding to join him at such a party; the Americans turn the offer down politely.[17]

---

17. *Proceedings of H. Kent Hewitt Inquiry on Pearl Harbor Attack, 1941,* via the Hearings Before the Joint Committee on the Pearl Harbor Attack, S. Doc. No.79–27 (1946).

# ALEWA HEIGHTS

## HONOLULU
## OCTOBER 11, 1941

Takeo Yoshikawa sits on a straw mat at the Shunchoro Tea House, gaze fixed on the lights of Pearl Harbor visible from the window. The first rays of dawn are starting to brighten the sky, and ship sorties from the port have just begun. The agent IDs the ships preparing to move, and by now he knows their basic deployment patterns and even the names of most of the officers onboard.[18]

The lady who owns the establishment, Taneyo Fujiwara, allows him to post up here through odd hours, drinking and watching the ships. And he doesn't have to ask for a place at the window anymore. The owner automatically seats him there.

The geisha girls, too, are cooperative without being overtly complicit. After a night of chatting up US servicemen, Yoshikawa gets a closing-time rundown. "I occasionally gleaned small bits of information—never with their connivance, however," he says. "It would have been too risky to confide in a woman, and, besides, the Japanese population of Hawaii we found essentially loyal to the United States."[19]

His alter ego, Tadashi Morimura, is getting a reputation at the consulate. He shows up around 11:00 a.m., doesn't do any perceptible work, and instead relishes his ability to wander Hawaii and run up bills. His fellow staffers don't appreciate it, but he also finds that the women at the consulate are attracted to island attitude and devil-may-care freedom.[20]

---

18. "My favorite viewing place was a lovely Japanese tea house overlooking the harbor. It was called 'Shunchoro.' I knew what ships were in, how heavily they were loaded, who their officers were, and what supplies were on board." Takeo Yoshikawa, *Japan's Spy at Pearl Harbor* (Jefferson, NC: McFarland, 2020).

19. Ibid.

20. "He was frequently drunk, often had women in his quarters overnight, came to work late or not at all, as he pleased, insulted the Consul General on occasions, and generally conducted himself as if he were beyond penalty." Report of Admiral H. Kent Hewitt to Secretary of Navy, July 12, 1945.

His relationship with his original contact, Third Secretary Seki, has fallen apart. Seki mistrusts and envies the dashing Morimura. They argued on the basics of the operation, with Seki advocating for recruiting more men to monitor other Hawaiian islands. Yoshikawa disagreed, seeing no reservoir of talent for this among the population. Vice-Consul Otojiro Okuda ended the debate in his own way: by ordering Seki to drop his involvement with the espionage effort.

New orders from Tokyo for freshly updated information on the fleet and local defenses have kept Yoshikawa busy. He feels like he's always on assignment: when he's walking the streets of Pearl City, practicing kendo, touring the island with a camera, picking up hitchhiking sailors or spending long nights at the tea house, watching the ships at Pearl Harbor.

Yoshikawa's taken up with a second consular secretary and owner of the Royal Taxi Stand, John Mikami, to keep from over-relying on Kotoshirodo. Mikami is a Japanese citizen whose contacts at the consulate trust him as a discreet driver. He figures out "Morimura's" priorities, and he's soon going out of his way to point out details of military significance.

He speaks lousy English and has little education, but Mikami is a natural when it comes to observing the fleet; he knows even more than Seki. Even better, the new driver enjoys mixing business with pleasure, and he helps recruit young women for their outings. Yoshikawa and Mikami had recently taken a consulate secretary, Sakae Tanaka, and her friend on a boat tour of Kaneohe Bay. Instead of peering through the glass-bottom hull, the men kept watch on the Naval Air Station's PBY Catalina seaplanes moored there.[21]

Mikami and Yoshikawa are confident to the point of recklessness. The driver once drives through the gates of Fort Shafter, the command headquarters of the US Army in Hawaii. They stroll around innocently before being asked to leave, which they do without giving any identification. Less productive—and not as daring—Yoshikawa also attends

---

21. Ibid.

religious meetings, where he rubs elbows with community leaders. "Those men of influence and character who might have assisted me in my secret mission were unanimously uncooperative," he says.[22]

Yoshikawa stays at the tea house until his eyes get heavy. Before he leaves Shunchoro for some sleep and tomorrow's bleary appearance at the consulate, Yoshikawa invites the geisha who's entertained him to join him on a tourist flight over the island. He wants to see the direction of the runways at Wheeler Airfield and count the hangars, and he could use some comely company. The young woman agrees, and their date is set for Monday, October 13.[23]

From: Harold Stark, Chief of Naval Operations
To: All Navy outposts in the Pacific
November 27, 1941

This dispatch is to be considered a war warning. Negotiations with Japan looking toward stabilization of the conditions in the Pacific have ceased and an aggressive move is expected with the next few days. The number and equipment of Japanese troops and the organization of the naval task forces indicates an amphibious expedition against either the Philippines, Thai, Kra Peninsula, or possibly Borneo. Execute an appropriate defensive deployment preparatory to carrying out the tasks assigned in War Plan 46 [the Navy's war plan]. Inform district and army authorities. A similar warning is being sent by the War Department.

Admiral Husband Kimmel reads the words "war warning" with genuine concern. It's unique language, and it indicates that fighting will start soon. And somewhere far away, apparently, since the warning doesn't list Hawaii among the possible targets.

22. Takeo Yoshikawa, *Japan's Spy at Pearl Harbor* (Jefferson, NC: McFarland, 2020).
23. Hearings Before the Joint Committee on the Pearl Harbor Attack, S. Doc. No.79–27 (1946).

However, like most commanders, he's grown numb to warnings from DC that never seem to prove true. Vice Admiral William Halsey calls them "wolf messages," cried too often to mean anything. As a result, in Hawaii the PBY seaplanes don't search the coastlines, the radar operators aren't briefed on the presence of a roaming Japanese expeditionary force and the military intelligence units aren't informed of the dispatch.

The day before, a Japanese strike fleet moved out of Hitokappu Bay, lights blackened and in total radio silence, now heading into heavy weather. It's a massive array of ships: six aircraft carriers, two heavy cruisers, thirty-five submarines, two light cruisers, nine oilers, two battleships and eleven destroyers. The carriers' target is Oahu.

# KALAMA BEACH

### OAHU
### NOVEMBER 28, 1941

Takeo Yoshikawa sets out in his sightseeing garb, first in a private taxi, then on foot. He's already aching from a day spent diving Mamala Bay to study submarine barriers at the entrance to Pearl Harbor. He didn't find them, despite long stretches spent swimming underwater to avoid being seen. It's been frustrating.

Since November 15, Yoshikawa has been trying to meet the demands of another cable delivered to him via the consulate. "As relations between Japan and the United States are most critical, make your 'ships in harbor report' irregular, but at a rate of twice a week. Although you already are no doubt aware, please take extra care to maintain secrecy."

Now, in seeming defiance of that last bit of advice, Yoshikawa's been tasked with delivering ten thousand dollars in cash to a Nazi spy.[24]

Consul General Kita has hired Otto Kuehn, a former German

---

24. Takeo Yoshikawa, *Japan's Spy at Pearl Harbor* (Jefferson, NC: McFarland, 2020).

military officer who lives in Honolulu, to spy on passing ships and nearby airbases for twenty thousand dollars. He's been on the consulate payroll before, delivering observations of the US Fleet between 1936 and 1939. Now the relationship is being reactivated.

It's not just information Kuehn is peddling, but a location. His two beach homes can be used to collect real-time information from the far side of the island. In the event of a war, the consulate is sure to be closed, and having a spy on the island would become more valuable.

Yoshikawa is here to deliver the spy his first payment, a stack of hundred-dollar bills in a cardboard envelope. He can still hear Kita's words when he handed over the cash: "Apart from you, I can't find anyone suitable to deal with this."

Yoshikawa arrives at and takes in Kuehn's two-story home. He must be a man of some means. The house sits on the beach, with a prominent, peaked dormer window facing the water. He can see the edge of a second, small building in the backyard.

A kid opens the door when he knocks.

"I am here to see your father," Yoshikawa says.

The eleven-year-old peers at the Japanese man intently for a moment, and Yoshikawa has the strange idea that he's being professionally examined. "One moment please," comes the reply, and the door closes.

The door opens and a broad but gaunt-faced man stands there, his son now nowhere to be seen. "I was in the back working in my garden."

"You are Otto Kuehn?" Yoshikawa asks brusquely.

"Yes," comes the reply. Kuehn's severely receded hairline and eyes set a little too far apart make him look like an aquatic predator.

"I have something for you from Dr. Homberg," Yoshikawa says, citing an alias previously used by Kuehn to launder money from the Japanese government.

"Come back to the garden house," the German responds.[25]

He's in the employ of the Nazis' Abwehr intelligence organization

---

25. Ibid.

and has scandalously close ties to Propaganda Minister Joseph Goebbels. Kuehn's daughter, Susie, was the media master's former mistress at age seventeen. Fearing Hitler's scorn, Goebbels arranges a faraway posting for the entire family.

The Kuehns have been in Hawaii since 1935. Kuehn's wife, Friedel, and her half brother, Hans Joachim, are also active spies here. Daughter Susie operates a beauty parlor—with the cheapest services in the city—and the wives of high-ranking military personnel spend hours there gossiping about their spouses' careers and deployments. At night, Susie romances US military personnel and gathers information about their jobs.

Young Hans, the Kuehns' son, is also an active member of the spy ring. The family dresses him as a US Navy sailor, and he walks the waterfront, drawing invitations to tour Navy ships. The young man would go aboard alone, trained to report on various items of interest.

This activity in Hawaii has already earned the family an investigation by the FBI. "The couple have large sums of money apparently at their command," says one memo to the FBI director, dated May 1, 1939. "They entertain frequently and lavishly, their guests are usually Army officers and their wives who are stationed at the various forts located within twenty-five miles of Honolulu and naval officers and their wives who are stationed at Pearl Harbor."

The conclusion in 1939 is damning: "It has been apparent for a long time that the purpose of this couple in their entertainment of Army and Navy personnel is to secure information regarding the secrets and movements of the Army and Navy."

The investigators seized the family's Honolulu bank records. There were seventy thousand dollars' worth of deposits between 1936 and 1939, but no one in the 14th District Intelligence Office could link the payments to the Kuehns' seeming attempts to collect information. For his part, the German claims he's enjoying a big inheritance. The money, carefully laundered, actually came from the Japanese Consulate and not the Abwehr.

Despite the near miss, Kuehn remains a bold opportunist. He sees the war clouds gathering, and a way to capitalize on them. In September 1941, he reaches out to General Kita at the Japanese Consulate, offering to be a set of eyes on the American forces.

In the garden house, Yoshikawa hands him the package and a letter from Kita. Kuehn pointedly opens the letter first, seeing typewritten words in English. "You know what this says?" Kuehn asks him.

He shakes his head, lying. It's a request to set up a shortwave transmitter at one of his homes and a date for a test transmission at a specific frequency. Yoshikawa has no desire to discuss these details with a stranger.

From the pinched and nervous look on Kuehn's face, the idea is dead on arrival. He scribbles a quick response by hand, slips it into the envelope and hands it back to the stoic Yoshikawa. "Give me some time and I'll bring in some alternatives."

"Not to me," Yoshikawa says, handing over the cardboard package holding the cash. "To Okuda."

"Do you know what's in here?" the German asks, now hefting the money. "Would you like a receipt?"

It's a borderline insult, reducing him to the status of an untrusted errand boy. "That won't be necessary, thank you," Yoshikawa says tightly, then motions to the typewritten, unsigned letter. "Please destroy that."[26]

On November 30, Kuehn delivers an envelope into the consulate with his secret communication scheme, as his wife waits in a running car. There are seventeen types of signals using bedsheets strung on clotheslines, lights in the windows of two different homes, flashing car headlights, particular flags flown on sailboat masts, all used in various combinations.

Okuda, Yoshikawa and Kita see right away that it's too complicated and ask for a revision. Kuehn's son delivers the details of a new system to Okuda on December 2. The system is now pared down to just eight codes: A light shining in the dormer window of the Oahu house from

---

26. Ibid, Yoshikawa. And "In the Matter of the Confinement of Bernard Otto Kuehn," Office of Military Governor, Territory of Hawaii, 1942, included as Exhibit 52 in the "Proceedings of the Army Pearl Harbor Board," which includes Kuehn's confession to the meeting.

9:00 to 10:00 P.M. means "carriers have sailed." A linen sheet hanging on a clothesline on Lanikai Beach between 10:00 and 11:00 a.m. means "battleship formation has left the harbor." And so on. There are also codes that can be inserted into newspaper classified ads, a clandestine communication system meant to hide in plain sight.[27]

The consulate now has surveillance outposts on the beaches of Lanikai and Kalema and a fail-safe spy network in place if the consulate is shut during a war. Kita sends word to Tokyo detailing the plan. Later that day, he receives a reply with even more mandates.

Cable Message to: Consul General Kita, Honolulu
From: Shigenori Tōgō, Minister of Foreign Affairs, Tokyo
December 2, 1941

In view of the present situation, the presence in port of warships, airplane carriers, and cruisers is of utmost importance. Hereafter, to the utmost of your ability, let me know day by day. Wire me in each case whether or not there are any observation balloons above Pearl Harbor or if there are any indications that they will be sent up. Also advise whether or not the warships are provided with anti-mine nets.[28]

# ALEXANDER YOUNG HOTEL

## HONOLULU
## DECEMBER 3, 1941

Captain Irving Mayfield cradles the phone to his ear and leaves a message for SAC Shivers at the Federal Building. One of his men heard a rumor

---

27. "In the Matter of the Confinement of Bernard Otto Kuehn," Office of Military Governor, Territory of Hawaii, 1942.
28. Hearings Before the Joint Committee on the Pearl Harbor Attack, S. Doc. No.79–27 (1946).

from an informant that the Japanese consul general in Honolulu is burning his papers; can he confirm it?

It's a call he wouldn't need to make until recently. But now that the FBI has tapped the consulate's phones, he's depending on their ears.

Mayfield doesn't know that the FBI's coverage is limited, as Shivers thinks the Navy has it covered. He and Shivers may have trust, but when it comes to eavesdropping on the consulate, coordination is currently lacking.

The effort fails from good intentions. In late November, Shivers learned that the Navy hadn't covered a phone line at the consulate, most often used by the cooks. He sends men to fill that gap, adding new wires to the already busy junction box.

Everything seemed fine until a telephone repairman arrived on a service call and saw a jumper wire from the FBI tap, opened the box and saw a nest of strange connections. He called his office, where a Navy contact tipped off Mayfield. He pulled the taps off the consulate on December 2, thinking that the FBI had its own taps on the consulate's phone lines.[29]

For Douglas Wada, it's the end of his personal window into life at the consulate. No great intelligence breakthroughs ever came from the Navy's tap, but he'll never again look at Kita's picture in the newspaper without imagining him secreting the maid into his quarters at night, thinking no one is noticing.

There are now twenty-five officers and thirty enlisted men at the 14th District Intelligence Office, yet Mayfield can't seem to keep up. In addition to running an intelligence organization, he's charged with recruiting and training all the personnel needed for radio and cable censorship. Complicating things, the new arrivals have little or no intelligence training. Support from

---

29. Shivers in the Clausen report to the 79th Congress: "The ONI, which for several years had covered what were supposed to be all telephone lines at the consulate, did not in fact cover one line to the cook's quarters; I therefore covered this line, which resulted in information as to the destruction by the consul of all his important papers on 3 December 1941, about which I have already testified that I assumed the ONI had all other lines covered up to and including 7 December 1941, and did not receive any information to the contrary until today, when it was stated that the coverage by ONI ceased on 2 December, 1941, at the order of the District Intelligence Officer; that had I known such ONI coverage had ceased, I would have caused FBI coverage in replacement."

the top remains lackluster. He endures frustrating meetings with Admiral Kimmel and General Short, who once called him "too intelligence-minded" to his face. The opportunity to pass off the high-risk, labor-intensive phone surveillance operation on the consulate was a welcome relief.

Three busy hours go by quickly, then the phone rings. It's Shivers, bearing news: an hour ago, the FBI intercepted a local telephone call from the cook at the Japanese Consulate saying that Consul General Kita is "burning and destroying all his important papers." Shivers adds that he's telegraphed Hoover with the news.

A grateful Mayfield hangs up, then tasks his own men to take a deeper look. He doesn't realize that Shivers confirmed the news by eaves-dropping on a phone conversation from the cook's quarters. Because the Navy never covered that phone, Shivers assumes that's the reason Mayfield missed it.[30]

By the day's end, his men report that Hawaii is not unique. A communiqué that day warned that Japanese diplomats in Washington, London, Hong Kong, Singapore and Manila were also burning their codes and documents.[31]

It's disturbing news for the counterintelligence operators in Honolulu, who must stand idly by as potential evidence goes up in smoke. At the same time, there's nothing specific that warns of an attack here.

Mayfield is still waiting for his gambit with RCA to pay off. Inside the consulate are reams of Kita's cables to and from Tokyo that he'll soon be able to read, at least the ones sent after December 1. However, the messages will arrive in code, and the ONI office doesn't have the ability

---

30. "The ONI, which for several years had covered what were supposed to be all telephone lines at the Consulate did not in fact cover one line to the cook's quarters; I therefore covered this line which resulted in information as to the destruction by the Consul of all his important papers on 3 December 1941, about which I have already testified that I assumed the ONI had all other lines covered up to and including 7 December 1941, and did not receive any information to the contrary until today, when it was stated that the coverage by ONI ceased on 2 December, 1941, at the order of the District Intelligence Officer; that had I known such ONI coverage had ceased, I would have caused FBI coverage in replacement." Robert Shivers testimony, *Proceedings of the Hart Inquiry*, April 13, 1944.

31. FBI Memo from December 6, 1941, "Proceedings of the Clausen Investigation," testimony to the US Congress delivered November 25, 1944.

to decipher it. The messages will have to be sent to Station Hypo for deciphering and translation.

It'll be two more days before Mayfield gets the first batch of cables and another week—December 11—before he will be able to read them.[32]

Office of Naval Intelligence

Washington, DC

December 4, 1941

Memo prepared by the Counter Subversion Section, Office of Naval Intelligence, from information received from various sources. Subject: JAPANESE INTELLIGENCE AND PROPAGANDA IN THE UNITED STATES DURING 1941.

Methods of Operation and Points of Attack

With tension growing between the United States and Japan, the Japanese Government decided its system for securing information was inadequate to meet a situation involving war. As early as February 1941 and coincident with the arrival of the new ambassador Admiral Kichisaburo Nomura, diplomatic and consular representatives were instructed to reorganize and strengthen the intelligence network in this country and to relax the former policy of "cultural propaganda and enlightenment."

Designed to continue in operation, even in the event diplomatic and commercial relations between the two countries were severed, an intelligence machine geared for war was put into operation . . . . The focal point of the Japanese

---

32. "Proceedings of the Clausen Investigation," testimony to the US Congress delivered April 13, 1944. "Q: Were copies of the messages transmitted by the Japanese Consulate General by cable or radio made available to your organization? Mayfield: They were not, until after the visit of Mr. Sarnoff, of the Radio Corporation of America. The Japanese Consul General sent its traffic using the various communication companies alternately. The Mackay Radio Company, according to my recollection, handled the traffic during the month of November; traffic was switched to the Radio Corporation of America as of December 1, 1941. Thereafter, I was able to obtain all of his traffic from R. C. A., but since it was all in code and I had no reading organization, it was necessary to submit this traffic to another organization to be read."

Espionage effort is the determination of the total strength of the United States. In anticipation of possible open conflict with this country, Japan is vigorously utilizing every available agency to secure military, naval and commercial information, paying particular attention to the West Coast, the Panama Canal and the Territory of Hawaii.[33]

# FEDERAL BUILDING

## HONOLULU
## DECEMBER 4, 1941

SAC Robert Shivers picks up his pen and regards the report he's about to sign, ready for Hoover himself. It contains 347 names of Hawaiians to be arrested if a war begins. All but nine are Issei "enemy aliens." The majority of those on the FBI- and Army-created pickup list are innocent of sedition, and Shivers knows it. But it's the best he can do and still fulfill his mandate to protect the nation from possible harm.

He signs the document and sends it to DC. Afterward, he asks John Burns, now the Honolulu police's acting chief, to visit the office for a discreet conversation. The policeman finds Shivers's face is grim. "Nothing I'm hearing gives me any hope. I think a Japanese attack in the Pacific will come within the week."

Burns doesn't reply, his own worst fears being confirmed by a well-connected federal agent. "I'm asking you to check all your best sources for any sign of suspicious activity. Anything. Strange boats, people using shortwaves, neighbors saying . . ."

Burns is listening, but his eyes are becoming moist. The police officer shakes his head but only says, "I'll look into it."

The next day, Hoover responds to Shivers: the pickup list is not only

---

33. "Japanese Intelligence and Propaganda in the US During 1941," declassified memo prepared by the Counter Subversion Section, Office of Naval Intelligence, December 4, 1941.

approved, the SAC should start preparing a joint FBI, police and military operation to make the arrests as soon as war is declared.

From: Consul General Kita, Honolulu
To: Shigenori Tōgō, Minister of Foreign Affairs, Tokyo
December 6, 1941

. . . investigations have been made in the neighborhood of Pearl Harbor, they have not set up mooring equipment, nor have they selected the troops to man them. Furthermore, there is no indication that any training for the maintenance of balloons is being undertaken. At present time there are no signs of barrage balloon equipment. In addition, it is difficult to imagine that they have actually any. However, even though they have actually made preparations, because they must control the air over the water and land runways of the airports in the vicinity of Pearl Harbor, Hickham, Ford, and Ewa, there are limits to the balloon defense of Pearl Harbor. I imagine that in all probability there is considerable opportunity left to take advantage for a surprise attack against these places. In my opinion the battleships do not have torpedo nets.

# PACIFIC OCEAN

## TEN MILES FROM PEARL HARBOR'S ENTRANCE
## DECEMBER 7, 1941

Ensign Kazuo Sakamaki[34] and Petty Officer Second Class Kiyoshi Inagaki feel the world tilt as their seventy-eight-foot-long submarine

---

34. US documents also list him as a "sub-lieutenant," which was between ensign and lieutenant in the Japanese Navy in World War II. In Sakamaki's memoir *I Attacked Pearl Harbor*, he gives his rank as ensign.

detaches from the hull of its mothership, a larger sub called 1–24. The two men are cramped inside a five-foot-wide hull of HA-19, a *Ko-Hyoteki* "midget" submarine. Now they're reeling as it nearly capsizes during its first moments of free sailing.

"Something's wrong with the trim," Sakamaki says to Inagaki after the mini-submarine rights itself. "You'll have to dump some of the ballast." There are lead weights for that very purpose stashed in the aft, and the teenage Inagaki starts to crawl to the rear of the sub.

It's midnight, just turned December 7. If all goes well, Sakamaki can expect to die gloriously before midday. He just turned twenty-three years old in November.

Sakamaki is one of ten sailors—evenly divided between young officers and petty officers, none of them volunteers—selected to attack the US battleships in Pearl Harbor with a flotilla of five mini-submarines. The battery-powered *Ko-Hyotekis* can navigate waters too shallow for conventional submarines, making them ideal for this secret mission. Or so the designers say—these are untested and experimental warships.

Inside the cabin, the crews have food, wine and maps of the harbor, including the names of the ships at each berth. The information has come from a spy working in the consulate in Honolulu—they don't know the name "Yoshikawa," but they're grateful to him. The information on the map was supplemented by the spy's latest report, the final one before the attack, delivered by radio on December 5 while the minisubs were still on board their parent submarine.[35]

The mission of all five minisubs is to sneak into the harbor and hide there until waves of Japanese fighters and bombers attack. Only then will they launch their two 1,000-pound torpedoes at the battleships moored there. This is not strictly a suicide mission—there is a

---

35. "If the Japanese maintained radio silence, how were these messages received? Radio silence doesn't include high and low frequency radio broadcasts to and from Imperial Naval Headquarters and Admiral Yamamoto. These so-called Tokyo Fleet broadcasts are designed to not give away the fleet's position, and hide the new messages amid old, useless broadcasts." Lieutenant Commander Philip H. Jacobsen, USN (Ret.), *Naval History Magazine*, vol. 17, December 2003.

rendezvous established in the waters outside of the small Hawaiian island of Lanai, and crews are issued escape and evasion maps of Oahu—but it is extremely high risk. The idea of dying in Hawaii has been instilled in the crews of the Third Submarine Squadron since they were chosen for the mission; having multiple siblings is a criterion. And Sakamaki is one of eight sons.[36]

He tries to put his family out of his mind. When they parted on November 18, Sakamaki felt torn apart. His parents and friends kept saying how proud they were, but he couldn't look them in their faces. Even now, the thought of never seeing home again nearly overpowers him.[37]

Death is more certain for himself and Inagaki than the eight other submariners in this secret flotilla. Before launching, submarine Captain Hakusa Hanabusa told him that the gyrocompass of H-19 wasn't working.

"Ensign Sakamaki, what do you want to do?" the captain asked.

"Captain, I am going ahead," came his immediate reply.

"On to Pearl Harbor!" the captain responded, pleased.

Now that he's in the water, the reality of his situation threatens his martial resolve. The submarine can't surface for fear of being detected. Nor can he truly steer without his gyrocompass. When he surfaces just long enough to risk a glimpse through his telescope, he's horrified to see they're going in the wrong direction, away from the lights of Honolulu. *Heaven,* he thinks, *is not on our side.*[38]

Sakamaki submerges and tries to readjust his course, fighting the rising fear of failure. He can only hope the other four minisubs in the squadron are faring better in their approach to Oahu, because it's too late to turn back. The attack on Pearl Harbor has begun.

---

36. Kazuo Sakamaki, *I Attacked Pearl Harbor* (Honolulu: Rollston Press, 2017). He identifies his squadron and submarine as A-24.
37. Ibid.; these are the words he used to describe his emotions.
38. Ibid.

# PART 5

# TWO WAVES

# JAPANESE AIRCRAFT CARRIER *AKAGI*

## PACIFIC OCEAN
## DECEMBER 7, 1941

Captain Minoru Genda is an avid customer of the intelligence gathered by Japanese spies in Hawaii, but he's never waited for a dispatch from them of such importance. This predawn report will be the last intelligence report from Honolulu, routed to them through the consulate. The details, delivered via coded messages from Tokyo scant hours before the operation starts, are just two days old.[1]

It's been a long road for Genda, one that's taken him from the family farm to the skies of an acrobatic military demonstration team and to England as an observer during the Battle of Britain. Now he's on the dark bridge of the flagship carrier of the Japanese strike force heading toward Hawaii, on the eve of a historic attack.

The *Akagi* is familiar to him—he served here as a pilot in 1931—but the circumstances are profoundly unique. What the Japanese Navy is now trying has never been done before, and much of the planning has been done by Genda himself.

He and Admiral Yamamoto have known each other since 1933, when they served together aboard the carrier *Ryūjō*. That was the same year that Genda started studying, on his own time, ways to attack the

---

1. See note above regarding this exception to the strike force's radio silence. Not only is it securely coded, but it's also not possible for the Allies to determine directional bearings from these transmissions.

US base at Pearl Harbor by air. Part of it was the professional challenge it represented—a remote target considered untouchable by warplanes.

In early 1941, when Yamamoto shared his overall plan to attack the base with a cadre of trusted officers, he tasked Genda with figuring out some of the thorniest technical details. Genda was responsible for training pilots on dropping new shallow-water torpedoes (a Japanese innovation involving breakaway wooden fins) and the virtues of level-bombing by tactical aircraft (lessons gleaned from fighting in Europe). He was an early advocate for a three-wave attack, with the third aimed at the farms of crude oil tanks and military repair facilities.

Now, after years of conjecture and months of hard work and intense planning, it's nearly time to launch. But what will they find when the warplanes arrive? That's hopefully what Admiral Chuichi Nagumo, the task force's commander, has read from the report from the operatives in Hawaii.

Nagumo reads the message aloud: "Vessels moored in harbor: nine battleships; three class B cruisers; three seaplane tenders, seventeen destroyers. Entering harbor are four class B cruisers; three destroyers. All aircraft carriers and heavy cruisers have departed harbor. No indication of any changes in US Fleet of anything unusual."

The news is unwelcome—it would have been ideal to unleash the dive-bombers on the carriers' vulnerable decks. Indeed, Genda secretly hopes the admiral will focus more deadly attention on the base's infrastructure and oil storage facilities now that the carriers are out of reach.

To the dismay of Genda—and Admiral Yamamoto—Nagumo seems uninterested in hitting the infrastructure that would cause long-term damage to the naval base. His priority targets are the battleships, which have status as the dominant weapons of naval warfare. If Japan strikes them hard enough, the Pacific Fleet can be called "crippled" and the American will to fight in the Pacific will be broken.

The intelligence from the spies in Hawaii is transformed into orders for the pilots. As other planes hit the airfields across Oahu, the first wave of attacking torpedo bombers is ordered to focus on the choice targets lined up along Battleship Row.

# KAMA LANE

### HONOLULU
### DECEMBER 7, 1941

Sunday morning for Douglas Wada is meant for fishing. He heads to Pearl Harbor nearly every weekend, joined by friends and family. He goes so often that he stashes a bait box of live shrimp beneath Pier 2.

Today's plan was supposed to be picking up the day's live shrimp at five o'clock, with plenty of time to meet up with two friends to fish *papio*, a juvenile ulua. But when Wada gets there, the bait box is gone.

Meeting back at Wada's house, the friends are disappointed but not deterred. They decide to buy California shrimp for bait and drive Wada's car to the beaches of Diamond Head, five miles away.

The trio leaves Kama Lane at 7:00 a.m. Just because the day started off on the wrong foot, that doesn't mean it's fated to be bad.

# USS *HELM* (DD-388)

### PEARL HARBOR
### DECEMBER 7, 1941

Lieutenant Commander Chester Carroll, captain of the USS *Helm*, watches from the navigation bridge as the destroyer moves into Pearl Harbor's West Loch at 7:59 a.m.[2] Sunday morning or not, she's got all hands on board. The Navy isn't entirely heartless; Carroll granted shore leave last night, but all hands had to be back early enough for the ship to be underway at 0700.

West Loch is the home to deperming buoys, floating stations where ships and submarines can wipe their magnetic signatures before leaving port. Carroll will order the *Helm* to sidle up to a buoy, where loops of electrical cable pulse at about two thousand amperes. This removes the

2. Ship's log, USS *Helm* (DD-388), December 7, 1941.

magnetic field that naturally builds up around a metal hull, which is what triggers the fuses of torpedoes and many undersea mines.

Carroll glances at his thirteen-year-old son, Chet, standing next to him and smiles. The boy is enjoying a morning cruise, watching the sailors scramble to their duties, feeling the energy of the machinery thrumming through the ship's metal bones and observing the status of his father, to whom everyone on board defers. The jaunt to West Loch should only take an hour.

There are cries on deck, and Carroll hears the buzzing of aircraft. There are dark shapes dropping fast onto Ford Island. Now Chet will really see something: returning US air groups practicing dive-bombing runs on Ford Island. But an object separates from the lead airplane when it pulls out of its dive. A dusty impact craters the runway, and when the second bomber pulls up, Carroll watches in horror as a hangar explodes.[3]

"General quarters!" Carroll orders, and the crew starts to scramble with purpose. One of the attacking bombers streaks toward the *Helm*, sparks of flame flickering from its wings. A stream of bullets rip into the water just a few feet from the destroyer.

"Why didn't we return any fire?" Carroll demands, realizing the forward guns should have had a shot. The delay has been spent cleaning grease from the guns, slathered on the metal to preserve them for action.

"Ensign, take him to the wardroom," Carroll says, motioning to his son. Ensign James Baker leads the wide-eyed Chet Carroll away. He'll spend the rest of the morning reading comic books "while the world was blowing up all around him," as Baker puts it.[4]

The sky is filled with smoke and silhouettes of enemy warplanes. The *Helm*'s guns have now been wiped clean of grease, and at 8:05 a.m., the destroyer's .50-caliber machine guns open fire on the attacking Japanese planes.[5]

---

3. Rear Admiral Victor A. Dybdal USN (Ret.), "What a Way to Start a War," *Naval History Magazine*, vol. 15, December 2001.
4. Ibid, with Dybdal quoting his shipmate's comments in "Remember Pearl Harbor," *Inside Worster*, December 1991.
5. Ship's log, USS *Helm* (DD-388), December 7, 1941.

A flock of torpedo planes come from Barber's Point, heading straight for them. Relief floods Carroll as he realizes they're not on a good approach to drop their weapons on the *Helm*. The planes roar overhead and keep to their heading. Those torpedoes are destined for someone else.

As the men finish readying her two five-inch guns, the *Helm* drives out of the West Loch into the main channel, where Carroll sees more enemy planes creasing the air. The forward machine guns rattle as the ship breaks into the main channel, and minutes later, when another group of torpedo planes cross the main channel, the *Helm's* big guns are ready to add to the reception.

Carroll feels a savage glee as the stream from one of his aft machine guns sweeps across the path of an oncoming plane, which lurches drunkenly in the air before catching fire. He sees it crash behind the trees of Hickam Field and marks the time and the responsible gun position, which he later learns is manned by gunner's mate W. C. Huff.[6]

Any satisfaction he feels vanishes as a massive explosion ripples across Pearl Harbor and a new pillar of billowing black smoke gushes into the air above Battleship Row. From the stern, the crew can see the aftermath of the explosion of the USS *Arizona*. The *Helm* steers away from the cataclysm behind them, heading toward the entrance of the harbor. Carroll can't fight in such a constrained space, and being sunk at the harbor's entrance would cause a nightmare.

The *Helm* reaches the harbor's entrance at 8:17 a.m., guns trained to the sky. But there are eyes scanning the water as well—and the cry soon erupts that a conning tower has been spotted to the ship's starboard side, right outside the channel. Carroll examines it under binoculars; it's a tiny version of what he's been trained to look for in an enemy submarine. It's not American and it's lurking near the harbor; Carroll knows what to do immediately.[7]

"Five-inch guns," he says, starting to order them to shoot.

Even as he says the words, the conning tower vanishes beneath the

6. Ibid.
7. "USS *Helm*, Report of Pearl Harbor Attack," *Naval History and Heritage Command*, December 11, 1941, https://www.history.navy.mil/research/archives/digital-exhibits-highlights/action-reports/wwii-pearl-harbor-attack/ships-d-l/uss-helm-dd-388-action-report.html.

waves. The gun crew fires anyway, geysers of water rising from the explosive impacts. The *Helm* passes the channel's entrance buoys and, free to maneuver, turns toward the sub's last known position, increasing speed to twenty-five knots. The destroyer is on the hunt.

The conning tower appears again 1,200 yards away, seemingly right on top of Tripod Reef. Carroll sees parts of the hull exposed to the breakers. They're foundering there, he sees, stuck on the reef.

The two five-inch guns swivel to a bearing of 290 degrees, the gunners taking aim at the oddly small submarine.

"Fire."

# TRIPOD REEF

## HONOLULU
## DECEMBER 7, 1941

Kazuo Sakamaki and Kiyoshi Inagaki know inglorious doom is approaching as their submarine lies grounded outside of Pearl Harbor.

The mission has been a disaster—the submarine's broken gyrocompass made safe navigation impossible through the reef-strewn waters. What good is a detailed map if they don't know the direction they're heading? They have struck reefs twice, and the third time left them stuck here outside the harbor to watch smoke rise as the air raid unfolded.

And now they're in the crosshairs of a US destroyer.

The impact of a five-inch shell resonates deafeningly through the hull. The next lands close enough to shake the sub, and the men feel a sudden lurch as HA-19 slips from the grip of the reef.

Sakamaki dives the submarine beneath the waves and steers it away from the wrathful destroyer.[8] He guides it along a sizeable curve, a course

---

8. Ibid. "0820: Opened fire on submarine off Tripod Reef, bearing 290 distance 1200 yards from buoy #1. No hits observed, but there were several close splashes. Submarine appeared to be touching bottom on ledge of reef, and in line of breakers. While still firing at submarine it apparently slipped off ledge and submerged."

that will take them away from the harbor but back to the shoreline. They've failed to do their part during the surprise raid, but they're not ready to give up. There must be a target outside the harbor worth ramming.

# 4401 KAHALA AVE

## HONOLULU
## DECEMBER 7, 1941

Robert Shivers is upstairs getting dressed, readying himself to play host to an emergency services meeting breakfast at his Black Point home. It's just after eight o'clock, and they're expected within the hour. Even now, Margaret and Sue are setting the table.

Then the phone rings, he hears Sue answer, and she calls for him. "It's the office," she says, handing him the receiver.

The student watches his face fall. "Send them here," he says, voice firm but hollow. "I'll be right down." And then he hangs up.

"The Japanese are attacking us, here," Shivers says. "When the men get here, tell them to come to the office. But feed them first; no telling when they'll be able to eat again."

Shivers is rushing out the door, spitting commands to his shocked wife and boarder. "Turn on the radio and keep it on."

A buzzing noise overhead draws their attention and a trio of warplanes cruises past. Sue sees "a big sun, rising sun," and the reality of the situation nearly makes her faint. After the planes pass overhead, the married couple quickly embrace before Robert Shivers dashes to his car. The FBI special agent in charge opens the door and pauses.

"Margaret, you take her wherever you go," he says. "Don't let Sue out of your sight."[9]

---

9. Interview with Sue Isonaga, *The Hawai'i Nisei Story: Americans of Japanese Ancestry During WWII*, a joint project between the University of Hawaii at Manoa's Center for Oral History and Hamilton Library and Kapi'olani Community College.

# JAPANESE CONSULATE

## HONOLULU
## DECEMBER 7, 1941

Yoshikawa is eating toast, coffee, eggs and papaya at the consulate, "still somewhat befuddled by my late work on the previous night," he would later remember, when he hears airplanes in the air, then the first distant *boom*.[10]

*It's some sort of training maneuver*, he thinks. Then his brain catches up. He rises and, before reaching the shortwave radio, more blasts reach the building and rattle the windows in their frames. Yoshikawa switches on the radio and peers out the window. There's already black smoke shrouding the harbor.

Consul General Kita hurries in, dressed for golf, and they silently listen to the 8:00 P.M. news on Radio Tokyo. Despite the rising chaos outside, the broadcast is routine. The two men eagerly await the weather report. "East wind, rain," the announcer says carefully.

For countless spies and diplomats around the world, it means that the imperial council in Tokyo has decided on war with the United States. ("North wind, cloudy" means war with Russia; "West wind, clear" means Britain.)

For the two Japanese men hearing explosions in Honolulu, it's more of an official confirmation than a news flash. They take to their feet wordlessly, stride to the consul general's office and collect the most recent code books and cable messages. The pair then head outside, spark a small fire and then hesitate as the moment sinks in. The pair grip hands, and Yoshikawa finds tears seeping from his eyes. Grip released, the pair start tearing the paperwork and dropping the remnants into the flames.

Outside, the first Honolulu police detectives are pulling up to the consulate. SAC Shivers placed a phone call within the first moments of the attack, asking local cops to put the consulate under surveillance. The

---

10. Takeo Yoshikawa, *Japan's Spy at Pearl Harbor* (Jefferson, NC: McFarland, 2020).

cops spot smoke curling from the yard. They report this immediately; it's either a smoke signal or the destruction of evidence. The orders come over the radio to intervene, and they rush to the front door.

Yoshikawa leaves the bonfire to head back to the consul general's office, where he needs to clean out the safe. Inside, among other sensitive diplomatic communiqués, are incriminating cables about Otto Kuehn that detail ways to pass signals and a newspaper code. The consulate's cipher clerk has the only keys to the safe, but by the time Yoshikawa finds him, the Americans are barreling into the building. The purge of documents is incomplete.

Yoshikawa slips away, wondering if he should try to flee. He has a plan to flee to Mexico and continue to spy on America from there. Now, with the entire consulate arrested within minutes, the chances of escape seem remote. He decides it's better—and less scary—to brazen it out as just another consulate worker.

The detectives are gathering the remains from the bonfire and looking for the key to the safe in Kita's office when everyone's heads turn to the northwest, drawn by the sound of fresh detonations. It's 8:50 a.m., and the second wave of the attack on Pearl Harbor has begun.

A sharp, nearby blast makes everyone jump. An American antiaircraft shell has landed nearby and exploded.[11] War has come to the streets of Honolulu.

# DIAMOND HEAD BEACH

### HONOLULU
### DECEMBER 7, 1941

Fishing gear and shocked friends inside the car, Douglas Wada puts some power into his Chevrolet, speeding through Waikiki on Kalakaua

---

11. More than forty people are killed by falling American antiaircraft shells.

Avenue. "Those idiots," Wada says of the Japanese. "Don't they know they're going to lose?"

"So you don't think this is an invasion?"

"I didn't say that," Wada says. "If they come, we're sitting ducks."

Red lights appear in his rearview—a Honolulu police cruiser. "Let me do the talking," Wada says, identification at the ready.

"You can't go any further," the officer starts to say, then sees the ID.

The HPD cop scans the name and says, "Go ahead. I think they're looking for you."[12]

# OVER THE NAVY YARD

### HONOLULU
### DECEMBER 7, 1941

Lieutenant Commander Takashige Egusa is probably the finest dive-bomber pilot in the Imperial Navy, and his men are considered to be elite. It's their job today to break the back of the US forces in Hawaii.

Of the 167 aircraft of the attack's second wave on Pearl Harbor, seventy-eight are dive-bombers and the rest are high-altitude bombers. There are no torpedo planes this time. The dive-bombers are fairly useless against battleships, which have deck armor that can withstand the 550-pound bombs. If aircraft carriers were present, the weapons would be perfectly suited to punch through their wide flight decks.

With them absent, the targets of choice are cruisers, and Egusa is leading a ten-plane sortie to the Navy Yard to find them. There's a low overcast cloud layer that makes identifying targets nearly impossible. The

---

12. MIS Veterans Club of Hawaii interview, in which Wada describes his feelings about the Japanese attack and chance of invasion, and relates the anecdote with the officer. The cop may have meant, "The Navy is looking for its own to report," or could have referred to radio reports looking for Wada specifically after he didn't appear for some time that morning. Mayfield later tells him he was ready to have him arrested.

sky is also black with smoke and, unexpectedly, thick blooms of antiair-craft fire that make approaches dangerous.

Egusa finally spots the outline of a priority target fifteen thousand feet below—the heavy cruiser *New Orleans*—and tips his airplane in a steep angle, soaring downward above the ship. At two thousand feet he releases the bombs, then feels the g-forces push him into the seat as he climbs away.

The bombs detonate in the water below, shameful white geysers marking their impacts. He's come all this way, only to miss.

His poor performance is repeated across the Navy Yard. Of the ten planes, only one cruiser, the torpedo-damaged *Raleigh*, suffers major damage. The exception is the USS *Nevada*, targeted by more than a dozen dive-bombing attacks as she limps away from the harbor. Hit by six bombs and on fire, yet somehow still afloat, *Nevada* ends her epic run by intentionally running aground.

Egusa flies back to the carriers, disappointed. American antiaircraft fire downed fourteen dive-bombers, in exchange for an underwhelming performance. Although the Japanese pilots will overinflate the damages, the reality is that the dive-bombers achieved a dismal 20 percent accuracy rate, mostly against stationary targets.

The second wave of the attack on Pearl Harbor ends at 9:55 a.m. There will not be a third—Admiral Nagano leaves the oil storage tanks and repair facilities untouched. When Yamamoto hears of this, he's incensed at the lost opportunity. The warships have been savaged, but the military port itself will recover all too soon.

Across Oahu, the fires burn. At Pearl Harbor Naval Base, eighteen warships are sunk or grounded, including five battleships. Frantic rescue efforts are underway—there are dying men trapped in the air pockets of overturned ships. Responders can hear them drowning as they cut through the decks to rescue them; they'll soon learn to fill the holds with gas to keep the ships afloat during the process.

The Japanese planes have left carnage across the island. Dive-bombers attacked Wheeler Field, finding 120 fighters parked in neat rows. Nearly half of the P-40s there are now destroyed and the hangars took a beating; thirty-three men were killed and seventy-three wounded. The raid caught other airplanes in the open at Hickam Field, as well: five B-17s, seven B-18s and two A-20s destroyed and another nineteen airplanes damaged. First- and second-wave attacks took out twenty-seven of the thirty-three PBY seaplanes at Kaneohe Naval Air Station. B-17s at Bellows Field were bombed and strafed.

Over an hour and fifteen minutes, 2,403 Americans are killed and 1,143 wounded. Of these, roughly forty-nine of the dead are civilians, many struck down by errant five-inch antiaircraft rounds fired by defenders.

Firefighters and volunteer workers were killed, caught in the second wave as they responded to the first. Japanese fighters also strafed John Rogers Field, Honolulu's airport, killing one, and fatally downed two people joyriding that morning in a Piper J-3 Cub plane.

From: Admiral Nagumo
To: Pearl Harbor Attack Force
December 7, 1941

Brilliant success was achieved for our country through the splendid efforts of you men. But we still have a great way to go. After this victory we must tighten the straps of our helmets and go onward, determined to continue our fight until the final goal has been won.

# ALEXANDER YOUNG HOTEL

## HONOLULU
### DECEMBER 7, 1941

Douglas Wada drops off his friends at Kama Lane and rushes inside to speak with Helen. She tells him that the phone's been ringing off the hook, and someone from his office said something about sending police for him if he doesn't turn up.

There's no time to eat, only to change from his fishing outfit into a uniform, embrace his wife and drive downtown. Wada reaches the Alexander Young Hotel just before noon. He can only hope the warplanes won't return to target government buildings. Or that warships are launching landing craft to occupy them.

Downtown Honolulu is an enraged beehive. The faces of those dashing in and out of the Alexander Young Hotel are fixed in confusion and frustrated anger. Guests and office workers each wear a unique but similar profile of shock and grief, but sooner or later each face turns in grim fixation at the columns of black smoke rising from the naval base.

Wada heads inside, bracing for his captain's reaction. Indeed, Mayfield storms over as Wada enters the sixth floor. "Where the hell have you been? I was ready to have you arrested."

"Fishing," Wada says simply. "Sunday, day off."

Mayfield shakes his head. "At least you found time to get your uniform. But none of us are going anywhere for a long time," he says. "You better get ready. We'll have plenty for you to look at soon.

"And Wada—sorry to interrupt the fishing."[13]

# FEDERAL BUILDING

## HONOLULU
## DECEMBER 7, 1941

Gero Iwai tries not to feel the other men's eyes on him as they gather in a conference room on the second floor. Most know him, but some do not. They're taking second looks at the only Japanese American in the room of Army intelligence agents and G-men.

---

13. The reaction to Wada's late arrival is described by Wada in his MIS Veterans Club of Hawaii interview; the latter half of this exchange is dramatized.

SAC Shivers is in charge. Army officials order their four commanding generals (and nine corps commanders) to work with the FBI to round up all persons on their detention lists. Shivers, Bicknell and Honolulu police acting captain John Burns sit down with a card file and make the final determinations on who's to be arrested. Personal friends and acquaintances are spared at the last moment, but the number still hovers at more than four hundred people.

The wheels to sanction these arrests have been spinning for hours. Just after the second wave, Lieutenant General Short stood in Iolani Palace to ask Hawaii territorial governor Joseph Poindexter to declare martial law. The governor called President Roosevelt, who advised him to follow the recommendation, which he did. By the rules drafted beforehand by Lt. Col. Thomas Green, this enables local military authorities to apprehend US citizens without cause.

Hoover telegrams his field offices: "Urgent. Immediately take into custody all Japanese who have been classified in the A, B, and C categories."

At just before 2:00 P.M., Shivers is handed a letter from Short authorizing execution of the arrests. By then, President Roosevelt has signed Proclamation 2525, classifying all Japanese aliens living in the United States or any of its territories as "alien enemies" subject to apprehension. Some arrests had already begun, but under martial law, the final official authorization had to be given by the Army.

Across Honolulu, FBI men, military intelligence agents and local cops gather the detainees and deliver them to the Honolulu Immigration Station. There are almost five hundred residents in Hawaii, citizen and alien alike, placed under armed guard that day: 345 Japanese aliens, twenty-two Japanese American citizens, seventy-four German nationals, nineteen citizens of German ancestry, eleven Italian nationals and two citizens of Italian descent.

Nearly every consulate support worker is seized, including Richard Kotoshirodo and John Mikami. (Of more than two hundred seized, only these two are actually guilty of abetting espionage.) Also detained are the Japanese language school teachers and religious leaders from Shinto shrines and Buddhist temples. Members of mainstream Japanese civic societies are hustled into cars and ferried away from their families.

Those detained are brought under armed escort to an immigration building next to the territorial government officers near Honolulu Harbor. The prevailing feelings inside the cramped quarters are disbelief and shame. These are the leading merchants, priests, teachers and social organizers in Honolulu, now rounded up with fewer rights than those afforded criminals.

# ALEXANDER YOUNG HOTEL

### HONOLULU
### DECEMBER 7, 1941

It's approaching midnight, but no one in the 14th DIO office is going home. Wada's day has not been spent chasing cases as much as enabling countless investigations. The documents come in, he translates them and he waits for another. There's plenty of slack time, when the minutes crawl and the banality of waiting for documents spars with the tragic drama unfolding outside the building.

His DIO colleague Ted Emanuel perks up suddenly. "Hey, Doug," he says. "You want to go drive around at night to see what's cooking?"

Wada weighs the options. He'd be venturing into an uncertain city, one possibly on the verge of invasion or bombardment. Paranoia is brewing in Oahu. There have been reports to the office of fifth-column behavior—cars blocking first responders in traffic, parked cars blocking roads and even unexplained gunshots at military personnel. None of the reports are substantiated. But even wearing a Navy uniform, which he still is, there could be confusion.

There's an expectation of further catastrophe, one that Wada shares. The Army is poised to respond to an invasion—the 24th Division guards the North Shore and the 25th Division protects Honolulu and the south. The personnel on guard duty are jumping at shadows, and antiaircraft crews are shooting at the flimsiest radar contacts. Army and Navy airplanes trying to land have been met with "friendly" five-inch gunfire, and Wada heard rumors of B-17 crews being slaughtered this way while approaching Oahu.[14]

However, all of this risk is balanced by the sheer boredom of waiting. Any action would also ease the discomfort of being away from his family during this crisis. And on top of everything, just a few blocks away, grim history is being made. Wada wants to bear witness and steady his resolve to what he knows are approaching hard times.[15]

"Okay," he says.

The pair of naval intelligence officers set out in a Jeep, rolling through civilian areas to seek a place with a vantage of the rescue operations. "What do you think the Japanese are thinking, attacking like this?" Emanuel asks on the way.

"They don't know that they can be beaten," Wada says. "Not yet."

Nearing the far side of the ships' berths, Wada can see the outlines of military guards on the other side of the wharf. He's happy to be wearing a Navy uniform. "You think they see us?"

"I don't know. If they do, they have to see we're in a Jeep."

"I'm not so sure," says Wada, watching the silhouettes raise what appears to be rifles. "Boy, let's get going!"

The crack of the rifles jars Emanuel from disbelief. He spins the Jeep's wheel and speeds away from the wharf, bright spots of muzzle flashes behind them. "Damn those buggers," Wada cries, feeling the adrenaline surge course though his shaking hands.

"They never even said anything," Emanuel marvels.

"Forget all this. Let's go back to the goddamned hotel."[16]

---

14. He mentions this in an interview, referring to an actual incident that was censored at the time.
15. MIS Veterans Club of Hawaii interview. "Q: At that time—Pearl Harbor attack—when Japan is the enemy, did you also feel that from now on it's going to be tough to be Japanese? Wada: Yeah, I realized it was tough for me."
16. Ibid.

# BELLOWS FIELD BEACH

### HONOLULU
### DECEMBER 8, 1941

The Army Jeep pulls to a halt in the sand, two soldiers quickly disembarking under morning light struggling to break through the clouds. One man is holding an M1 Garand rifle, the other a M1911 .45 pistol. Both weapons are loaded.

Hawaii Territorial Guard Cpl. David Akui takes in the stretch of beach near Bellows Field, where his company is bivouacked. They're responding to a report of a strange shape wallowing in the surf, possibly an enemy landing craft or submarine. More likely, more hysteria.

Akui knows the island well. The twenty-one-year-old Nisei was born in Hawaii and enlisted in 1940, before the entire National Guard was ordered into federal service. He's now assigned to the 298th Infantry in a heavy-weapons platoon. Like the other 350 Nisei guardsmen in Hawaii, he responded for duty after the Sunday-morning attack. Company G's camp is at the end of the runway of Bellows Field, now strewn with burnt airplanes and pockmarked hangars.

The man with the rifle is Company G's commander, Lt. Paul Plybon. He's from Greenwood, Mississippi, and has a nickname that plays on the letters of his last name: "Playboy." He was at the base during the raid the previous day and watched helplessly as unarmed B-17s returning to Bellows Field got ambushed by Japanese fighter aircraft. Plybon was under the Japanese pilots' guns as they strafed the base. "All of them were grinning," he later seethed. "They waved at you as they pulled up."[17]

The pair take in the surf, scanning for anything peculiar. There's no submarine, but they spot an odd shape at the water's edge and are shocked to see they have found a corpse. During the grim walk closer,

---

17. Jim Schlosser, "Once-Quiet Sunday Turned World to War," *Greensboro News & Record*, November 30, 1991.

the details of a naked Japanese man appear. There's a lanyard around his neck with a stopwatch dangling from it.

When the "corpse" stirs, the weapons rise. The bedraggled man on the beach opens his eyes and twitches convulsively as he sees Akui standing over him with the pistol aimed at his head. "I'm cold," the man says in broken English.

Kazuo Sakamaki, commander of the Japanese mini-submarine HA-19, has just become the United States' first prisoner of war of World War II.[18]

# IOLANI PALACE

## HONOLULU
## DECEMBER 8, 1941

Iolani Palace was the royal residence of Hawaii's kings and queens until 1893, when it became the provisional government's headquarters, followed by the territorial government. If local advocates have their way, it may one day be the statehouse. The message behind operating out of the ornate building remains the same over the years—the people in charge of the islands dwell here.

So, it's fitting that Lt. Col. Thomas Green, now the Hawaiian Department's judge advocate, moves into Iolani Palace the day after Pearl Harbor. The man who wrote the rules governing the military administration is on hand to direct martial law operations.

At 12:30 P.M., Green switches on the radio to hear President Roosevelt address a joint session of Congress.

> Mr. Vice President, and Mr. Speaker, and Members of the Senate and House of Representatives:
>
> Yesterday, December 7, 1941—a date which will live in infamy—the

---

18. When the Office of Naval Intelligence agents come to collect him, Plybon lets his vengeful feelings slip: "You're taking him to the fucking Alexander Young Hotel?"

United States of America was suddenly and deliberately attacked by naval and air forces of the Empire of Japan.

The United States was at peace with that Nation and, at the solicitation of Japan, was still in conversation with its Government and its Emperor looking toward the maintenance of peace in the Pacific. Indeed, one hour after Japanese air squadrons had commenced bombing in the American Island of Oahu, the Japanese Ambassador to the United States and his colleague delivered to our Secretary of State a formal reply to a recent American message. And while this reply stated that it seemed useless to continue the existing diplomatic negotiations, it contained no threat or hint of war or of armed attack.

It will be recorded that the distance of Hawaii from Japan makes it obvious that the attack was deliberately planned many days or even weeks ago. During the intervening time the Japanese Government has deliberately sought to deceive the United States by false statements and expressions of hope for continued peace.

The attack yesterday on the Hawaiian Islands has caused severe damage to American naval and military forces. I regret to tell you that very many American lives have been lost. In addition American ships have been reported torpedoed on the high seas between San Francisco and Honolulu.

Yesterday the Japanese Government also launched an attack against Malaya.

Last night Japanese forces attacked Hong Kong.

Last night Japanese forces attacked Guam.

Last night Japanese forces attacked the Philippine Islands.

Last night the Japanese attacked Wake Island.

And this morning the Japanese attacked Midway Island.

Japan has, therefore, undertaken a surprise offensive extending throughout the Pacific area. The facts of yesterday and today speak for themselves. The people of the United States have already formed their opinions and well understand the implications to the very life and safety of our Nation.

As Commander in Chief of the Army and Navy I have directed that all measures be taken for our defense. But always will our whole Nation remember the character of the onslaught against us.

No matter how long it may take us to overcome this premeditated invasion, the American people in their righteous might will win through to absolute victory.

I believe that I interpret the will of the Congress and of the people when I assert that we will not only defend ourselves to the uttermost but will make it very certain that this form of treachery shall never again endanger us.

Hostilities exist. There is no blinking at the fact that our people, our territory, and our interests are in grave danger.

With confidence in our armed forces—with the unbounding determination of our people—we will gain the inevitable triumph—so help us God.

I ask that the Congress declare that since the unprovoked and dastardly attack by Japan on Sunday, December 7, 1941, a state of war has existed between the United States and the Japanese Empire.

Green switches the radio off. The reality of his position washes over him like a wave—with the war official, the martial law over Hawaii is good as permanent. Now the Army must run *everything*. All civilians need to be registered and fingerprinted. Manpower is needed to censor the press, long-distance telephone calls and all civilian mail. The Army must police the ban on liquor sales. The list seems endless.

Emergency medical facilities fall under direct Army control. That includes the Japanese Charity Hospital—the military took control of over half of the hospital's facilities in the aftermath of the attack. The day before, eight hundred volunteers from the United Japanese Society in Honolulu, freshly trained to respond to medical emergencies, went straight from their graduation ceremony to tend to the wounded.

Of all the challenges Green faces, creating a functioning justice system is the thorniest. It's not easy to replace the civil system with military courts overnight. Easing his job is the lack of impediments: the writ of *habeas corpus* remains suspended, search warrants are unneeded and even written charges are optional. Being tried before a military court will be a shadow of the former process—presided over by a sole officer, who'll be encouraged to sentence offenders the same day of their arrest.

Japanese Hawaiians are subject to special restrictions. For them, meeting in groups of more than ten is forbidden. Being outside during the nightly blackouts is cause for detention. The entire community is ordered to turn in all firearms, flashlights, portable radios and cameras.

At his home on Kalama Beach, Otto Kuehn hears the rap on his front door, blood frozen. The military police hustle him, Friedel, Hans Joachim and Susie into a truck. All are held in cells at the US Immigration Service's detention center in Honolulu, held for the crime of being German in Hawaii.

# ALEXANDER YOUNG HOTEL

---

## HONOLULU
## DECEMBER 8, 1941

All eyes on the sixth floor are fixated on the young Japanese man, wrapped in an Army blanket and flanked by two Army guards. It's the Office of Naval Intelligence agents' first close look at the enemy who attacked their city. The prisoner has no shoes and is bare-legged— Douglas Wada realizes the man is naked under the blanket.

"Look at his face," says Gero Iwai. The prisoner is a young man, seemingly well built, but his vacant expression, under regulation-cropped black hair, makes him appear ghostly. Wada recognizes the man is physically healthy but shattered by psychological trauma, but that inspires little pity. He recognizes similar pain behind the eyes of many in Honolulu today.

This time it's Iwai who's been summoned to help interrogate the survivor from a sunken Japanese submarine that attacked Pearl Harbor yesterday.

The prisoner is taken to an office, the door closes and the sixth floor returns to its buzz of activity. Agents are chasing leads from the intelligence trove taken the day before, with the goal of unraveling any spy networks and safeguarding the island.

Captain Mayfield waves for them, and they feel the pressure of eyes following their progress across the office. "He won't give his name but says he swam ashore, we're assuming from somewhere off Bellows Field," Mayfield says. "He stopped speaking English once he got to Fort Shafter, but the guys who caught him say he can, a little."

Mayfield shows them a stopwatch on a lanyard. "He was naked when they found him. This was all he was wearing."

Wada examines the piece; it's stopped at 0201, beads of saltwater trapped behind the glass. He turns it over in his hands and sees Japanese characters scrawled there.

"'Watch, Type 1, Navy #296,'" Wada reads aloud, then looks at his commanding officer. "Imperial Navy issue."

"I need you two to get this guy talking. Right now, he only says he's ready to kill himself," Mayfield says. "We need to know where he came from and if there's anyone else out there we have to worry about. Get him talking in Japanese and hand him off if he really can speak English." Mayfield pauses. "You two are about to lead the first POW interrogation of this war. Do it right."

They bark a sharp, "Yes, sir," and walk, almost dazed, to the office where the prisoner awaits. Wada feels his mind focus, the way it used to when he stepped up to the plate, blocking everything but the task at hand. He and Iwai take deep breaths and open the door.

The man looks pathetic in his blanket, shoulders hunched and head hung low. The pair of military intelligence agents make respectful, traditional introductions. His eyes don't hold theirs for more than a moment, and waves of shame seem to radiate from him, but the prisoner responds to the polite approach.[19]

The prisoner identifies himself. He's Ens. Kazuo Sakamaki, twenty-three years old, from the Okayama Prefecture, graduate of the Imperial Naval Academy. The preliminaries now behind them, they'll see how cooperative he really is. As per ONI best practices, they take no notes, just talk.[20]

"Ensign, we must know what kind of ordeal left you naked on the beaches of Hawaii."

The response is flat, emotionless. "I commanded a small submarine, and we ran aground offshore. We swam for the shore, but I lost him in the surf. I was the navigator, but the compass was broken. We couldn't access the harbor, and we couldn't avoid hitting reefs."

"A two-man submarine, that's ingenious. How far did you travel in that little submarine?"

Cold eyes, a mouth twitch.

"It couldn't have been more than a hundred miles," Iwai prompts.

"It was more than a hundred miles," Sakamaki says softly.

"On diesel engines?"

Sakamaki opens his palms and remains silent. There are limits to what he'll share. He knows he's being pumped for information. The conversation continues, but he won't speak about the mothership that delivered him, even its tonnage. The man seems to be on the verge of a catatonic depression.

"Ensign," Wada tries. "You were part of a magnificent success for

---

19. The agents are just the first Americans to take advantage of how the psychology of *bushido* produces broken, pliant prisoners. As US diplomat Ulrich Straus will note in his book, *The Anguish of Surrender*: "Silence is by far the best weapon a prisoner determined to divulge no information can wield. It seems clear, however, that virtually none of the Japanese POWs availed themselves of it" (Seattle: University of Washington Press, 2005).

20. The ONI favors a light approach to interrogations in its training manual: "The use of high-pressure methods is discouraged, not only because these tactics may reflect against the Service, but also because, in investigative work, force is a poor substitute for brains." This is vintage Cecil Coggins.

your nation. We must compliment your military on the success you achieved yesterday."

The man's eyes rise from the table, and the two intelligence agents don't see pride, they see anger. "What happened was not the success we imagined."

"You caught the entire US Army and Navy by surprise," Iwai asks, genuinely surprised. "What did you expect?"

"What was expected, what was asked of us, was to deliver a fatal blow," he responds. "We did not. I did not. Now I'm disgraced. I ask you not to share news of my survival with my government. And I ask for the opportunity to commit suicide."

"I don't understand how you feel that you failed." Best to play on the man's fatalistic mentality and shredded ego.

"We did not enter the harbor during the attack. And when we finally had the chance to attack a capital ship, I couldn't even see it well enough to aim the torpedoes," Sakamaki says, reliving the experience to the first people who are able to listen. "I opened the conning tower hatch to see for myself, but the sea was rough. The water rushed in and ruined our engine. The fumes were choking us.[21]

"We were helpless, out of control, and we crashed on another damned reef. I set charges to blow up the submarine, then we stripped and jumped into the heavy surf. I never saw him again."

He stops, eyes unfocused.

"There was just one crewman besides yourself?" prompts Wada.

A curt nod. "Petty Officer Kiyoshi Inagaki. I think he must be dead, drowned."

"But you successfully scuttled the sub?"

"The charges never detonated, and it's probably still there to be found," says Sakamaki bitterly, but then adds, "There's no paperwork or anything inside. It's really just a two-man torpedo."

"What happened when you reached the beach?"

---

21. Batteries emit hydrogen and chlorine fumes when in contact with seawater.

"I was exhausted and half-drowned. When I opened my eyes, a soldier was standing over me with a pistol. That's when I knew I failed my nation by not committing suicide. I asked for this honor, on the beach with the soldiers."

Wada asks what the response was. "They laughed. My greatest mistake was being captured. This is the first time I have failed."

"You spoke to the men in English; you must have been trained for this. Why?"

"A little English, I took it in school, but transferred to Chinese classes." Even this educational history is bathed in pathos. But there's no indication of a looming invasion where English would be needed during an occupation.

"Let's hear some English," Iwai prompts.

After a while, a pair of ONI agents slip into the room and insert themselves in the conversation. The POW is now talking; Iwai and Wada are a success. The official Navy report includes no names but credits "two competent interpreters" for starting the difficult process of opening the prisoner to sustained questioning.[22]

At the end of the session, Sakamaki is escorted from the hotel, back to his cell in Fort Shafter. He seems genuinely sad to have to leave. In a report he sends later that day, 14th District Intelligence head E.T. Layton remarks that "it is evident that the officer appreciated the treatment afforded him by the naval questioners to that of the Army. It is felt that with proper handling further information might be derived from this officer."[23]

Sakamaki's information prompts a hunt for the minisub and the missing Japanese sailor. Both are found wallowing lifeless on the beach later that day. (The submarine had been bombed by Navy planes, which dislodged it from the reef and freed it to wash up on shore.) The

---

22. The report details the interrogation and serves as the basis of the dramatization. It's included in the Proceedings of the Hewitt Inquiry, United States Congress, 1946.
23. Layton's memo is also included in the Proceedings of the Hewitt Inquiry, United States Congress, 1946.

paperwork found inside HA-19 is delivered to the Alexander Young Hotel, where Wada and Iwai are waiting to examine it.

Among the small cache is a damaged navigational chart with a course on it, directions on how the sub could best get into Pearl Harbor. There are time schedules, landmarks and labels with the berths of the warships of the US Navy there. There are also diagrams of coastal defenses across the island.

The map is freshly updated, the most obvious proof being the absence of the recently departed aircraft carriers. "Let's get the ship schedules," Wada says. Using that, they calculate that the mini-submarine commander received intelligence reports as late as December 5.

Wada and Iwai are now among the first in the United States to realize the scope of the spy operations that prepared the Japanese Navy for the attack. And with that revealed, the US intelligence community's failure to prevent it.

"My god, they were accurate," says the Army intelligence agent.

"Some good spy work," Wada responds coldly.[24]

"Professional," agrees Iwai. "And, I'd bet, straight from the consulate."

# FEDERAL BUILDING

## HONOLULU
## DECEMBER 9, 1941

Douglas Wada stands next to Gero Iwai and stares down at the collection of consulate documents, spread out on the table in front of them. There are several garbage bags with more in the interrogation room.

"You called me over here for *this*?" Wada asks his friend.

Iwai shrugs. "What else you have going on?"

Wada can't help but laugh. In truth, he is a huge help because Iwai

---

24. The MIS Veterans Club of Hawaii interview includes his reaction to the quality of the information in the submarine.

has never lived in Japan and there are words and phrases that the Army intelligence officer may not be familiar with.[25]

One bag of the documents has been emptied on the table, forming a bird's nest of shredded paper. "I guess the consulate people had a chance to rip up everything."

"And burn it too," Iwai says. "The police didn't mention this to us when they said they were coming."

"This must have come from the unopened safe," says Iwai, seeing a stack of cables from Kita to Tokyo. The lines are broken into ten five-letter segments. In any language, it makes no sense. "It'll have to be sent off to be decoded."

"Now we both have to piece the rest of this stuff together," Wada says, looking forlornly at the pile of torn paperwork. They form two mounds of paper shreds, one for larger pieces that they have some hope of identifying. But these documents have been shredded expertly and mixed in a bag, leaving the remains indecipherable.

After spending time arranging sections from several bags, no part of any of the jigsaw puzzles come together. "I don't think we'll be able to do this," Iwai concedes.

"Well, I'm taking some larger pieces back with me," Wada says, plucking a few off the table. "It'll show Captain Mayfield what you got me into." [26]

# KAMA LANE

## HONOLULU
## DECEMBER 10, 1941

After three days of continual service, and no invasion coming, Douglas Wada is given permission to go home. He's relieved but also feels dread.

---

25. This conversation is dramatized, but in his interview with the MIS Veterans Club of Hawaii, Wada makes the point about Iwai relying on him during translations because he never lived in Japan.
26. MIS Veterans Club of Hawaii interview.

Helen must be terrified and confused after a morning of phone calls from authorities followed by days of silence from her husband.

Wada is ready to park outside his home when he's taken with a sudden urge. He pulls to the end of the street, where his parents' home and the Kotohira Jinsha shrine are located. There are lights on in the Wada family home; all's well as can be. Other Shinto carpenters are listed on some pickup lists, but Wada knows Shivers wouldn't arrest his father. Still, the lights are reassuring.[27]

But the shrine's gate is shut and the lights are dark. By the next morning, people will gather there to leave hand-sewn hospital slippers to send to those injured by the attack. But Kotohira Jinsha will remain closed.

Rev. Misao Isobe, who married Douglas and Helen Wada, has been detained.[28]

---

27. Others in his neighborhood are not so lucky. At least seventeen people within a mile and a half of Wada's home were detained that day, according to FBI records collected and analyzed by Matt Parsons and Victor McPherson.
28. "Isobe, Misao," *Hawai'i Internee Directory*, https://interneedirectory.jcch.com/jp/internee/isobe -misao.

# PART 6

# HUNTING GHOSTS

# ALEXANDER YOUNG HOTEL

## HONOLULU
## DECEMBER 11, 1941

Irving Mayfield spends his early morning reading Consul General Kita's pre-attack cable messages, first delivered to him by RCA before the attack and decoded for him by Station Hypo cryptologists, who delivered it today. Just in time to be worthless. "They have not set up mooring equipment, nor have they selected the troops to man them," he reads. "Furthermore, there is no indication that any training for the maintenance of balloons is being undertaken."[1]

His coffee tastes especially bitter this morning. His office had the leads needed to crack this espionage ring three days before the attack on Pearl Harbor.

Three messages are particularly suspect: on December 4, the consulate messages detailed ship movements, and Tokyo responded that day with a request for more information the next day. Kita and his spies responded with details of the fleet anchored at Pearl Harbor as of the afternoon of December 5.[2] The attack force came to Hawaii armed with fresh information, courtesy of the consulate's spies.

---

1. He doesn't read an accurate translation today. Station Hypo personnel deciphered the message and handed it over to Navy Lieutenant Joseph Finnegan, a Japanese translator assigned to Station Hypo, immediately after the attack. He produces a translation that doesn't accurately include the comment at the end of the first paragraph that there's "considerable opportunity left to take advantage for a surprise attack against these places." The erroneous Japanese-language decryption of "Morimura's December 6 message" was made public in 1946 by a Pearl Harbor investigation conducted by Admiral Henry Kent Hewitt.
2. T. S. Wilkinson, "ONI Memorandum to the Secretary, Subject: Espionage in Hawaii," January 13, 1942.

Another curious find is a dispatch sent from Tokyo on December 3 containing an odd system of signal codes meant to convey the movement of US Navy ships. The clandestine system involves lights in two houses on Kalama and Lanikai Beaches, garments on clotheslines, flags on ships, newspaper classified ads—lots of details that can be used to narrow down locations and find the spies.[3]

This is evidence of an active espionage ring operating beyond the confines of the consulate, something more insidious than a phony diplomat gathering photos available to a tourist. This is bloody collaboration.

Mid-morning on December 11, the FBI, Army and ONI leadership—the familiar trio of SAC Shivers, Army Lt. Col. George Bicknell and Mayfield—huddle to form a coordinated response to the information. The FBI assigns a pair of agents to Kalama Beach to identify the house with the dormer window so prominently mentioned in the Japanese dispatches. For its part, the Army posts sentries along both Kalama and Lanikai beachheads, scanning the shoreline and seascape to watch for the enemy's flashing lights.

The Navy tasks Douglas Wada to look for suspicious ads in Japanese newspapers, but he's looking for a needle in a haystack as other agents do the street work. The ONI sends agents Joe McCarthy, Fred Paoa and Albert Kai to Lanikai that afternoon.

Geography guides their search for the spy's home. There are seventy houses along the shoreline, but after scanning them during beach strolls, only two are shown to have clotheslines suitable for the signaling the scheme describes. The owner of both homes is Otto Kuehn, a German national currently in detention in an immigration cell.

The navy intelligence agents spend more than a week scouring Lanikai for clues. They interview every neighbor on the beach, including two spooked Navy lieutenants who rent the homes. (Lieutenant Chapman and Lieutenant Stubby are both attached to the hospital at Schofield and

---

3. Ibid.

had no communication with the owners.) No one reports any suspicious lights or boat traffic. In fact, many locals debunk the idea that a sailboat had been signaling to enemies before or during the raid, given the weather. With water too rough for sailing, seeing such a boat offshore would have attracted attention.

Less helpfully, reports of emergency flares, mysterious blue lights and shoreline fires distract the agents in Lanikai. These come from volunteer shore spotters, military personnel and police officers alike. None are verified to be real.

Meanwhile on Kalama Beach, FBI agents are building off their earlier investigation into the German national. A drive past the Kuehn home quickly confirms it has a dormer window. They canvas the neighborhood and dig deeper into the family's finances.[4]

After seven days of investigation, Otto Kuehn and his family are squarely in the crosshairs of US counterintelligence.

# DEPARTMENT OF THE NAVY

## WASHINGTON, DC
## DECEMBER 15, 1941

Secretary of the Navy Frank Knox stands before the assembled press to tell the media what he found during a whirlwind tour of Hawaii. He knows congressional investigations are coming, and he wants to see the situation for himself to get ahead of them.

He tells the assembled media that both the local Army and Navy commanders failed to prepare for a Japanese attack. There is blame to go around, as long as it's focused on those in Hawaii. But the headlines are made when a reporter asks Knox about the role played by local collaborators. "I think

---

4. "In the Matter of the Confinement of Bernard Julius Otto Kuehn," *Order to the Provost Marshal by the Office of the Military Governor, Territory of Hawaii*, November 7, 1942. Included in the *Proceedings of the Army Pearl Harbor Board* as Exhibit 52.

the most effective fifth-column work of the entire war was done in Hawaii with the possible exception of Norway," he responds.[5]

The comment is also damagingly vague. Entirely lost—or intentionally obscured—is the distinction between fifth-column activity, abetted by a wide section of Oahu's population, and a compartmentalized intelligence operation run by government agents.

To many, the comparison to Norway is laughable. In 1940 fascists there under Vidkun Quisling paved the way for German invaders by seizing Norway's nerve centers, spreading false rumors and occupying military bases. In other words, nothing like the situation in Hawaii.

If Knox only meant the consulate's spy ring, his language blows their numbers way out of proportion. *The Times* of San Mateo on December 18 makes the handful of spies sound like an army: "Secretary of Navy Frank Knox brought back word from Hawaii that the fifth column had played a large part in the attack on Pearl Harbor by giving the Japanese information regarding the hours of American air patrol the territory and local of military and naval centers." Other West Coast newspapers run alarmist headlines like "Fifth Column Prepared Attack" and "Secretary of Navy Blames Fifth Column for Raid."

At the root of fifth-column fears, Kita's men in Hawaii have managed to besmirch the entire Japanese population in America. The impact of their actions will be arguably more damaging to the United States in the long term than the information supplied to Nagumo's attack force.

Knox never walks back his blanket statement. Likewise, nothing's done at the highest level of the Roosevelt administration to repudiate it or to publicly affirm the loyalty of the ethnic Japanese in America.

Since December 8, the number of arrests in Hawaii have slowly crept upward. By December 16, the total is 543, the elite of the traditional Issei community leaders among them. The reaction from the Nisei population is to push back with volunteerism, public loyalty rallies and other forms of conspicuous patriotism.

---

5. *The Press Democrat*, December 16, 1941.

Civic groups, presciently organized before the war, are working to ease tensions. Members of the Citizen's Council go to the FBI office to "offer their assistance in putting into operation the plans they had helped to evolve during the months preceding the outbreak of hostilities." Shivers's prewar community relations campaign is paying off.

The fate of Japan rests largely in the hands of the new Army commander in Hawaii, Lt. Gen. Delos Emmons. General Short's job as commander of the Hawaiian department ended ten days after the attack on Pearl Harbor. He reverted to his permanent rank of major general since his temporary rank of lieutenant general was contingent on his command.

FDR has brought in a distinguished man to become military governor. Emmons, age fifty-four, is one of the Army's most experienced leaders. The West Virginian graduated from the United States Military Academy in 1909 and transitioned from the infantry to aviation during his steady rise through the ranks. His last position was chief of the Air Force combat command. Emmons and his subordinate Lieutenant Colonel Green—with the new title "Executive, Office of the Military Governor"—have their hands directly on the mechanisms of martial law.

Now Emmons has a choice to make. There are two visions of Hawaii, and they're in direct opposition. Either it's the hotbed of possible sedition that needs to be secured for the good of an existential fight, or it's a potential wellspring of patriots who prove the American experiment is strong enough to withstand the stresses of war.

On December 17, the day he assumes command, Emmons makes his first speech as the preeminent power in Hawaii. It's an eagerly awaited event, carried live on the radio for the entire city to hear.

Emmons says his own initial examination of the attack has concluded, and he reports that "no American citizens or alien Japanese residents of Hawaii were involved in any acts of hostility against the US forces." He takes a bigger step, getting ahead of the cries coming from the mainland. He tells the crowd, the city and all the islands that he's not contemplating either mass imprisonment or forced removal of all Japanese Americans from Hawaii.

It's a promise that will be tested.

# JAPANESE CONSULATE

## HONOLULU
## DECEMBER 18, 1941

After more than a week spent locked up inside the consulate, Takeo Yoshikawa is pretty sure his cover identity is holding.

So far, his strategy for interrogations has been simple—stick to his script. When questioned, he's just a pencil-pushing clerk working on expatriation paperwork. But the timing of his arrival and close relationship with Kita will clearly mark him as a person of interest. And that's assuming that no one knows about his excursions across the island.

Most worrying, Yoshikawa has to assume that his accomplices Mikami and Kotoshirodo will be taken in for questioning, along with all the others working as hired help at the consulate. The incriminating trips he's taken with them have not come up in questioning, but the spy feels like he's living under a guillotine blade.

Consul General Nagao Kita himself is still among the 250 staffers and their families, and that bodes well for Yoshikawa. It's his name on the intelligence communiqués to Tokyo, his office that held the incriminating documents. If Kita vanishes, Yoshikawa will know to be on guard for his own seizure. He's sure that the Consul General will sell him out.

His worries increase when their wardens order Kita and a handful of his closest staff, a total of sixteen adults and five children, to a separate detention center. Among those chosen are Otojiro Okuda, Kokichi Seki and "Tadashi Morimura." Yoshikawa feels a creeping dread. US government officials have segregated the diplomats involved in the Pearl Harbor attack from the other consular Japanese staff.

The Japanese prisoners are loaded clandestinely aboard a US Coast Guard vessel at the Honolulu pier, bound for San Diego and an uncertain future.

# FEDERAL BUILDING

## HONOLULU
## JANUARY 1, 1942

Kimie Doue graduated from McKinley High School in 1937. When the young Nisei woman heard of a job working as a receptionist at the Japanese Consulate, she figured it'd be more interesting than other offices around town. Now she's seated before three intelligence agents, under suspicion of being a traitor.

Only, Doue isn't cowed. This earns respect from the men, FBI agent Fred Tillman, Naval Intelligence agent Lt. George Kimball and Capt. Frank Blake from Army military intelligence. They'll note in their report, "She appeared slightly above-average intelligence for a Japanese girl of her class and impressed the agents as being entirely frank and cooperative."[6]

The FBI is busy filling in the blanks of the consulate's operation. The diplomats have been removed from Hawaii, but there are plenty of support staff left to interview. Today is the start of the investigation of consular secretaries and locals hired to work at the consulate.

Doue worked there as a receptionist, an obviously perfect position for watching visitors and snooping on the staff. There's a baseline of people coming and going at any office; receptionists are in tune with this and can pick up on events that stand out.

The agents ask for Doue's instinct, and she comes up with a name. Tadashi Morimura. It's one consulate staffer who Army intelligence has

---

6. Hearings Before the Joint Committee on the Pearl Harbor Attack, S. Doc. No.79–27 (1946).

segregated from other detainees due to his being suspicious, both for the timing of his arrival and his habit of touring Oahu's heights with a camera.

"And what makes him stand out?"

"He comes into work at about 11:00 a.m., two hours after the doors open, and I almost never saw him at his desk in the afternoons," she says. "There was one week in the fall when he didn't come to work at all."

"Where did he go? Any idea how he got around? He have a car?"

"Taxis," she says immediately. "We usually call the owner of the Royal Taxi Stand, and he used that a few times. But I've seen him drive off with consular secretaries, which is odd because the staff usually looks down on the secretaries."

"You recognize anyone he was with?" Tillman asks.

"Richard Kotoshirodo also has a car, and when they'd leave in it, they'd be gone all day."

"You happen to know the make, model?"

"Ford sedan," she responds. "Must be a '37."

"Thank you for being so observant, Miss Doue; it's extremely helpful and appreciated. Anyone else?"

"He's friendly with John Mikami, I know that," she says. "They've taken girls out together."

The interviewers know an investigative gold mine when they see one—an observant, collaborative witness. "Did anything else strike you about Morimura that was odd or out of place?" Tillman says hopefully.

"Well, there was his map," Doue says. "I'd see a big map of the island spread out on his desk, where he'd mark it up with a pencil."

"He was writing notes on a map of Oahu?" Kimball asks.

"In Japanese, yes, sir," she says firmly. "I'd see it when I'd bring mail to his desk. That was the only time I was ever close to him."

The receptionist has already produced the names of a Japanese official and two American citizens who may have formed a spy ring that prepared the attack on Pearl Harbor. The agents hope that she has more to add, this time about visitors to the consulate. Tillman asks if any struck her as engaged in anything beyond the routine.

Doue can only think of one, a strange *haole* man who showed up in November. She never heard his name, but she remembers his "Jewish look" very well. The man must have been secretly spirited into the Consul General's private office upon arrival; she only spotted him while he was exiting. Pressed, she says his most recent visit was toward the end of that month.

"I think he might be a spy," Doue adds, warming to the reaction of the agents.

Tillman absorbs this and takes a hopeful leap. He knows that in the room next door Special Agents J. Sterling Adams and George Allen are interviewing a German named Otto Kuehn. This is the second day he's been fetched from US Immigration Station detention to be grilled. So far, he's denying being a spy for the Japanese or anyone else.

The FBI agent excuses himself and confers with his boss. SAC Shivers, who's supervising the interviews, smells blood in the water and accompanies him to the interrogation room. Doue's basic description of the strange man matches Kuehn's. A positive ID could sink the man's stubborn denials.

"I want to know if you can do something for me," Shivers says to the former receptionist. "Can you observe a certain person and tell if you've seen him before? He's in the room next door. He'll be surrounded by agents."

She agrees, nervously, and the agents take her to a stenographer's room and place her behind a desk. The FBI agents walk in, keeping Kuehn distracted with a conversation. Doue reacts immediately, gasping and slapping a piece of nearby carbon paper to her face to stay hidden.

"It's him," she says when the men leave the room. "It's the Jewish man."[7]

With Otto Kuehn identified—awkwardly, given his Nazi roots—as

---

7. Ibid.

the consulate visitor, the FBI agents have new leverage to apply to pry a confession from him. He admits that he created the series of signals found in Kita's office and transmitted to the Japanese government. But he denies sending any signals in support of the December 7 attack—it took him entirely by surprise, like everyone else.

One spy has been nabbed. It's now time to shine a light on Morimura's role by grilling Richard Kotoshirodo.

# FEDERAL BUILDING

## HONOLULU
### JANUARY 4, 1942

Agents Tillman, Blake and Kimball sit across from Richard Kotoshirodo, regarding the man with cool eyes. The dual citizen has a thin mustache and full head of hair swept back in something close to a pompadour. He's kept up some of his style while imprisoned at Sand Island, but his eyes and body language are anything but devil-may-care.

There's nothing that inspires more confidence in an interrogator than having specific details they can use to grill a suspect. And they have a trove—dates, times, destinations, parties, women. They have a series of suspicious payments in his account at Yokohama Specie Bank.

Since speaking to Doue, the trifecta of government agents has taken statements from half a dozen secretaries and staffers, all of whom describe Morimura's suspicious activity, loafing at work to travel around the island with drivers like Kotoshirodo.

Everyone in the room seems to tacitly know that they've got him. But they still start lightly, by asking him to describe—in numbing detail—the procedures behind logging and sorting the mail coming into the consulate. It's not as innocent as it appears—the line of questioning leads to the connection between Kotoshirodo and Kokichi Seki, who had actually opened the mail that the secretary delivered to him.

When the conversation turns to the couriers used by the consulate, Kotoshirodo's responses come quickly and confidently. He and Seki's contacts with a salesman (along with the testimony of a confidential informant called "J-1") land a man named Tomoaki Nakamura in the Sand Island camp. "There was no evidence that he had purpose other than that of selling office supplies," one ONI report later admits.[8]

Kotoshirodo becomes more guarded when the agents mention Morimura. He describes an innocuous car trip with him just after the staffer arrived in March 1941. But as the interrogation continues, he begrudgingly but steadily describes a series of expeditions: specific trip itineraries, dates travelled, directions taken, evenings out with women, bills paid in cash directly supplied by Seki.

He also discloses some tension between Seki and Morimura, as the two sparred over a trip across Oahu. He knows about it only because he was supposed to drive them on the cancelled trip. When it comes time to interview the consulate treasurer, he may be willing to implicate someone he doesn't like.

The interrogation ends with Kotoshirodo's signed statement. That day, SAC Shivers sends a memo to the Alexander Young Hotel's sixth floor summarizing what the trio of agents discovered.

MEMORANDUM TO OFFICE OF NAVAL INTELLIGENCE
January 4, 1942
Attention: Captain I. H. Mayfield
Re: Japanese Consulate activities
—Confile; Espionage—

During investigations conducted by ONI, G-2 and the FBI, Special Agent F. G. TILLMAN and Lt. GEORGE KIMBALL of ONI have developed the following information which it appears

---

8. Results of the Clausen Investigation, Hearings Before the Joint Committee on the Pearl Harbor Attack, S. Doc. No.79–27 (1946). https://www.google.com/books/edition/Hearings/P0LkOsQtAbkC?hl=en&gbpv=0.

may be of immediate interest to you in defense of these islands.

During the course of an interview with RICHARD MASAYUKI KOTOSHIRODO, a former clerk employed by the Japanese Consul-General at Honolulu, it was developed that TADASHI MORIMURA, who is registered with the Secretary of State as the Chancellor of that Japanese Consulate, is without doubt the person charged by the Japanese Government with the collection of military information in the Territory of Hawaii. This is substantiated by the statements of other members of the clerical staff of the Consulate, and by MORIMURA's apparent activity.[9]

Kuehn is a Nazi snake and an opportunist, but Morimura is a *bona fide* foreign agent intimately involved in an attack that killed more than two thousand Americans. Kita can't be viewed as anything but the ringleader, with Okuda acting as his accomplice and two consulate secretaries acting as flunkies.

All of these men are in US custody. The diplomats are locked up in San Diego. John Mikami is detained and interrogated on January 6. He tries hiding behind his poor education and broken English but ends up corroborating Kotoshirodo's more effusive details. The pair remain locked up in Sand Island, the newly created internment camp in Honolulu.

J. Edgar Hoover is eager to punish the spies of Honolulu. The State Department disagrees, fearing that Japan would retaliate against American diplomats and citizens under its jurisdiction—or in areas soon to be occupied.

The Navy, FBI and Army counterintelligence agents have uncovered the spy ring that paved the way for the attack on Pearl Harbor. The question for the Roosevelt administration has become what to do with the perpetrators.

---

9.  Clausen Investigation Hearings, 79th US Congress, US Government Printing Office, 1946.

# ALEXANDER YOUNG HOTEL

## HONOLULU
## JANUARY 5, 1942

Today's newspaper has news that Wada doesn't want to read: the War Department has changed Nisei draft classification from 4-A, eligible for military duty, to 4-C, designating an alien. The Selective Service now deems them "not acceptable to the armed forces because of nationality or ancestry."

The question is, what will become of those already in the armed forces? Iwai and his Army friends are convinced they'll be fired. When they tell Douglas Wada, he believes it too. The news today is a confirmation to him that the United States is rejecting the service of loyal Nisei.

With a head full of steam, he approaches Captain Mayfield as soon as he spots him in the office. "The Army is discharging all the Nisei, and I think you have that in mind too."[10]

Mayfield blinks at this sudden approach. "What are you talking about? Who told you that?"

"Any time you have in mind, let me go."

"Calm down, Wada. That's not happening, and there's no way we're letting you resign. So take a deep breath and stop lipping off." Mayfield pauses, controlling his temper. "None of us thinks it's the right thing. Not in here."

Wada has been in the Navy long enough that a dressing-down has the desired calming effect. "Okay sir, but what are we going to do about it?"

Mayfield smiles. "We haven't been spending all this time with your lawyer friend Marumoto and his pals for nothing. There's more than just military intelligence in this city to press the case, but they'll need us to prove it. And there's someone I think you should meet."

A few days later, Wada sits down in an office with a forty-year-old man with keen eyes and a lean frame. He introduces himself as Lt. Cecil

---

10. Wada details this exchange in his MIS Veterans Club of Hawaii interview.

Coggins, from the staff of the commander of the Pacific Fleet. He's been in Hawaii working counterespionage since 1940. As the spymaster with the 14th Naval District, he personally selected and trained nearly a hundred counterespionage agents—most of them Nisei—to watch for suspicious activity within the Japanese community in Hawaii. Wada has been kept away from these kinds of operations to preserve his identity and those of the informants.

Coggins is a Missourian, born in St. Louis in 1902, and attended the University of Missouri and Jefferson Medical College. He became an amateur spy hunter while working as an obstetrician in California, when he monitored suspicious Japanese fishing boats on his own, eventually presenting his data on their clandestine signaling schemes to an impressed Navy department.[11]

"So," Coggins says with no preamble, "how loyal are the Nisei?"

"Just as loyal as I am," Wada says, returning his frankness. "Forget the draft; ask for volunteers. If you ask for two hundred, you'll get four."

"You're sure?"

"If you're not sure, what about me?"

Coggins laughs. "You? You're special."

"What about Iwai?"

"Oh, you two are both special. Being in the service long enough will do that." Coggins pauses. "What if I were to send a wireless back to Washington, telling them to recruit these available Nisei soldiers to work in the European area?"

"Fighting *Germans*?"

"Fighting for their country," Coggins retorts. "In the Pacific area they'll be mistaken by Marines and shot to hell."[12]

"Well, sir, you know the psychology."

Soon after his meeting with Wada, Coggins emerges as a behind-the-scenes defender of the Nisei in Hawaii. What the naval intelligence agent

---

11. His techniques became the basis of the official *Manual of Investigations of the Office of Naval Intelligence*, the one quoted earlier in this book.
12. MIS Veterans Club of Hawaii interview.

told him has been repeated by military and law enforcement—the closer to Hawaii an official is, the more convinced they are of Nisei loyalty.

Coggins meets with members of the Honolulu Civic Association, previously the Hawaiian Japanese Civic Association, and together they draft a statement of Japanese American loyalty. It declares that "to deprive us of the sacred right to bear arms in defense of our country is contrary to the principles upon which American democracy is founded."

The statement is presented to the highest-ranking military personnel in charge in Hawaii, Lt. Gen. Delos Emmons and Adm. Chester Nimitz, at a luncheon organized by Hawaii businessman Walter Dillingham, the transportation building's namesake. Once a skeptic of the Japanese population—plantation strikes prompted his support of the Johnson-Reed Act—the powerful businessman is now an unlikely but welcome champion of their cause.

The message delivered is clear: there's a groundswell in Hawaii in support of the Nisei right to prove their loyalty in uniform. Only time will tell if the effort is enough to convince the Roosevelt administration to reverse course.

## SAN PEDRO YMCA

### SAN PEDRO, CALIFORNIA
### JANUARY 29, 1942

Kenneth Ringle holds a copy of his latest report on the "Japanese problem" and can only hope for the best. It's been freshly submitted to his superiors, and it'll soon be shared and debated nationwide. His nation is on the edge of a historic mistake, and this document is Ringle's way of trying to avert the fall.

Last week, Congressman Leland Ford introduced a bill calling for the internment of all US residents of Japanese extraction, citizens included. He's the first congressman to do so, but he's following the lead of a delegation of West Coast mayors who have been advocating for mass removal.

Ringle's report convincingly argues against mass incarceration in Hawaii. It argues that the vast majority of Japanese Americans are at least "passively loyal" and that any potential saboteurs or enemy agents could be individually identified and imprisoned, "as in fact most already have been."

Ringle wrote his report to be persuasive. "The entire 'Japanese Problem' has been magnified out of its true proportion, largely because of the physical characteristics of the people," it reads. "It is no more serious than the problems of the German, Italian, and Communistic portions of the United States population and it should be handled on the basis of the individual, regardless of citizenship, and not on a racial basis."

The report in no uncertain terms reserves the right to crack down on Japanese institutions, specifically cultural societies, athletic clubs, Buddhist temples and Shinto shrines, all of which he presents as extensions of the Japanese Consulate. Yet it estimates the actual number of saboteurs or agents who pose a threat "to be less than 3 percent of the total, or about 300 in the entire United States."

In such small numbers, any Japanese nationalist groups can be handled: "The membership of these groups is already fairly well known to the Naval Intelligence Service or the Federal Bureau of Investigation and should immediately be placed in custodial detention, irrespective of whether they are alien or citizen."

The report's ultimate solution for America's Japanese population is to "indoctrinate and absorb these people, accept them as an integral part of the United States population, even though they remain a racial minority, and officially extend to them the rights and privileges of citizenship, as well as demanding of them the duties and obligations."

The Ringle Report becomes a clarion call for all those lobbying against mass internments in camps. One of the most prominent voices speaking against internment is J. Edgar Hoover. His trusted Honolulu SAC, Shivers, and other G-men on the front lines of counterintelligence have convinced the director that it's folly.

On February 5, Los Angeles mayor Fletcher Bowron makes a speech calling for the immediate removal of the Japanese Americans from the West Coast. He suggests putting them in camps and putting them to work for the war effort.

FDR now has two visions he can follow—one of paranoia and fear, the other of acceptance and self-confidence.

Ringle, Shivers and Hoover lose the debate on February 19, 1942. That day, Roosevelt issues Executive Order 9066, authorizing military commanders to remove anyone deemed a security threat without a hearing.

Although the language of the order doesn't specify any ethnic group, it's immediately applied to Japanese in America. The Army soon announces mass evacuations of all Japanese residents in designated "military zones" in California, starting in late March. It's the start of something worse.

## FRENCH FRIGATE SHOALS

### TERRITORY OF HAWAII
### MARCH 5, 1942

Lieutenant Hisao Hashizume eases his Kawanishi H8K seaplane onto the water, creasing the surface with a thick, white wake. When the speed decreases enough, he steers toward the two whale-like humps jutting from the water nearby—Japanese refueling submarines, waiting for his arrival.

These are brand-new warplanes, and this is the H8K's first combat sortie. They're built for long-range maritime patrols, big enough to travel long distances and armed to put up a fight against US Navy fighters. They are envisioned to fly alone, but their first operation is a special case.

A second seaplane lands close by and heads for one of the submarines.

Each flying boat carries four 550-pound bombs and a ten-man crew. The pair took off from the Wotje Atoll in the Marshall Islands, about 1,900 miles away. This rendezvous will ensure they can reach their target: Oahu.

The French Frigate Shoals in the Northwestern Hawaiian Islands make a good, remote meeting spot. The area is marked with a twenty-mile reef, dozens of sandbars and a 120-foot-high pinnacle, remnants of an ancient volcanic explosion. It's also only 560 miles to Pearl Harbor, close enough for these high-endurance seaplanes to reach from this refueling rendezvous.

Hashizume and the other crewmembers are in the midst of an armed reconnaissance mission over Pearl Harbor. With just two airplanes, it's not meant to damage much more than morale. But any information the Imperial Navy can glean on the US Navy's dockyard preparations is as valuable as the expected emotional upheaval they'll surely cause by launching another aerial attack.

The refueling is well-practiced and quick. It's a moment of extreme vulnerability, so everyone is motivated to act fast. The submarines are already submerging as the seaplanes take off, heading into the cloudy skies to the east.

In some ways, the flight is a success. No one expects the seaplanes and they soar, unimpeded, to Oahu. The cloud cover helps them evade detection but also makes their own observations nearly impossible. Confused and nervous, Hashizume drops his bombs on a mountainside—the unpopulated slopes of Mount Tantalus, it turns out—and the other airplane follows suit. The impacts wake locals, who curse the Army for an early antiaircraft drill, but the bombs hurt no one.

The mission is a dud, but the aircraft don't go unnoticed. Adm. Chester Nimitz, commander of the US Pacific Fleet, mines parts of French Frigate Shoals and posts ships there to watch for submarines. When Admiral Chuichi Nagumo asks for more seaplanes to track the American Fleet in Hawaii, his fleet won't have this option for armed recon.

The raid is destined to be a historic sidenote, but it's one with ramifications. For Station Hypo codebreakers in Honolulu, it's a moment of vindication. They warned that the Japanese were considering refueling at French Frigate Shoals in preparation of a disruption raid, and now it's happened. Confidence in their cryptography skills will mean a lot as the Pacific War enters its next, pivotal phase.

There is a big battle brewing, and it'll be won and lost on the use of naval intelligence. The US Navy for months has gathered evidence of sizeable numbers of enemy units and equipment moving, signs of a major offensive. The critical source of the information is intercepted messages to and from staging areas in the Marshall Islands. But where will the Japanese attack?

In early March, the designator "AF" begins appearing in coded messages as the target. On March 13, American cryptanalysts break the Japanese Navy's general-purpose code. Now they're able to build the case that "AF" means the American island garrison at Midway.[13]

# TRIANGLE T GUEST RANCH

### ARIZONA
### MARCH 14, 1942

Takeo Yoshikawa takes in a lungful of the dry desert air. Around him are vistas worthy of a Hollywood Western, from the boulder-strewn landscape to the humped silhouettes of mountains on the horizon.

The Imperial Navy spy has studied the United States and understands, academically, how many square miles comprise the US mainland. But travelling from the bustling shores of San Diego to this wasteland,

---

13. Japan wanted to conduct another seaplane overflight of Hawaii on May 30 before attacking on Midway. The submarine refuelers aborted the mission when its captain saw American ships guarding their meeting spot. Blind to the location of American carriers, Admiral Nagumo stumbled into the US trap at Midway, turning the course of the war in the Pacific.

and knowing it's a just small percentage of the overall nation, gives him real perspective.

Not that the group of Japanese diplomats had a chance to sightsee. The entire journey had been taken in secrecy, under armed guard of plainclothes US Border Patrol agents. They had been taken directly to and from the docks of San Diego to a hotel room and then to a train station, speaking to nobody, using side entrances, taking up entire trains with cars emptied of routine passengers. The few who attended them, including the Border Patrol agents, assumed that the group were VIPs.

The final stop was here, at the Triangle T Guest House in Arizona. It's as remote as a Pacific atoll, a cluster of cabins set off from the highway near the almost-town of Texas Canyon. There's a new fence surrounding the cabins, patrolled by Border Patrol agents. No one ever leaves and no guests are permitted. Each week a government official drives to Benson, fifteen miles away, with a shopping list. A local doctor visits only when needed. The ranch manager, staff and the Border Patrol don't know why they're being housed here.[14]

For a secret prison, it's fairly benign. The children seem happy and the adults are slowly acclimating to the alien surroundings. The Americans are friendly, enough so that they play baseball and tennis matches together. The consul general's staff even receives their personal belongings, sent from Hawaii in simple wooden crates.

For all this courtesy, Yoshikawa isn't content. Even though he finds life on the ranch "quite comfortable," he knows federal agents are gathering evidence against him in Hawaii.

The FBI interrogators plague him, Kita and Seki. They come with new names and details, clearly obtained from Otto Kuehn, Mikami and Kotoshirodo. During questioning, the interrogator tends to offer cigarettes, which he always accepts. He tries to keep with the same strategy: evade, evade, evade. Reveal nothing.

---

14. Takeo Yoshikawa, *Japan's Spy at Pearl Harbor* (Jefferson, NC: McFarland, 2020).

As the noose seemingly tightens, the tension within the ranch increases. One day, Kita pulls him aside for a quiet word. "This might not come as a surprise, but we're all starting to think about whether you might be willing to take responsibility on your own," he says. "That way, all the rest of us could go free."[15]

Yoshikawa nods wordlessly, having no intention of doing any such thing. Now he has something else to worry about. If pressured too hard, Kita may be the one who cracks.

# DEPARTMENT OF AGRICULTURE

### WASHINGTON, DC
### MARCH 18, 1942

Milton Eisenhower is packing up his office, mulling over how much has changed this week. He's just arrived back in the capital after a trip to Abilene, Kansas, to bury his father, who died on March 10. He travelled there to attend the March 13 funeral.[16] His brother, Army Brig. Gen. Dwight Eisenhower, is busy working for Army Chief George Marshall in the War Plans Division and couldn't attend but sent a eulogy that he wrote in a spare half hour.[17]

And then, the president called. There's to be a mass evacuation of Japanese population in California. There will be more than a hundred thousand people in need of food, shelter and employment in a matter of weeks. Until today Milton Eisenhower's served as director of information at the Agriculture Department, a job best known for cheerleading Roosevelt's New Deal policies. Now he's to become the head of the freshly created War Relocation Authority.

15. Ibid.
16. *The Kansas City Star,* March 10, 1942.
17. Michael Korda, *Ike: An American Hero* (New York: HarperCollins, 2007).

The WRA is to "take all people of Japanese descent into custody, surround them with troops, prevent them from buying land, and return them to their former homes at the close of the war." It's a daunting task, and he'll need help.

One of the biggest influences on his thinking is the Ringle Report, and Milton Eisenhower has the discretion to recruit whatever staff he wants. So, he writes to its author.

The letter reaches Kenneth Ringle as he's ready to quit intelligence work and get onto the bridge of a warship. He's filling out a request for transfer when Eisenhower's letter arrives. It begins with admiration for his work and clarity of vision for the Japanese. The head of the WRA then says he thinks internment is a mistake, one that needs to be mitigated for the sake of 120,000 human beings on the West Coast who are about to be housed in government camps.[18]

Ringle has lost his battle, at least in the mainland. His son describes him at this time as "drained, depressed and feeling somehow an inadvertent accomplice to the betrayal of America's Japanese." But he agrees to help the WRA.

He begins to expand his January report to a fifty-seven-page manual on how to run the internment camps and, even more importantly, designs plans for reintegration. He also lays the foundation for military recruitment of internees.[19] It'll be Ringle's final work in intelligence; he keeps his transfer for combat duty ready to file later this spring.

But Ringle has one final bow planned before leaving the stage—leaking his revised report to the press, including the parts detailing the overall loyalty of the Japanese in America.[20]

---

18. The WRA doesn't cover the two thousand people of German and Italian ancestry who are interned; separating Japanese from this pool for more rapid release is one of Ringle's suggestions.

19. In an interview with the authors, his son, Kenneth Ringle Jr., said he was motivated by Eisenhower's plea for humane treatment.

20. Ibid. Ringle leaks the report to *Harper's Magazine*, and it runs in October 1942 under the title "The Japanese in America—The Problem and the Solution." The byline is attributed to "An Intelligence Officer." Ringle's son recalls the worldly man's grounding in Midwestern morality. "My father had that lowercase-*d* 'democratic' heritage of growing up in Kansas. He didn't like Harry Truman, but the two were remarkably similar in many ways."

# THE PRESIDIO

## SAN FRANCISCO
## MARCH 29, 1942

It's a grim day for history when Lieutenant General John DeWitt of the Western Defense Command issues Public Proclamation No. 4. The government has mandated the forced evacuation and detention of all Japanese Americans on the West Coast. They'll be jailed within forty-eight hours.

It's been a bad month for those who lobbied against this move. On March 21, Congress passed Public Law 503, which made violation of FDR's Executive Order 9066 a misdemeanor punishable by up to one year in prison and a five-thousand-dollar fine. Now the White House's dictate authorizing military commanders to remove anyone deemed a security threat without a hearing has sharper legal teeth.

The FBI's crackdown on nationalistic Japanese groups continues, but instead of soothing nerves, it seems to stoke fears. On March 27, agents organize with local police in San Joaquin Valley, California, and arrest thirty-eight suspected Japanese residents. Several, including a Japanese language teacher named K. Honma, admit to being part of the Black Dragon Society.

There's no bigger hobgoblin than the Black Dragon Society (or *Kokuryūkai*). Founded in 1901 by martial artist Uchida Ryohei, its public goal was to keep Russia out of East Asia. Despite its prominent members, the group adopted organized crime to further its goals. The society was instrumental in fueling the rise of the ultranationalists in Japan in the 1930s and was blamed for murders of moderate politicians there.

The Black Dragons also established tendrils abroad, forming groups to promote Japanese interests in China and the Philippines. The group has been visibly active in the United States. One of the earliest examples came in 1924, when the Black Dragon Society led protests against the Japanese Exclusion Act. More worrisome are the actions of Japanese Col.

161

Satokata Takahashi, who emigrated to Canada under the name Naka Nakane, snuck into the United States and held joint meetings with anti-government African American groups in Chicago and Detroit. The non-whites, he argued, needed to stick together in a global struggle.

When the draft started in 1940, the Selective Service registrars kept close tabs on who was refusing. They noticed African Americans in Chicago and Detroit were declining to register under religious grounds, describing themselves as Muslim. The FBI had been tipped off that Takahashi was back, and immigration officials already had him in custody before the attack on Pearl Harbor. These seeming signs of Black Dragon Society activity have the FBI on edge.

It doesn't take much to inflame the jingoistic media, and any threat the Black Dragon Society actually poses is inflated to damn the entire Japanese population in America. Pundits declare a fifth column operating from fishing boats, shrines and plantations.

"There are just enough half-truths in these articles and statements to render them exceedingly dangerous and to arouse a tremendous amount of violent anti-Japanese feeling," warns Ringle in his second report.

Many national columnists, radiomen and local politicians prove eager to inflame their readers. "I know this is the melting pot of the world and all men are created equal and there must be no such thing as race or creed hatred, but do these things go when a nation is fighting for its life?" writes Seattle newspaper columnist Henry McLemore. "Not in my book."

He lobbies for the removal of all Japanese from the West Coast. "Personally, I hate the Japanese," McLemore concludes. "And that goes for all of them. Let's quit worrying about hurting the enemy's feelings and start doing it."[21]

This is the environment in which Lieutenant General DeWitt decides to go ahead with his drastic move. He's using the presidential executive order and Congress's new law as the basis to relocate every one

---

21. Henry McLemore, "This is War! Stop Worrying About Hurting Jap Feelings," *Seattle Times*, January 30, 1942.

of the 120,000 individuals of Japanese descent from the West Coast. They are to be held in ten "assembly centers" in remote areas of Arkansas, Wyoming, California, Utah, Arizona, Colorado and Idaho. It's a euphemism for fenced and guarded prison camps. Nearly 70,000 of those to be locked away are American citizens. The government makes no charges against them, nor can those being held appeal their incarceration.

Hawaii's fate is different. The response there echoes the recommendations of the Ringle Report. The local political leadership has been sidelined by martial law, but the local FBI, Army and Navy personnel step up to lobby the Army for a different approach than what's happening in California. Ringle's colleagues in Hawaii, including Mayfield and Shivers,[22] have convinced Lt. Gen. Delos Emmons to resist the idea of mass incarceration. And he sticks to his guns, despite Roosevelt administration pressure.

The detentions that do occur in Hawaii ensnare innocent community leaders, athletes, farmers and journalists, but at least they are subjected to criterion based on more than just race. It's a decapitation strike against all Issei leaders.[23] They end up in the detention camp on Sand Island, once used for ship quarantines. From there, most are shipped to mainland camps.

Despite this, volunteerism in Hawaii continues to soar, with Japanese in the islands serving as block wardens, Red Cross workers, firefighters and ambulance medics. The Kiawe Corps on Oahu clears thickets for military camps, builds trails and strings barbed wire along the coastline. The police reserves are at work on the streets and police stations.

The new, key liaison between people of Japanese ancestry in Hawaii and the military government is the Emergency Service Committee, chaired by Masaji Marumoto. The Morale Section of the Military

---

22. Also worthy of mention is the Army G-2 Colonel Kendall J. Fielder.

23. "The outbreak of the war and its progress removed leadership by the Issei both in the Japanese homes and the community. Some persons of community prestige were interned. In fact prestige was, one might almost say, a criterion of the American authorities for internment." Bernhard L. Hormann, "Postwar Problems of Issei in Hawaii," *Far Eastern Survey* 15, no. 18 (September 11, 1946), Institute of Pacific Relations.

Governor's Office approved its formation in February. Marumoto, with his prewar connections to the FBI, is the ideal front man for an organization meant to promote loyalty in public and enforce it in private. His commitment to promoting Nisei military service is deep enough that he plans to volunteer for the Army once the situation in Hawaii is stabilized.

His leadership comes from the forceful dissolution of the existing Japanese societies and institutions, something Marumoto and other Nisei power brokers endorse and in which they actively participate. The Emergency Service Committee pressures interned trustees of Japanese language schools, Shinto shrines and other organizations to voluntarily dissolve.

The Committee runs "English only" campaigns that replace Japanese signs and rename landmarks, efforts that are done both publicly and less amicably behind closed doors.[24] It's severe self-censorship, done out of unfair but seemingly undeniable necessity. It's also a generational purge that solidifies the Nisei power structure in Hawaii.

The blood donations, war bond drives, networks of informers installed by Shivers, work of military intelligence agents like Gero Iwai and Douglas Wada, police volunteers working to secure the island and freshly uncovered details of the centralized spy ring in Honolulu all argue against wholesale internment. Another factor that limits the detentions is purely practical. Of a population of 423,000 in the Hawaiian Islands, there are 157,900 of Japanese ancestry, about one-third of whom are Japanese citizens. The economy of Hawaii would likely crumble if such a sizeable portion of its population were to be locked away.

Despite the low percentage of internment—about one percent of the Japanese population—the social damage to Hawaii is incalculable. Under military rule, expressions of Japanese culture are all but forbidden. Teaching the Japanese language leads to internment, and the shrines are closed. Kendo is also banned, most of the founders jailed or deported.

---

24. Shigeo Yoshida, "Emergency Service Committee," 100th Infantry Battalion Education Center, 30th Anniversary Reunion, June 1972.

Members of the Army arrive at gyms, gather the tatami mats and kendo swords and burn them in piles.[25]

Within days of Pearl Harbor, the US Army took over the Yokohama Specie Bank, froze its assets and interned its officials. It now uses the Renaissance-style building on Merchant Street as a military police station. In February 1942, the US Department of the Treasury began to liquidate the bank's $3 million in assets, including deposits.

Hisakichi Wada has lost his savings.[26]

# ALEXANDER YOUNG HOTEL

### HONOLULU
### JUNE 3, 1942

In May, Cecil Coggins appears at the Alexander Young Hotel on one of his sporadic visits to the sixth floor, now entirely taken up by more than one hundred Navy intelligence personnel. "Hey Doug, remember that wireless? Well, they're going to do it. Training up an all-Nisei outfit."[27]

His word precedes the announcement by days. The ban on new recruits is still in place, but the Army has activated Nisei troops already in service and formed the 100th Infantry Battalion. Many of its 1,400 second-generation Japanese American members are Hawaiian Territorial Guard soldiers, men who suffered the indignity of having their weapons taken away after the Pearl Harbor attack after spending the day collecting the wounded and clearing wreckage.

Wada feels a welcome shift in Honolulu, happy to feel less like an oddity. "Upon formation of the 100th Infantry, the feeling of the community changed," he would later remember. "I'm not saying that the

---

25. Despite all this, Henry Okazaki will soon help to develop the United States Army's field manual on hand-to-hand combat.
26. He's not alone: two other Japanese bank branches, the Pacific Bank ($2.8 million in assets) and the Sumitomo Bank (nearly $2 million), are likewise dismantled.
27. MIS Veterans Club of Hawaii interview.

Japanese here were unpatriotic, only that they were not able to understand why Iwai and I were the only Nisei serving in such a vital aspect of the military service."[28]

In Wada's eyes, Iwai's counterespionage work scrutinizing the Japanese population cleared the way for the 100th to be formed: "Largely as a result of Iwai's investigation and report, allegations of espionage and disloyalty by Japanese American residents in Hawaii were proven to be wholly unfounded and false."[29] The effort was bigger than just one man, but there's no doubt the counterintelligence agent's lonely work helped ease fears in Washington, DC.

On June 5, the 100th Infantry boards the USS *Maui*, bound for California. It'll take five days to arrive, then another two to reach their training base in Wisconsin. The morale on the *Maui* is high—the Nisei have something to prove, once they're given the chance to fight.

# HOTEL PENNSYLVANIA

## NEW YORK CITY
## JUNE 11, 1942

US Border Patrol Agent Reed Robinson sits in a chair in the seventh-floor hallway of the Hotel Pennsylvania, thumbing through a recent issue of the *New York Times*. He's catching up on the news after a multiday train ride from Arizona to New Jersey and then New York, spent guarding his Japanese prisoners from Hawaii.

The two-dozen consular staffers and their families had arrived at Penn Station that day at 11:00 a.m., where they were secreted across the street to the Hotel Pennsylvania. Robinson is now guarding the room—not so much to thwart an escape as to prevent a random act of violence

---

28. "Letter from Douglas T. Wada to Commander, US Army Intelligence Center," January 9, 1993.
29. Ibid.

against them—as fellow agents Pettengill and Panther rest. He'll be relieved at 8:00 P.M.

The must-read newspaper story is the eyewitness account of Ensign George H. Gay Jr., shot down at the Battle of Midway. He watched the Navy savage three Japanese aircraft carriers from the water and was later rescued to provide the first eyewitness report. "For twenty-four hours Ensign Gay drifted in the seas and obtained one of the most amazing eyewitness stories of a major naval engagement in the history of sea warfare," the *Times* says.

What he saw on June 4 was the Navy's revenge for Pearl Harbor. With Navy cryptanalysts predicting the Japanese fleet's movements, naval aviators were able to get the drop on them as they attacked the base at Midway. Waves of Douglas SBD Dauntlesses from the USS *Enterprise* and *Yorktown* bombed the carriers *Kaga*, *Akagi* and *Soryu*. All three were fatally damaged.

The tide of the Pacific War seems to have turned, if the Navy's crowing is to be believed. Robinson only hopes the news of the damage is as significant as reported, and then idly wonders if his Japanese detainees would believe the news if he could tell them.

The next week is spent at the hotel, visiting with the personable prisoners between duty shifts. Encouragingly, 123 pieces of their baggage arrive, causing a surge in their morale. They are in good spirits, knowing they're heading home. After Midway, with America sure to go on the offense, Robinson thinks that it may be safer for them to stay in the United States.

On June 18, Robinson's final duties with the distinguished prisoners begins when he trundles them out a back entrance and into a car. They head through Manhattan, heading west. Along Pier 97 is a massive white ship, the words "Sverige" and "Diplomat" painted in prominent black letters on its port and starboard. The hull is also painted with an enormous Swedish flag. Everything about this vessel says, "Don't shoot me." And every belligerent in World War II has agreed, even amid the savagery, to allow this ship to cruise unmolested.

The MS *Gripsholm*, built in 1925, was the first diesel-powered cruise ship to cross the Atlantic. Now the US government has chartered the *Gripsholm* (and its sister ship, the *Drottningholm*) to use in prisoner exchanges between Germany, Italy and Japan. This is to be the *Gripsholm's* first trip in its new role as an internationally recognized mercy ship.

On the docks are more than a thousand people, mostly Japanese officials and businessmen and their families, filing up the gangplanks to board the luxury liner. The numbers of transportees make Robinson wonder why his prisoners were treated so differently than the others on board. But if the agent was supposed to know, he figures they'd have told him. That's life during wartime.

Robinson and his two men shake hands with Kita and some of the other prisoners, wishing them luck on the voyage. They are still officially detained by the US government, but they're no longer the Border Patrol's responsibility. It's time to head back to Arizona, where the war is increasing tensions along the US-Mexico border.

Yoshikawa watches the Border Patrol agents leave and feels a weight lift from his shoulders. He and Kita share a hopeful look and the pair board the *Gripsholm*. Until he's in Japanese custody, he'll remain Morimura. Still, the spy's paranoia eases again when the ship pushes away from the pier, leaving the continental US behind.[30]

The mercy ship is surprisingly luxurious, and the crew explains the décor is modeled after a Swedish castle.

The mood among many passengers is merry, enjoying the relief of leaving detention. But also onboard are nine from Hawaii who are being forcefully repatriated to Japan.[31] One of them is Rev. Isobe, of the Kotohira Jinsha on Kama Lane. For those like Isobe, it's not a return. It's an exile.[32]

---

30. Takeo Yoshikawa, *Japan's Spy at Pearl Harbor* (Jefferson, NC: McFarland, 2020).

31. Researcher Matt Parsons cross-referenced records from the FBI and Japanese Cultural Center of Hawaii to compile a full list of those sent to Japan on mercy ships.

32. Authorities arrested 234 Issei Buddhist priests in Hawaii and the mainland during the war, as opposed to thirteen Nisei priests. Kelli Y. Nakamura, Bishop Mitsumyo Tottori, "Patriotism Through Buddhism During World War II," *The Hawaiian Journal of History* (vol. 51), University of Hawaii Press, 2017.

On the bridge, the mood is tense. Oceans are now battlefields, and any big ship is a potential target for submarines. To avoid misdetection, the *Gripsholm* is outfitted with massive floodlights that illuminate the words on her hull and make the white vessel practically glow on the waves. No ship *wants* to be seen these days, making any competent submarine captain pause before attacking.

It takes more than a month for the *Gripsholm* to reach the Portuguese-controlled port of Lourenço Marques, on the southeastern coast of Africa.[33] There, the passengers are traded for 1,554 Allied civilians who had been picked up in Japan, Hong Kong, Singapore and Vietnam. The first US prisoner swap of World War II has been accomplished.

Almost no one beyond military intelligence agents in Hawaii knows what just happened. The spies who the US government knows facilitated the attack on Pearl Harbor—Kokichi Seki, Nagao Kita, Otojiro Okuda and "Tadashi Morimura"—have all been released.

---

33. Now Maputo, the capital of Mozambique.

# PART 7

# THREE YEARS LATER

# KAMA LANE

At age sixty-nine, Hisakichi Wada sits on his front porch and takes in the darkened Kotohira Jinsha shrine next to his house. The gate's closed, the lights extinguished, the priest deported. Behind him, 1042 Kama is just as tomb-like. For the first time, the elder Wada's home is empty but for him.

Chiyo Wada was hospitalized in Honolulu's Kuakini Hospital and died on April 25, 1944, at age sixty-two. Hanako Wada moved out before her mother's death, marrying Tokiharu Ota on April 8. He's a grounds-keeper who works and lives at the largest freshwater fishpond in Oahu. Cut from Hisakichi's traditional cloth, Ota prefers palm frond brooms to modern designs. The couple's new home at 1930 Ualakaa Street is literally in a swamp.

Even with Itoyo and her family living next door, and Douglas and Helen nearby, Hisakichi can't help but feel left behind. His son helps support him financially, but Douglas's work—the hours, secretive nature and military crackdown on his art and religion—stands like an unseen barrier between them.

The military fist around Hawaii is unclenching, at least a little. Martial law eased in March 1943, when some functions of civilian governance returned to Hawaii. (One of those pressing for this was Neal Blaisdell; Wada's former baseball coach "Rusty" is now mayor of Honolulu.) Two years later, however, the General Orders remain in effect, *habeas corpus* remains suspended and the arrests of the supposedly disloyal continue.

Even worse, the US Army last year condemned the Damon Estates in Moanalua Gardens in order to build a $16 million hospital complex. The two-story Japanese tea house Hisakichi Wada built and (until 1942) maintained has been torn down. It's the literal destruction of his legacy in Honolulu.

Douglas Wada sees the damage this does to his father and curses the military and territorial government for their wantonness. "The damn fools!" he calls them.

Hisakichi Wada's never been detained or even questioned. Other shrine carpenters in Honolulu can't say the same—most are in internment camps. Given his son's job, this is not too surprising. He feels grateful and guilty.

There is little relief for other Buddhists and Shintoists in Honolulu, who petition the Army for permission to reopen their facilities for meetings.[1] The requests are routinely denied, and the only religious services allowed are those that commemorate fallen soldiers. Over the years these gatherings have morphed into an almost faith-healer-style movement, led by the fringe sect called Seicho-No-Ie. Devout Issei gather by the hundreds every week with photos of their sons, which the priests and priestesses bless in order to protect them on the battlefield.

Despite the proximity of the Pacific War, this spring's offensive in northern Italy is even more personal to Hawaiians. There, Nisei boys of the 442nd and 100th are bloodily pushing the German Army across the Senio River. The reputation of the unit is one of courage and casualties, and those at home fear the grim, proud tradition of sacrifice will continue.

Hawaii was an epicenter of the national struggle to once more allow Nisei to enlist. Local Army and Navy leadership advised Washington, DC, to let it happen after being approached by patriotic groups, one of them being the Japanese Hawaiian Civic Association.

---

1. It's not easy to find those who can officiate, and those who remain are largely American born. Authorities arrested 234 Issei Buddhist priests in Hawaii and the mainland during the war, as opposed to thirteen Nisei priests. Kelli Y. Nakamura, Bishop Mitsumyo Tottori, "Patriotism Through Buddhism During World War II," *The Hawaiian Journal of History* (vol. 51), University of Hawaii Press, 2017.

The Army was ready to act. One reason for their choice was the work of Gero Iwai, who delivered a secret report to Lieutenant General Emmons that detailed the agent's exhaustive work seeking subversives and saboteurs. He found few of the former and none of the latter. Emmons forwarded the report up the chain with his endorsement to form a Nisei infantry unit.

In February 1943 the Army created the 442nd Regimental Combat Team and solicited volunteers. The initial goal was three thousand enlistees from the continental US and 1,500 from Hawaii. More than ten thousand Nisei men volunteered from Hawaii. Barely one thousand volunteered from the US West Coast states—universal detention clearly dampened enthusiasm in the mainland. In Hawaii, 2,686 were accepted to the 442nd.[2] (As Douglas Wada reads the recruitment numbers, he recalls his comment to Cecil Coggins, and smiles.)

While the new recruits trained, the 100th Infantry deployed to the Mediterranean in August 1943. The battalion, dubbed the "Purple Heart Brigade," was awarded six Distinguished Service Crosses during the first eight weeks of combat in the Italian campaign. The 100th went on to be officially integrated into the 442nd Infantry Regiment, which together are participating in more blood-soaked victories across Europe.[3]

The Issei parents of these soldiers are gripped with fear and have no spiritual outlet, and so many turn to Seicho-No-Ie for comfort. While this new religion spreads, innocent shrines remain shuttered.

As if a sign of the times that year, then-sixty-eight-year-old Hisakichi Wada also mangled his hand. The injuries, their cause only listed in media accounts as "a machinery accident," couldn't be crueler to a *miya-daiku* carpenter.[4] Hisakichi's left hand is now missing most of four of its fingers, digits that he spent a lifetime training to carve intricate designs

---

2. One of them is Douglas Wada's colleague from the Customs Office, Noboru "Hunchy" Murakami.
3. The 442nd would become the most decorated unit in US military history, earning more than eighteen thousand individual awards.
4. *The Honolulu Advertiser,* August 12, 1961.

and mount sturdy wooden frames. The injury compounds the loss of his now irreplaceable masterworks on the Damon Estates.

But the arrival of more grandchildren elevates Hisakichi's mood. Helen and Douglas welcomed Gail Wada in 1944, and Hanako gave birth to Craig Ota this year. But even they are reminders that the new generation is born to a changed Hawaii, a place that's rejecting the generation of immigrants who chose to venture here to begin with.

The human price of the war in Honolulu can be seen in Hisakichi Wada's tired face. He walks the streets a free man, his family growing and his son not serving overseas, but these hard years are nevertheless destroying him.

# SUGINAMI WARD

## TOKYO
## MARCH 10, 1945

The walls of Obihiro-Kōsei General Hospital tremble as the bombs rain down on Tokyo. Takeo Yoshikawa steps away from the window, where he can see flashes across the dark horizon.

He feels dread, but not disbelief. He saw the military and government collapsing before he resigned from the Imperial Navy, and the analyst in him knew the arrival of bombers was inevitable. But as an expecting father, he's burdened with a whole new level of fear. His wife is, even now, between waves of contractions. His child has an ironic sense of timing, Yoshikawa thinks, to be born during a nighttime air raid.[5]

After returning from Hawaii, Yoshikawa returned to Navy General Staff. He worked with the Third Bureau's 5th Section, under Rear Admiral Kaoru Takeuchi, to analyze enemy fleet movements. Part of his

---

5. Takeo Yoshikawa, *Japan's Spy at Pearl Harbor* (Jefferson, NC: McFarland, 2020).

intelligence work involved interrogating American prisoners of war held at a secret detention site in Ofuna, outside Tokyo.[6]

Yoshikawa knew at the time that this violated international law, but he doesn't stoop to torture, preferring a more unexpected, humane approach. He heard the POWs' stories of mistreatment firsthand, and some unexpected kindness can go a long way to win over a previously abused prisoner.

But Yoshikawa also understands why his intelligence-section colleagues sometimes lost their tempers and beat "self-confident and proud" prisoners. The results, he says, were bruised faces and broken teeth. (Surviving POWs describe their treatment there as worse.)

Yoshikawa lost his faith in the Japanese government shortly after Prime Minister Hideki Tojo was forced to resign in July 1944. His successor, Kuniaki Koiso, took to the airwaves crying, "Victory is right before us!" even as the losses mounted.[7] Military intelligence units fed the disastrous war effort with clearly erroneous reports. Yoshikawa was disgusted by this and resigned from the Navy, preferring to build airplanes than help bring the ruination of Japan.

Tonight's air raid is not the first the couple has endured. The bombing of Tokyo has become a steady menace since November 24, 1944, when 111 B-29s raided the Nakajima Aircraft factory. This is where Yoshikawa works, and it's located in his neighborhood in Suginami. Various sections of the city have been struck by high-altitude bombers looking to destroy the remains of Japan's defense industry. Their aim is dubious, but at least they were aiming at military targets.[8]

Firebombing has proven to be more indiscriminate. A first wave of

6. Stephen C. Mercado, "Intelligence in Public Media," *Studies in Intelligence* 64, no. 2 (June 2020).

7. Admiral Takijiro Onishi argued the Japanese "would never be defeated if we were prepared to sacrifice twenty million Japanese lives in a 'special attack' effort." He later followed his own example by committing suicide rather than surrender.

8. In November, Commanding General Hap Arnold responds to a request that the USAAF symbolically bomb the Imperial Palace on December 7. "Our position—bombing factories, docks, etc.—is sound," he replies. "Later, destroy the whole city." Quote from Michael S. Sherry, *The Rise of American Air Power: The Creation of Armageddon* (New Haven: Yale University Press, 1987).

bombers drops explosives, and follow-on aircraft then drop the M69 bombs to ignite the remains. In a city like Tokyo, with residences made primarily of wood and paper, the resulting firestorm spreads damage far beyond the points of impact.

The M69 is not one incendiary bomb but many: thirty-eight bomblets packed inside a single casing. Each bomblet is a hexagonal steel pipe, three inches wide and twenty inches long, packed with about five pounds of napalm and a timing fuse. Each B-29 can carry forty of these cluster bombs, amounting to 1,520 bomblets per aircraft. The munition opens at two thousand feet, releasing a three-foot streamer that points the fuse downward, ensuring it triggers on contact. The fuse burns for five seconds before setting off a black powder charge, creating a burst of napalm that can spray flaming gel up to one hundred feet.

The firebombing raids start as high-altitude daytime missions striving for precision strikes against priority targets but largely fail. Tonight, the attacks have shifted to nighttime. Overhead, 279 Boeing B-29 Superfortress bombers are targeting East Tokyo in an attack focused on destroying civilians and breaking the government's will to resist.

Emi and Takeo Yoshikawa see dawn with a baby girl in their arms. As they leave the hospital, a stream of horrifically wounded are arriving. An estimated one hundred thousand Japanese people have been killed and one million left homeless. Survivors are calling it "the Great Tokyo Air Raid," and they're not exaggerating. It's the most devastating single air attack of the entire war.

Yoshikawa's district, in Western Tokyo, has been largely spared the worst of the bombing raids so far. But as hundreds of thousands of refugees stream out of the stricken Shitamachi Ward, one place they go is unscarred Suginami.

They bring details of the Great Air Raid devastation with them, news that the papers and radio broadcasters are studiously ignoring. The gale-force winds drove the flames ripping through homes, choking people to death as they sought refuge in shelters or killing them while working futile bucket brigades. Those who survived are the ones who fled.

Well-founded fear grips Tokyo. More than eight hundred thousand residents flee between the March bombings and April; the train stations are packed. There are scenes of heartbreak as parents, obeying government orders to help hold the city together, watch their children board trains to the countryside. The people of Tokyo are being chased away by a grim word being used by those emerging from the rubble and ashes, one usually reserved for slash-and-burn agriculture: *yakenohara,* "torched field."

On April 13, the bombers return and Yoshikawa, Emi and the baby hustle into an air raid shelter, doubting its ability to protect them but having no other refuge. He wonders if this raid is a way to commemorate President Roosevelt, who died today. Yoshikawa knows a lot of people celebrated after hearing the news on the radio; they certainly aren't so happy now.[9]

The Army Air Force calls the raid Perdition, the largest incendiary attack on Tokyo, and it was planned well before FDR's demise. Over three and a half hours, 327 B-29s drop 2,120 tons of high-explosive bombs on Tokyo. Firefighters focus their efforts on factories, which have a chance to be saved, and leave the wooden homes to burn. Relatively few bombs fall in Suginami, but a firestorm crosses into the neighborhood from the east.

The city is ravaged. About eleven square miles of Tokyo are now *yakenohara*, flattened and spread with the immolated remains of 170,546 buildings and 2,459 people. Incendiaries also torched several buildings within the Imperial Palace, which wasn't even supposed to be a target. Residents shocked by the carnage in the densely packed city somehow find a reserve of moral outrage when they spy fires raging behind the palace walls.

Yoshikawa ventures into the wastes after this second firebombing raid. He finds Tokyo "transformed into a giant ruin that stretched out as far as the eye could see. A putrid stench floated in the air everywhere you went." People on the streets are scrambling for food, turning to the black market in desperation. Hunger has been a problem in Tokyo for a while, but the nightmare of starvation is looming.

---

9. Takeo Yoshikawa, *Japan's Spy at Pearl Harbor* (Jefferson, NC: McFarland, 2020).

An additional 640,900 homeless now wander Tokyo, staggering to air raid shelters, seeking space with relatives or desperately trying to leave the city before it becomes a necropolis, a place for the dead.

Yoshikawa is stubborn and will stay in Tokyo. The *bushido* code, eroded by war, remains at his core. And at her insistence, Emi and the baby will also stay. She tells him that she wants to do her part in the "final battle for the mainland" that the government is talking about on the radio. When people ask him about his wife's choice, he proudly says she "has a taste for extreme hardship."[10]

# ALEXANDER YOUNG HOTEL

## HONOLULU
## JUNE 20, 1945

"Okinawa," says Bradford Smith smugly. "Mass surrenders. A population calm and under control."

"Congratulations, sir," says Douglas Wada to the psychological warfare expert. "You're not actually surprised, are you?"

"Of course not!" the man spits out. "This is our business, and we know it well. They're approaching seven thousand prisoners taken, men who were committed to dying who decided not to. That's not bad for a bunch of 'paper bullets.'"[11]

It's a moment of glory for the chief Office of War Information (OWI) unit located here in Honolulu. Better known for the propaganda it produces for a domestic audience, there are those within the OWI who are creating leaflets aimed at Japanese soldiers and citizens.

Smith, chief of the OWI Central Pacific Operation since 1942, uses his knowledge of Japan from five years as a teacher at St. Paul's University

---

10. Ibid.
11. Wada said in interviews that he worked with this unit and helped design pamphlets. Smith's comments are adapted from an interview with Smith in *Honolulu Magazine*, "How Propaganda Leaflets Prepared in the Islands Helped End World War Two," February 1947.

in Tokyo to guide his strategy. In December 1944, he formed a cadre of almost a hundred writers, artists, translators and printing specialists to create propaganda aimed at Japanese citizens. The OWI is a joint Navy and civilian outfit when it's founded, bringing Wada into its orbit when it opens shop in Honolulu.

Working with the OWI is a welcome break from his daily duties, which largely are dedicated to reading and censoring the mail heading from Hawaii to Japan. This is a distasteful chore, and Wada prefers his other duty, translating radio intercepts. They come in wax cylinders, where he pieces them together and sends the transcripts up the chain. "All those cylinders," Wada says. "I don't know what happens to those cylinders after I get through them."

But even these have become routine, especially as the war winds down to its inevitable conclusion. The order to help Smith and his psychological warfare unit is a welcome opportunity to hasten its closure.

The OWI branch in Honolulu prepares the leaflets, but the bulk of the printing is now done on the island of Saipan, near Guam. There, they're loaded into Army Air Force B-29 bombers and dropped wherever General of the Army Douglas MacArthur wants. There are a variety of messages, aimed at civilians working at military factories ("Stay home and survive") or soldiers being given examples of honorable surrender in Japanese history ("Why do the militarists abandon the tradition of surrender established since the Meiji era?") Propagandists sometimes call their ordnance "thought bombs."

The battle of Okinawa is the first major military action that comes with a propaganda campaign built into its plan. There are reports of mass suicides and doomed charges into American guns, but there are also newsreels showing Japanese soldiers grouped by the hundreds who've opted to follow the directions of the air-dropped pamphlets. Now, even the State Department is lauding the results.

This leaves Smith in the enviable position of being proven right. "We printed more than six million this month alone," he says. "And there's a lot more coming. We both know what's next."

"Invasion of the mainland. And Tokyo."

"Exactly. We are to crack the 'unbreakable will of the Japanese people.' What do you think of this?"

He passes Wada a ten-yen note, but on one side there's nothing but a message in Japanese: "Your money would soon be as worthless as this leaflet if the militarists continue this hopeless war."

Wada smiles. "You keep those artists busy," he says. "It's not likely to go unnoticed."

Smith lifts another, shaped and colored like a leaf. Wada envisions the sky and ground littered with thousands of them, dropped in spring, conjuring the superstition that a premature fall is a bad omen. On one side there's a Japanese character that signifies the word *thought*.

Japanese character for the word *thought*.

Wada turns it over and reads the words there: "American bombs bring misfortune."[12]

# OKINAWA

### OCCUPIED JAPAN
### JUNE 30, 1945

It takes a lot to defeat a Willys MB, but Masaji Marumoto may have found a road that the Jeep just can't handle. And even if the vehicle can endure the pockmarked, muddy stretch ahead, the attorney isn't sure his body will be as resilient.

Marumoto isn't in uniform, but he's a private in the Army. And not just that—he's a military lawyer tasked not with warfare but rebuilding.

The influential attorney's road from Honolulu to war-torn Okinawa

---

12. Wada says he was involved with the manufacture of propaganda leaflets for Smith's outfit. The conversation is dramatized; all of the leaflets described existed.

began with a failed attempt to join the 442nd. Although he's thirty-seven, he wasn't rejected due to his age but because he was born with a slightly deformed foot. Undaunted, Marumoto pivoted and volunteered with the experimental Military Intelligence Service (MIS) language school in Minnesota, where he served as an assistant director and teacher to future frontline translators and code breakers. One of them is Wada's friend from his undercover customs assignment, Noboru "Hunchy" Murakami.[13]

Marumoto's first overseas assignment came on the heels of graduation from JAG school: go to Okinawa to help the occupying military leaders (mostly Navy) form a civilian government.

This is not a desk job, as is evident by today's testing of the limits of a Jeep. One of his duties is canvassing the refugee camps and surviving villages for Japanese civilian leaders to incorporate into a new regime. There are three hundred thousand civilians on Okinawa, most of them starving. The United States has inherited a humanitarian catastrophe and is relying on organizing the civilians to help prevent more suffering—and to preserve resources for an ongoing war.

Through his travels, Marumoto becomes quickly acquainted with how modern warfare can shatter human infrastructure and ruin native beauty. "The beach we have beats Waikiki any day," he writes his wife from Okinawa. "The scenery is beautiful here. It is a shame that the natural scenery should be devastated as much as it has been."[14]

He's also nervous since there are still Japanese soldiers, hunted and unsupported, lurking in the hills. The US forces had landed here in April and killed an estimated one hundred thousand Japanese troops in three months. They also lost 12,500 men, including Gen. Simon Buckner, killed by an artillery shell the week before Marumoto arrived.

Movement in Marumoto's peripheral vision makes him reach for

---

13. MIS's language school graduated more than six thousand linguists. Major General Charles Willoughby said of them, "The Nisei shortened the Pacific War by two years and saved possibly a million American lives and saved probably billions of dollars."

14. Dennis M. Ogawa, *First Among Nisei: The Life and Writings of Masaji Marumoto* (Honolulu: University of Hawaii Press, 2007).

the pistol on his belt, but it's just a mother and son, walking through the mud under heavy bundles that are larger than their bearers. Marumoto looks at the child and sees his son, Wendell, safe at home in Honolulu.

Thinking of home is a source of both pride and heartache, and he can't say that he misses the politics and compromise he faced while leading the civilian war effort there. Marumoto rode the line between the community and military through his prominent role on the Emergency Committee, but his portfolio of societies and social groups also had to be managed, converted or dismantled.

The fate of the Japanese Hospital fell on him, as the only remaining Japanese Benevolent Society board member not in detention. Despite the staff's courageous actions on December 7, 1941, the large hospital lost its core identity. He presided over its name change to Kuakini Hospital, the conversion of all Japanese signage and the forced rental of a large percentage of its floor space to the military.

What Marumoto wanted more than anything was to serve away from Hawaii, as he so forcefully advocated for others. He got his chance when he signed up for MIS, but that didn't mean Honolulu stayed out of mind. Marumoto visited friends being detained on Sand Island and was shocked to see how "they were being treated as POWs rather than internees . . . I found the conditions appalling. The internees were shabby and unshaven."

He knows that they are still there or relocated to mainland camps. The situation in his hometown is still painful to contemplate, even surrounded by the bigger sorrows of Okinawa. Marumoto is rebuilding a civilian government here, one recruited official at a time, even as Honolulu remains under military control. It's almost perverse.

If surviving this road, and all the other roads ahead, means Marumoto can in some small way help end the war, then it's time to keep moving. He works the gearshift and eases the Jeep forward, rattling across the broken, washboard surface. The silhouettes of the two civilians vanish in the rearview, and he makes his way back to military government offices.

His body is sore from the road's abuse, and the appearance of the child has made him glum. When he arrives back to camp, there is the usual bad food, canned water, no showers, epic dust clouds kicked up by truck traffic and cramped quarters. The grit in the air coats his skin with grime and wears away at his law books.

Yet Marumoto's still happy to be here, seeing the war's impact somewhere other than his home. He writes his wife on July 1: "Despite the inconveniences, I feel much better than when I used to sit at a fancy desk in more civilized surroundings."

# ALEXANDER YOUNG HOTEL

## HONOLULU
## AUGUST 14, 1945

Douglas Wada twitches involuntarily as the sirens blare across the city. He checks his watch—it's 1:45 P.M., a good quarter hour before President Harry Truman's address to the nation. Someone either jumped the gun or wants to make sure every radio is turned on to hear the coming announcement. But for many in Honolulu, including him, the sirens are an unwelcome reminder of December 7, 1941.

Cheering and car horns quickly drown out the sound. There are already hundreds gathered in the streets downtown. Around Wada are throngs of people, military and civilian, waving homemade flags and clutching each other. Faces and waving hands appear on every balcony and rooftop. Cars pass laden with girls in bikinis and shirtless boys. Bottles are being passed around in the streets. The people of Honolulu, like elsewhere in the United States, are unilaterally declaring this Tuesday a holiday.

The city has been alive with rumors for days, and the buildup is intolerable. For many, the parties began on Sunday. A growing tidal wave of glee is sweeping Honolulu as the war seems, at long last, to have reached an end.

The summer has been a bloody grind as the United States tried to convince Japan that it must surrender without conditions. This has been the demand since the Potsdam Declaration, an ultimatum issued by the United States, Great Britain and China on July 26, 1945.

But the amount of pain the Japanese leadership is willing to endure is mind-boggling. US warplanes firebombed Tokyo and other cities between February and April. The world then witnessed the first use of an atomic weapon on August 6, 1945, when Hiroshima and roughly 150,000 of its residents were destroyed by a single bomb. Nagasaki suffered a similar fate on August 9.

This afternoon's address from the White House can only mean one thing: Japan has given up.

At 2:00 P.M. sharp, 7:00 P.M. in Washington, Truman takes to the air: "I have received this afternoon a message from the Japanese government . . . in reply to the message forwarded to that government by the Secretary of State on August 11. I deem this reply a full acceptance of the Potsdam Declaration, which specifies the unconditional surrender of Japan. In the reply there is no qualification. Arrangements are now being made for the signing of the surrender terms at the earliest possible moment . . ."

That's all Wada is able to hear before the crowd in the street detonates in an explosion of euphoria. Every window starts to spew sheets of white paper, some shredded but mostly whole, creating a spontaneous rain of ticker tape. The buildings empty, streams of people transforming from office workers and uniformed military personnel into revelers. The throngs form parades that wander aimlessly, joyously through the city. "There wasn't a quiet spot, an uncrowded niche from Punchbowl to Aloha Tower, from Advertiser Square to Dillingham Boulevard," one newspaper reporter from the *Advertiser* relates.

Even the ONI releases most of its personnel to revel for the day. Wada now faces a gauntlet of happy mayhem to make it back to Kama Lane, where relief must be mixed with confusion. The streets are jubilant now, but who knows what kind of mischief may develop later, especially directed toward Japanese in Honolulu. With Helen and little Gail at home, it's the only place Wada wants to be.

There's a river of humanity surging down King Street, and he follows its flow north toward home. It's a blizzard of noise and flying papers. He sees the bars are still closed, for now, but the restaurants are open and overwhelmed. There's no menace in this crowd, no hint of violence. Some go out of their way to shake his hand or slap his back. Many others don't.

Passing the Kapalama Canal, the crowds thin, but there seem to be roving parades along most blocks. Even so, there is now room for carloads of revelers to roar past, streamers flying from their windows. There are also trucks loaded with sailors and women, dancing, hoisting bottles and waving flags. One shirtless guy sits atop the cab of one such party wagon, smashing a pair of trash can lids together like cymbals. Wada sees this is part of a wider war against the sanitation department, as many residents seem to be tying metal trash cans to their vehicles, noisily dragging them through the city.

The V-J parties continue for days.

The war is over, Sand Island internment camp will close and those Hawaiians shipped away will return. Wada can't help but think that the traitor Kotoshirodo could be among them. The damage done to the Japanese community in Honolulu is deep. Wada just last week spotted the August 5, 1945, comic strip in the *Honolulu Advertiser* featuring a bucktooth caricature standing in the fiery, corpse-strewn remains of Tokyo, asking, "Is all gathered to dedicate new Shinto Victory Shrine . . . where is?"

In the newspaper's front-page V-J celebration coverage, reporter Elaine Fogg notes: "On December 7, 1941, what is now the Victory Club was still the House of Mitsukoshi. We watched the escalator stagger yesterday under its load of joy-rising GIs—and felt very happy indeed over the change from then to now."[15] How can the Japanese population here recover with sentiments like that in the mainstream *haole* thinking?

---

15. *The Honolulu Advertiser*, August 15, 1945.

There's also the matter of his own community's reaction to his wartime service. It's something he and Iwai discuss on occasion. How will returnees from internment camps regard those who aided the apparatus that confined them? Iwai, being with the Army and directly responsible for developing pickup lists, seems more vulnerable to being ostracized, no matter how hard he worked to prove the population's loyalty and promote Nisei military service.

"You know," Iwai says, "they may not want me to live here when this is all over."

"Like hell," replies Wada, trying to make him feel better. "You've been here your whole life. Where else would you go?"

Talk of leaving reminds Wada of his own professional uncertainty. His entire career has been focused on the threat posed by Japan. As a Nisei, he had a unique utility here in Hawaii. Without the war, what role will he play? It occurs to him that his language training in Korean and Chinese could take him far away from Honolulu, home for his entire adult life. The idea is depressing.

# TOKYO STATION

### TOKYO
### SEPTEMBER 5, 1945

Takeo Yoshikawa releases Emi from a tight embrace, barely hearing the noise of the makeshift train station swirling around them. Tokyo Station is smashed—the roof, ornate cupolas and red-brick façade have been blown apart by bombs and gutted by fire—but some trains still run from makeshift platforms.[16]

Yoshikawa's wife and daughter ready to board one, the first step on

---

16. In his memoir, Yoshikawa specifically says his wife and daughter left from Tokyo Station, which suffered major damage. Takeo Yoshikawa, *Japan's Spy at Pearl Harbor* (Jefferson, NC: McFarland, 2020).

their journey to their mutual family village near Matsuyama, on the island of Shikoku. But he's not going with them, which he says is "breaking his heart."

Since the formal surrender three days ago, Yoshikawa's learned to look over his shoulder. He's afraid the ceremony held in Tokyo Bay means it'll be open season on Japanese military men facing charges of war crimes. He meets with Rear Admiral Kaoru Takeuchi, his superior while serving with Section 5, who has stayed in touch out of veteran comradery and shared self-preservation. The man tells him that he's planning to go underground.

Yoshikawa likes the sound of this. It's a passive-aggressive way of resisting the occupation while not actually putting himself in harm's way. It requires a sacrifice—sending Emi home to Shikoku. She's of course obediently leaving, but she's also made very clear that she's not happy about it. There's been too much shared hardship and danger to simply abandon her husband. But he says he's to be hunted down and his life depends on his ability to vanish. With her safe, he'll be able to do that.

It's a tragic parting . . . except as soon as his family leaves, Yoshikawa feels "like I had become much lighter." Without them, he can leave "Takeo Yoshikawa behind and assume any identity." In a sense, he's hiding from the humiliating defeat by reliving the role he associates with his glory days—the undercover operative who's smarter than everyone else.

He takes twenty thousand yen from his savings account, and Yoshikawa is gone. He invests in a load of rice and peanuts, purchased outside of Tokyo and brought in on a rented black-market truck. But fears of a coming crackdown seem confirmed on September 11, when General Douglas MacArthur orders the arrests of dozens of Japanese officials, including former prime minister Hideki Tojo. It could be the start of an overall roundup—rumors are flying that the occupying Allies are seeking members of his interrogation unit for prosecution.

Yoshikawa has more than just the abuses of Section 5 to worry about.

If a tribunal gets their hands on him, investigators are likely to figure out that they have "Tadashi Morimura" in their hands, the spy who doomed Pearl Harbor. "When that time came, I was certain that I would suffer their retribution."[17]

Working the black market in Tokyo is a great way to attract attention, but he needs money to support Emi and to support his life on the run. So he expands the venture into vending fuel, forming a loose cadre of disbanded military men to make pickups from Atsugi air base, located just outside of town. It's great income, but he knows it can't last.

Over drinks one night with his former boss Kaoru Takeuchi, the former admiral says he's heard their former commander at Section 5 has been detained. The two men agree it's time to disappear. They shake hands and go their separate ways.

Yoshikawa sends the bulk of his black-market profit to his wife and heads to the train station. There are American soldiers there, being loud and crass. "All that was left to me was to hold my temper and get aboard a train that was leaving the capital," Yoshikawa would later write.

He gets off three hours and 110 miles later at a place he's never been and where he knows no one: the city of Shizuoka on the south coast of Japan. Yoshikawa wanders aimlessly, his psyche reeling from recent events. He takes in the beauty of the place, its views of Mount Fuji and the imposing ancient remains of Sunpu Castle. But the streets are filled with gaunt, scarecrow people scrounging for food, "their faces . . . old, darkened and frail. You only had to look around to see the omnipresent scars of war."

At least he has money for a room in an inn. He spends a long night of tortured self-reflection. There's only one source of hope he's seen in Shizuoka—Ryutaku-ji, the Buddhist monastery. So the next day, he presents himself to a local temple and offers to sweep it. He becomes a fixture, meditating with the priests between his work of cutting firewood, cleaning the temple and begging for temple alms.

---

17. Ibid.

He also adopts a monastic name, *Hekishu*. It combines the Japanese characters for "boat" and the rock "jasper." The monks ask him for an explanation. "If you made a boat out of jasper, it will sink and never surface again," he says.[18]

## HONOLULU STAR-BULLETIN
## SEPTEMBER 17, 1945

### NAVY HONORS DOUGLAS T. WADA

Pearl Harbor (Sept 17, 1945)—The first civilian of Japanese ancestry to receive the navy's Civilian Certificate of Merit is Douglas T. Wada of 1042 Kama lane, Honolulu [...]. Mr. Wada was presented the certificate and citation by Vice Admiral Sherwoode A. Taffinder, USN, commandant 14th naval district [. . .]. Among those attending the ceremony were: Capt. Peyton Harrison, USNR, district intelligence officer; Cmdr. Denzel Carr, USNR, in charge of the intelligence office's foreign branch; and Lt. Cmdr. Yale Maxon, USNR, chief translator.

The citation reads: "For meritorious conduct in the performance of his duties as senior translator, district intelligence office, 14th naval district, from December 7, 1941, to August 14, 1945. By his initiative, diligence and faithful devotion to the best interest of the navy in the translations of Japanese documents, interviewing Japanese nationals and preparing propaganda for distribution, Douglas T. Wada contributed materially to the prosecution of the war against the Japanese empire."

---

18. Ibid.

# ALEXANDER YOUNG HOTEL

### HONOLULU
### SEPTEMBER 20, 1945

"I guess you've heard Truman made up his mind about the war crimes trial," says Lt. Cmdr. Denzel Carr.

Wada regards the 14th District Intelligence linguist, knowing what he's talking about but unsure why he chose the topic. After some wrangling, President Harry Truman decided that the Imperial Japanese military officers and government officials will appear before a newly formed international criminal court rather than MacArthur's military one. "Just like they're setting up in Nuremberg."[19]

"Not exactly," says Carr. "Now listen. I've been assigned to assist the prosecution of Japanese war criminals. I'm shipping out to Tokyo. I'll be back to the city, after all these years. And Maxon is going too."

"Well, congratulations are in order for you both," Wada says diplomatically. It sounds like a nightmare assignment. "At least you'll get a chance to hang the guys responsible for all of this."

"I'm glad you think so," Carr says, smiling. "You're coming with us."

Something in Douglas Wada's stomach drops, and the weight stays there as Carr spills the details. It's being called the International Military Tribunal for the Far East, charging Japan's top-tier leadership with war crimes. He and Wada are not only to help translate evidence and sit in on interviews, but they are also going to establish an entire translation unit to handle the flood of necessary work. "It's just three-month temporary duty."

"Which top-tier war criminals will we work on?" asks Wada.

"All of them, from Tojo on down."

The endorsement of his current boss for this task means a lot to Wada, as much as he doesn't want to go. This is a prestigious posting, of

---

19. The Nuremberg Charter, a decree issued by the European Advisory Commission, was signed on August 8, 1945.

historic importance. He'll be expected to excel and, in a high-pressure situation, be called on as a mentor, administrator and leader.

If that's not daunting enough, Wada must now go home and tell Helen that, even though the war is over, he's deploying to Japan.

Carr then says, in a different tone, "There's another thing we can do, since we'll be there. Some people in the building say we should try to look up an old friend."

Wada thinks for a minute. "Someone from the consulate who liked to take pictures of the base?"

"The same," Carr says. "The spy."

"Tadashi Morimura." Wada says the name with some venom. Like the rest of the military intelligence and FBI men in Hawaii, he was loath to see the consulate staff returned to Japan without paying for their roles in the Pearl Harbor attack. He's not a "top-tier" war criminal that they'll deal with, but there's nothing stopping them from identifying him for extradition by another war crimes commission.

"Okay," Wada says. "Let's try to find the bugger."[20]

---

20. MIS Veterans Club of Hawaii interview. Wada says he was tasked with finding Morimura but declines to say who did the tasking. This dialogue is dramatized, with reactions based on Wada's description of his initial feelings about the assignment. He calls the spy a "bugger" in the interview.

# PART 8

# JUS POST BELLUM

1. *Jus post bellum* loosely translated from Latin as "justice after war," a term used to describe the morality of how wars should end with the responsibility to rebuild.

# ICHIGAYA WARD

## TOKYO
## NOVEMBER 18, 1945

Seen from the seat of a Jeep, postwar Tokyo becomes a series of flickering images that create a disjointed patchwork in Douglas Wada's mind.

There are patches of life and normalcy in Ichigaya. He sees pairs of GIs and young Japanese women sitting on the grass talking, as if they were in downtown Honolulu. There are trees, intact buildings, streets lined with vendors and servicemen. But then he steers the Jeep onto an unpaved, ash-dusted road that cleaves through a blanket of rubble. He rumbles past gaunt Japanese residents pulling carts or walking the edges with haunted eyes, the road a nightmarish thoroughfare between living and dead parts of Tokyo.

"*Yakenohara*," he says softly.

Nothing remains of this neighborhood, formerly within one of the world's most densely packed cities, except the humps of formless debris and the occasional telephone pole standing mutely among the remains. God knows how many corpses remain buried in the desolate plains that surround him—or immolated to the point they've been incorporated into the soil.

Wada sees an undamaged hill rising from the gray waste. It's his destination: the Yasukuni Shrine. The large complex was founded by Emperor Meiji in June 1869 to commemorate those who die in service of Japan. The tradition morphed into a symbol of dedication to the emperor during the war. When kamikaze pilots told each other they'd "meet again at Yasukuni" before taking off, they meant this place.

Such a prominent hill made the shrine a clear target for the B-29s, but it had been spared, as one of several large buildings in Tokyo scouted as possible headquarters for an occupation. Now it stands abandoned and empty—General Headquarters last month announced plans to burn down the Yasukuni Shrine and build a dog-racing track. That plan has been scrapped, after religious leaders in Tokyo like Catholic priests Father Bruno Bitter and Father Patrick Byrne objected.

Wada is greeted by a sign at the entrance of the Yasukuni Shrine grounds: "Off Limits to All Allied Personnel and Vehicles." All he can see is a broad, paved street, lined with trees that seem to never have seen war, even though they are planted in a place that glorifies it. A large wooden torii gate stands sentinel, its base lost behind a rise that blocks his view. The ornate main shrine is obscured.

An older couple walks past the Jeep, eyes cast down. They're unnaturally thin and likely younger than they appear. He sees his father and deceased mother in each slow step. Wada is wearing his Navy uniform—when ordered to active duty, reserve personnel wear the same uniforms as the rated Navy. What will they think of a Japanese man wearing the enemy's dress? But they don't even spare him a look, as if he's the ghost here. The pair reach the entrance, pause and bow three times. Then they shuffle forward, past the sign and toward the torii gate.

Wada watches them with something more than just sadness. By exploring the ruins of Tokyo, he regains something that he finds necessary for his current assignment—anger. The Japanese leadership knew they were beaten and were too prideful to submit. And their people paid the price.

It takes a half hour to drive back to his Ichigaya office. It was the unified command building of not only the Japanese Ministry of War but also the Army General Staff Office and the Ministry of the Navy. Now it serves as the courtroom and offices for both the prosecution and defense of the International Military Tribunal for the Far East. This building, of all places, was spared the firestorms.

Wada pulls up to a gate, identifies himself and drives to the motor pool. The building has a dramatic art-deco feeling, something he feels he might've seen in the old movie *Metropolis*.[2] There's a white stone arch at the entranceway, familiar to him from Japanese newsreels and newspaper photos. It was a popular backdrop for images of Prime Minister Hideki Tojo greeting visitors to his wartime headquarters. Now, tribunal president William Flood Webb, of Australia, operates from Tojo's office.

Wada heads to the third floor, home of the International Prosecution Section.[3] Attorneys from eleven nations are gathering to tackle an epic task—investigate more than a hundred suspects to determine who should be named as a defendant in upcoming war crimes trial. Statements from victims, witnesses and perpetrators need to be taken and transcribed. War diaries, military orders and captured documents need scrutinization. There are affidavits and depositions, court exhibits and reams of documents generated by the defense teams that all need to be processed by linguists.

Two men can't do this alone, and Wada and Carr arrived before the attorneys to establish a core of trained translators to handle the workload. They'll have nearly a hundred men assigned to the task, one of the unseen flywheels of the war crimes trial.

The spy hunting has gone poorly. A spy in the US Navy would likely have naval training, so he checks Japanese military records. There's no Tadashi Morimura listed. His records in Japan don't exist, as if the man were an invention.[4] Without a name, it's impossible to find a person in this ravaged country. And he may very well be dead. The hunt is stymied.

In a search for justice, Wada must content himself with his job. He's only been here a few weeks, but the initial distaste he felt for the assignment is wearing off. He's growing to appreciate his chance to punish those who led the Japanese people to such indescribable suffering, even

---

2. *Metropolis* was released in 1927.

3. The courtroom is on the first floor; the second floor has offices for judges.

4. Wada says to the MIS Veterans Club of Hawaii interviewers: "When I went to look for him in Japan after the war, I couldn't find him. I checked with the Navy Department, and they said they [didn't] have a guy by that name. What the hell!"

when defeat was inevitable. Morimura may be out of his reach, but Tojo and the rest aren't.

And any time he feels his professional resolve erode, he can make a foray into the ruins of Tokyo to regain his motivation.

# FORMER JAPANESE MINISTRY OF WAR

## TOKYO
### NOVEMBER 28, 1945

Naval Technical Mission
Interrogation No. 10
Date: November 28, 1945
Place: Fleet Liaison Officer with the Supreme Commander for the Allied Powers[5]
Subject: Pearl Harbor Attack

Personnel Interrogated: Captain Minoru Genda, Air Operations officer on staff of Admiral Nagumo during attack on Pearl Harbor

Interrogators: Captain Robinson and Captain Peyton Harrison, USNR

Interpreter: Douglas Wada

Minoru Genda is small in stature, but his presence still seems to fill the interrogation room. His body is still but his eyes move around the room quickly; he's not nervous, just naturally observant.[6]

"The idea of the surprise attack originated with Admiral Yamamoto

---

5. FLTLOSCAP is representative of the Commander in Chief, US Pacific Fleet in Japan with the staff of the Supreme Commander, General Douglas MacArthur, while handling matters connected to the surrender.

6. Later, one Caucasian interviewer would note that "he thinks much more quickly and more to the point than the average Japanese."

during a conversation at the start of February 1941, with Admiral Onishi, of the 11th Carrier Division," Genda says. "I was present."[7]

For Douglas Wada, seated next to him, the war has come full circle. Since December 7, 1941, it has upended his life and the lives of his family and city. Now he's face-to-face with one of the main architects of the raid on Pearl Harbor.

The attack was a seeming breach of international peace that the Americans are eager to include on the list of Japan's war crimes. Genda's testimony could be pivotal in linking leadership to the surprise attack, but he's also going to make a deposition for the defense.

"I remember the admiral saying, 'If we have war with the United States, we will have no hope of winning unless the US Fleet in Hawaiian waters can be destroyed,'" Wada says, as he translates Genda's words. "And we discussed this. He directed Admiral Onishi to draw up a plan for an attack. And I was called in to evaluate it."

"You were one of very few people to know this was being planned," Wada now translates a remark from Captain Peyton Harrison, the naval reservist from Salt Lake City who's leading the interrogation.

Genda ticks off the names and ranks of the fourteen architects of Pearl Harbor attack: "Admirals Yamamoto, Ugaki, Nagumo, Yamaguchi, Okusaka; Captains Onishi, Kuroshima and myself; Commanders Kusaka and Ono; and on the Navy General staff, Admiral Fukudome, Captains Sanagl and Tomioka and Commander Miyo."

Genda goes on to say these men sat down on September 1 to scrutinize the attack with "map games" done in secret at the War College in Tokyo. On November 15, Admiral Yamamoto finally approved the plan and gave it to Admiral Nagumo.

On November 22, the striking force rendezvoused at Etorofu and departed on its mission on the morning of the 26th. They maintained a speed of twelve to fourteen knots and refueled at sea whenever the weather permitted. "The tanks were always to be kept full," he says.

---

7. *Pearl Harbor Attack: Report of the Joint Committee on the Investigation of the Pearl Harbor Attack*, Doc. 244, 79th Cong., 2d session, Part. 13, Exhibit No. 8, pp. 391–4.

Storms complicated these operations, but it was the promise of bad weather that helped cover their approach. "We didn't expect to meet any shipping, and fog and stormy weather would impair visibility conditions," Genda notes.

Wada's ears pick up when the conversation steers to intelligence about Oahu. "Twice after departure, information was received from Naval General Headquarters in Tokyo giving the dispositions of the US Fleet in Pearl Harbor," Genda says.

"When did these arrive, sir?" Wada says quickly, both anticipating the follow-up and eager to hear these details about the Honolulu spy ring.

"The second dispatch on this subject was received three days before the attack, on December 4."

Wada now hears the other side's details of how Pearl Harbor was struck. The strike force launched its airplanes about two hundred miles north of the western tip of Lanai. Three submarines were placed in a line a hundred miles ahead of the carriers for the final dash southward. Surface speed of these submarines was twenty-three knots. If they sighted any planes or ships, they were to submerge, get clear and surface only when it was safe.

As the mission approached, Genda and the staff felt more confident that they'd maintained the element of surprise. But the orders were clear—even if the Americans were found to be on alert, the attack was to proceed. Wada also finds it interesting that Genda says that just thirty-nine fighters were left to protect the Japanese carriers from an aerial counterattack.

These men remained in the flight-ready rooms; the surprise was total, and the fleet escaped unmolested. "Everything," Genda says softly, "went off according to plan."[8]

The hint of bitterness they detect doesn't need explanation. The intelligence, planning and early execution of the Pearl Harbor mission were nearly perfect. Yet the most important targets had been missed, the naval base was not crippled and the sleeping American giant had been hurt just enough to fully awaken. Genda knows this better than anyone.

---

8. Ibid.

The interview winds down with some historically useful housecleaning: a recital of the Imperial Navy order of battle on December 7. Genda notes that the Japanese lost twenty-nine aircraft, mostly in the second wave when the Americans were shooting back.

The men finish up with an exchange of polite goodbyes, when one of the captains says, "Doug, ask him if he has any regrets about bombing Pearl Harbor."

Genda offers a sad smile and a quick reply.

"He says," Wada notes, "'We shouldn't have attacked it just once.'"[9]

## INTERNATIONAL MILITARY TRIBUNAL FOR THE FAR EAST

### TOKYO
### APRIL 29, 1946

The International Prosecution Section gives its opening statement, but it'll take a week for the trial to begin. At this rate, Douglas Wada thinks bitterly, he'll be stuck in Tokyo until 1950.

The prosecutors narrowed down the list of Class A defendants to a group of twenty-eight.[10] The strategy here is not to convict every Japanese leader who participated in war crimes. The prosecution is trying to establish a pattern of similar abuses in various places, the core of any argument that the top leaders knowingly used war crimes as part of their expansionist strategy. The reams of battlefield orders his sections have transmitted now make more sense.

The Tokyo Trial's top-tier approach means that many Japanese

---

9. Genda would say this on many occasions in his life. Many agree that more attacks would have damaged the infrastructure at Pearl Harbor, especially the oil tanks, altering the course of the war by shutting the base down entirely for a long time.

10. Class A: Charges against Japan's top leaders alleging crimes against peace. Classes B and C: Charges against Japanese of any rank who covered conventional war crimes and crimes against humanity.

leaders responsible for the worst war crimes are not to be punished. Even high-ranking military figures are to be spared prosecution. Minoru Genda is one of the unprosecuted. He supplies depositions for both the prosecution and defense teams.

Prime ministers, top military commanders and foreign ministers are charged with fifty-five separate counts, including waging wars of aggression, murder and crimes against humanity, such as torture and forced labor. The prosecution must prove that war crimes were systematic, that each of the accused knew that troops were committing atrocities and that they had authority to stop them.

The trial is not the only punishment MacArthur has in store for the militarists of Japan. He orders the Japanese Army dismantled and all former military officers prohibited from taking positions in any level of government. MacArthur also takes aim at landowners who supported Japanese expansionism and the *zaibatsu* (business conglomerates) that helped build the imperial war machine.

Here, MacArthur's name is synonymous with power. Wada sees elements of local emperor worship aimed at the general; every day, crowds of Japanese citizens wait for a glimpse of him outside the Dai Ichi Building, just as they used to linger outside the Imperial Palace.[11]

One thing Wada didn't expect—or want—from the war crimes trials is how damned long they are taking. It's going to take nearly two hundred days in the courtroom for prosecutors to present their case. That alone might take the proceedings into 1947.

He and Carr are responsible for a sprawling but efficient translation machine. They have four sections with one hundred translators in each section. These are positions held by Tokyo residents, making him an unlikely boss of hundreds of Japanese citizens. Each section also has three Nisei monitors to correct the translations, most of them being MIS school graduates. (Alas, Hunchy is not one of them.)

Wada is the second in command of all the sections. Documents

---

11. As described by *The New Yorker*, October 19, 1946.

come to him, and he assigns them to each section with a deadline. After the monitors hand in the work, Wada double-checks it and hands it to Carr to send to the prosecutors.

His contact with the Japanese makes him empathize with them, at least on some points. When it comes to Russia having any say over war crimes proceedings, he agrees that they don't belong here. When he has to provide translations for Russians in Tokyo, Wada holds up the paperwork, and this delights his Japanese employees.

The three-month assignment stretches long past the original timeline, month by month. As it does, Wada watches Tokyo slowly recover. Residents are returning in droves, eager to find a place in the reconstruction. The rubble is cleared within months, although Wada often hears the distant booms of damaged buildings being brought down by controlled demolitions. Other times, the promising sound of construction noise fills the air.

It occurs to him that part of the life cycle of a "burned field" is its regrowth.

Yet, it's hard to watch the occupation forces' cavalier attitude toward the suffering Japanese people and the exploitative way the troops prey on desperate women. The Japanese population is proving just as predatory, as black marketeers and criminal gangs flourish.

Wada's unease at being stuck in Japan crests in the fall, when his temper boils over during a clash with an Army colonel. It's a matter of pride, and he tells Carr that the officer has a habit of "telling me what to do."

"I don't work under him, he can't boss me around like that," he complains.

"Is he interfering with your actual work?"

"No, but the guy is trying to run me."

"Doug . . ."

"We were only supposed to be here three months, and it's going on seven. I've had it. I'm going back to Hawaii. They hate my guts here anyway."[12]

---

12. Using Wada's quotes and language from his MIS Veterans Club of Hawaii interview, in which he describes his conflict and his complaints about it.

Wada is happy but not too surprised to hear in November, even as the prosecution still labors in the courtroom, that the Navy is reassigning him to Hawaii. He'll have to read about the tribunal's conclusion in the newspapers.[13]

It's time to head back to Honolulu; Helen; his two-year-old daughter, Gail; and a waiting job with 14th Naval District Intelligence.

## ALEXANDER YOUNG HOTEL

### HONOLULU
### FEBRUARY 18, 1948

Douglas Wada sets the phone in its cradle, dazed. A source has called with a name from the past. He doesn't divulge his source, even in classified memos, but someone has told him that Richard Kotoshirodo has resurfaced.[14]

Hunting Pearl Harbor spies is not his mandate. These days he's focused on ferreting out Communists from those who have access to the Pearl Harbor Naval Base, mostly merchant marines. He's striving to make more of the position by becoming an expert on local Communism. Like everything else in Hawaii, the history of socialism here is different than the mainland.

Understanding Japanese Communists requires knowledge of the sugar plantation strikes of the 1920s, when Socialists finally found a toehold in Hawaii. The direct connection is news to the intelligence

---

13. The prosecution's presentation continued until January 24, 1947. On December 23, 1948, General Tojo and six others were hanged at Sugamo Prison. Sixteen defendants were sentenced to life imprisonment. The Tokyo War Crimes Tribunal gave no clear-cut ruling on whether or not the surprise attack on Pearl Harbor was a breach of international law.

14. This tip could have come from a police officer or a neighbor who knows Wada works for the Navy; he doesn't operate informants but certainly is open to an approach of someone with information. In his confidential ONI report, he only cites "a reliable source." Given his unique status as the only Nisei in Navy intelligence, Wada is obviously a unique intelligence bridge to the Japanese community.

community, which has not yet delved into this local labor apocrypha. He's already started compiling his findings in a tome he's dubbed *A Brief History of Communism in Hawaii.*

Wada is well-regarded in the service, and publishing such an examination will propel him to better assignments. He knows the Navy is happy with him—his superiors shuffled the internal paperwork to keep him in naval intelligence. His designation as a reservist and special agent enables him to conduct investigations as either a civilian or a military officer, as needed.[15]

Wada's friends and colleagues notice that he more often presents a military persona, which makes sense because most agents don't advertise their position if they can help it. Also worth considering is the atmosphere in Honolulu. Being a naval officer isn't associated with pickup lists and late-night detentions, as is the case for Army intelligence officers.

However, there's only so much distance Wada can gain between his wartime service and his city. These same work friends have heard that Wada has been shunned by some in his community. There's a lot of bitterness on the streets, particularly among internment returnees and religious Issei.

Wada has some bitterness, too, when it comes to the spies who walked away from their Pearl Harbor operation. It's been a while since Wada's given thought to the former consular secretary, the traitorous enabler who admitted to driving Japanese consulate spies around the island. Kotoshirodo and his wife, Joan, spent the war in a mainland camp in Utah. He confessed his involvement in Pearl Harbor to the FBI and an internee hearing board. Yet, he's never been charged with any crime, even after much investigation and deliberation by the military investigators and the FBI.

In December 1945, Richard and Joan Kotoshirodo returned to Hawaii—or rather, the feds returned them—and the couple decided to

---

15. A confidential March 17, 1947, document about his hiring as "a civilian ONI agent" that year shows his annual salary was four thousand dollars.

stay in Honolulu. They lived in a neighborhood adjacent to Kapalama. She was pregnant with their first child. (Wada doesn't know it, but ONI vowed in a 1946 memo to the FBI to investigate Kotoshirodo's "activities" with a complete report. Two years later, none has materialized.)

Wada learns that the man, as befitting a lifetime of steady drinking, now works as a bookkeeper at the Pacific Liquor Company here in Honolulu. Recordkeeping there seems like a contact sport: that year a federal lien for $183,900 in back taxes was filed against the company.

None of this is newsworthy, in and of itself. But Pacific Liquor's president and chief stockholder is Takaichi Miyamota, a well-heeled businessman who owns several liquor distribution and sales outlets across the Islands. Miyamota is also, in the words of local newspapers, "a political associate" of the mayor.

Long-standing power broker John Wilson is amid his third go as mayor of Honolulu, serving from 1920 to 1927 and from 1929 to 1931 and taking office again in 1946. He's a Democratic party stalwart, born in Honolulu in 1871. As a Hawaiian with a Scottish and Tahitian bloodline, he's helped ease tensions between his political party and ethnic groups in Hawaii. His relationship with Miyamota is a living part of that effort.

Wada doesn't see much to be done but chronicle the development and move on with his other duties. So he turns back to the typewriter, inserts a page with a "FOURTEENTH NAVAL DISTRICT" letterhead and starts to work the keys.

The curt report, just three paragraphs long, is processed by the 14th DIO and forwarded to the FBI.[16] The counterintelligence ties between civilian and military government agents, forged during the war, remain in Hawaii and are ready for the Cold War.

Wada's update will be the last thing in the FBI's file on Richard Kotoshirodo, besides a 1958 request to see it by a US Air Force Office of Special Investigations special agent who's probably conducting a

---

16. His memo is included in Kotoshirodo's FBI files via National Archives, accessible via: https://archive.org/details/RichardKotoshirodo.

background check. The promised ONI "comprehensive report on Kotoshirodo's activities" never appears in the espionage enabler's FBI records.

# KAMA LANE

## HONOLULU
## MARCH 4, 1949

The news travels through Kapalama like a gust of wind: the federal government is attempting to sell the Kotohira Jinsha property. The news appears in local newspapers and spreads by outraged word of mouth.

In December 1947, Hawaii's Kotohira Shrine was finally allowed to reopen its doors, along with the other closed Buddhist and Shinto shrines. Rev. Isobe was still deported, so the religious services were nonexistent. As the shrine struggled to find its footing, the Justice Department swept in. In April 1948, citing the Trading with the Enemy Act of 1917, the government seized Kotohira's assets. The Act cited was passed into law to confiscate German American property during World War I. Other shrines across Hawaii also had their assets seized, including the Izumo Taishakyo Mission, Hawaii Daijingu Temple and Wahiawa Daijingu.

Upon hearing of the move to liquidate the land, the Kotohira Jinsha solicits the services of the law firm Robertson, Castle & Anthony, which files suit on March 31, 1949, against the United States attorney general, the State of Hawaii and the Federal Alien Land Office. They're challenging the apparent misuse of the Trading with the Enemy Act.[17]

It's the first such lawsuit initiated by a Japanese organization, and many eyes across Hawaii and the mainland are eagerly watching to see who wins.

---

17. *Kotohira Jinsha v. McGrath*, 90 F. Supp. 892 (D. Haw. 1950).

# US DISTRICT COURT,
# DISTRICT OF HAWAII

### HONOLULU
### MAY 18, 1950

Judge Joseph McLaughlin knows the value of a good legal fight. That's why he refuses both the plaintiff and the defendant requests for a summary judgment in *Kotohira Jinsha v. McGrath*.

It would have been easier to just rule from the bench and save months of judicial headache. The shrine wants its property back, and the government just wants the whole matter ended. But some scraps are worth having in the open forum.

Several trial dates were set and changed, delayed by both sides' trips to Japan to gather evidence. The trial began on March 27, paused as attorneys travelled to Japan and resumed on May 3. The trial ended May 17, after a "two-day argument upon the facts and the law," as the court puts it.

Today, McLaughlin dismantles the government's case one blow at a time. His ruling finds the government presented no justification for Kotohira Jinsha's closure. "The evidence does not establish any Japanese governmental control, direct or indirect, of this plaintiff, nor any direct or indirect doctrinal or financial control by any state shrine in Japan," he states in his decision. "Nor is there any evidence upon which I could possibly find or hold that the national interests of the United States required that this little insignificant shrine in Hawaii, with not more than five hundred members, should be deemed to be an economic, military, or even ideological threat to the United States."

The judge includes a pocket history of how the imperial government used religion to foster war. "To accomplish the ends desired by the militarists of Japan, Shinto was distorted and state Shrine loyalty became a test of patriotism and the false doctrine of Japanese supremacy and eventual world domination was fostered, which led to its ultimate defeat in World War II."

He reserves some editorial commentary to the shrine's form of Shinto, finding an umbrella approach to spirituality confusing. "Plaintiff and its members did not even understand what it was they believed or why," he writes in the court's ruling. "I am not even prepared to find on this evidence that this plaintiff, operating in the United States of America, held beliefs which could be agreed to constitute a religion . . . Its members practiced by way of prayers and ceremonies a primitive mythology known as Shinto or Way of the Gods, with special attention to three gods, but whether the plaintiff's tenets were the same as state Shintoism in Japan, or even Sect Shintoism in Japan, has not been established by either party."

Aside from these sharp elbows under the robe, the ruling is an unambiguous victory, not just for the shrine but for the democratic system tested by governmental overreach. "We have not yet come to the point nor will we ever while 'this Court sits' where the government can take away a person's property because it does not approve of what that person believes in or teaches by way of religion or philosophy of life," Judge McLaughlin writes. "The First Amendment forbids."[18]

The property is returned to the shrine. Getting legal permission for its leader, Rev. Isobe, to return from Japan will take longer. But the legal victory paves the way for more lawsuits and more overturned seizures. More importantly for the residents of Kapalama, the Kama Lane complex is free to reopen.

Soon after the judge's ruling, the shrine announces plans to hold an autumn festival in October, its first religious celebration in nearly nine years.

For the Wada family, it's a welcome return to normalcy. Hisakichi Wada still lives at 1025 Kama Lane. Leaving the swamp, Hanako Ota and her groundskeeper husband, who has a new job with the city, now live at 1045 Kama. They have their second daughter on April 1, 1950, giving the old man one more grandchild to dote on.

But Douglas Wada has moved on from Kama Lane. He, Helen and

---

18. Ibid.

daughter Gail now live at 1339 Alapai Street, a few blocks from Iolani Palace in downtown Honolulu.[19] Wada also expands his extracurricular activities, with a focus on developing the next generation. He's involved in the Lions Club of Honolulu, as he had been since before the war, but now also serves as an advisor to the Kapalama Community Club for Boys and donates his time to the Boy Scouts of America.

Wada's also opened his home to his nephew, Leslie Kowanoto, who's come from Japan. It's a very personal way to help his extended family recover and for the agent to push back on the dark memories of war-torn Tokyo. More selfishly, it's nice to have an impressionable twenty-year-old man around the house.

# MOUNT TANTALUS

## HONOLULU
## JUNE 26, 1950

Robert Shivers takes in the view of jungle canopy from the porch of his second home on Oahu and inhales deeply. There's a fragrance to the air here in the rainforest above Honolulu that he's never found elsewhere. At age fifty-six he feels older than he should, but even this makes him appreciate life's everyday pleasures. In Hawaii, there are many.

He found it hard—impossible—to stay away from Oahu. The FBI special agent in charge only left his post for the mainland in April 1943 after suffering chest pains, likely a small heart attack. But by 1944 he was pining for Hawaii, and Shivers pulled strings with friends of Eleanor Roosevelt to receive an appointment as collector of US Customs in Honolulu. He works out of the Post Office, Custom House and Court House building in Honolulu and lives in the upscale and *haole*-dominated Kahala neighborhood near Diamond Head.

---

19. US Census, 1950.

One joy of Honolulu is living close to their former exchange student, Sue Kobatake, who is still considered part of the family. The home holds sharp memories for her: she and Margaret stayed here for weeks, under armed guard, after the attack on Pearl Harbor.

This jungle getaway remains the family's haven, now from the stress of the city and its politics. There's a schism in the Democratic party, and everyone realizes that Governor Ingram Stainback won't be in office forever. He's been repeatedly appointed territorial governor since 1942, although his first two years were purely as a figurehead since the military ran the government.

Robert Shivers is a leading candidate for the job as territorial governor. This May, political operative Harry Krunick—a backer of Stainback—put the odds of Shivers's appointment at five to one, the leading contender next to the current occupant. The rumor is that Stainback may resign if he's sure the party won't fall into local left-wing or Communist leadership. (The governor was a staunch "cold warrior" before George Orwell popularized the term *cold war* in 1945.) Shivers can maintain a tricky progressive but conservative Democrat coalition, hence the good odds.

The year has been promising. One of Shivers's backers also just wrested control from the local unions, which won't push them from Stainback immediately but sets up the former SAC for their support. John Burns, the former police captain and current Democratic party chairman, already spent two months in Washington lobbying for Shivers.

He and Connie have been in the Tantalus house for weeks, sensing this phase of their lives may be the calm before a coming storm of hard work, political power and backroom intrigue. But they wouldn't want to be anywhere else.

As he sits quietly on the porch, inhaling the fresh Hawaiian air, sudden and severe pain shoots through his chest and arm, familiar but much worse than his attack in 1943. He cries out for Connie. She drives him six miles through the center of the city to Queen's Hospital, where

Shivers is diagnosed with having a major heart attack. "His friends are asked not to call because of his condition," the *Honolulu Star-Bulletin* warns ominously.[20]

Robert Shivers survives until June 28. He's buried in Diamond Head Memorial Cemetery, where Sue Kobatake can often be seen tending to the grave.

# ROYAL HAWAIIAN HOTEL

## HONOLULU
## AUGUST 31, 1951

Douglas Wada takes in the view of Waikiki Bay from the top floor of the Royal Hawaiian, recalling the sight of black smoke seeping into the air above Pearl Harbor almost ten years ago. If someone told him that Sunday morning that he'd one day serve as bodyguard to a Japanese leader in Hawaii, he'd probably have punched them.

"I think that it's time that I paid respects to the war dead," says Prime Minister Shigeru Yoshida, standing behind him.

Wada turns, face impassive but blood pressure ticking up a few points. At age thirty-nine, he's proven himself to be more than just a translator. He's been chosen for this escort duty for his knowledge of Japanese language, culture and etiquette. Wada is reliable and easy to talk to and knows his way around a golf course. He can charm Hawaiians, mainlanders and Japanese with a culturally flexible but authentic charm.

"Sir," he responds, "I respect the idea, and I'm sure the rest of the city would appreciate it. But I am responsible for your personal security, and from that vantage it is not a good idea."

"You have worked here a great deal of your life and were born here. Do you perceive a threat to me or to my family?"

---

20. *Honolulu Star-Bulletin*, June 27, 1950.

The naval agent glances at Yoshida's daughter, Kazuko, who's watching avidly. "Sir, with the peace treaty not yet signed, there's too much at stake to risk such an outing. I've been ordered to recommend you stay here."

Yoshida regards him with cool eyes. The prime minister is on his way to San Francisco to normalize relations between Japan and the United States. The nation is still, technically, at war with the US and will be until the Treaty of San Francisco is signed. It's a vanquished enemy, but an enemy nonetheless. "Did the reception at the airport today make you think there is a credible threat?"

Wada can't help but relax his face a little, almost smiling. The number of flower leis hung around Yoshida's neck on the way from the airplane to the car nearly blocked his vision. He's regarded as a peacemaker and a sign of a return to normalcy. "It only takes one person who disagrees strongly enough, sir. Again, the risk is too high, given your mission."

"Given my mission," he says, "the risk is too high not to do this. Please get a car ready. I am bringing the family with me."[21]

The National Memorial Cemetery of the Pacific is located five miles from the hotel, at the Punchbowl Crater, inside the towering, circular ruins of an ancient volcano. Everyone ignores the sight of antiaircraft batteries and pillboxes. Wada also knows that there is a secret signal collection station on the crater's heights, having visited once during the war.[22]

Instead, he plays the role of amiable tour guide and goes into the crater's ancient lore. Its Hawaiian name, Pūowaina, means "Hill of

---

21. Kazuko relates this conversation in an interview published in the *Bungei Shunju* monthly magazine weeks after the trip. Wada became a go-to tour guide to Japanese government officials like House Speaker Naka Funada, Chief of National Police Asonuma and Parliamentary Members Ohira, Kishi and Furuya. He also showed US Defense Secretary Dick Cheney around Honolulu.

22. "You guys know that we had a small wireless station up [in the] Punchbowl? They made me go. It was secret," Douglas Wada says in the MIS Veterans Club of Hawaii interview. It's an intriguing statement that he's not asked to expand on. In May 1944, a new monitoring station opened on the Punchbowl, including a rhombic antenna for communicating with San Francisco using Telefax equipment. Since translations were done in California, it's unknown why Wada got this tour. Given the OWI is one of the parties using the intercepts from the station, perhaps it was related to his relationships with them. But that is conjecture.

Sacrifice." This was once an altar for human sacrifice and punishment for violating taboos. This history holds some grim analogs, so he adds that Kamehameha the Great would fire the pair of cannons mounted at the rim to salute distinguished visitors. "If he knew you were coming, we'd hear them now," Wada says.

The graveyard ceremony is brief and solemn. Reporters watch as Yoshida lays flowers at the cemetery, a moment described in countless newspaper reports that warm the nation for the events in California. Wada is impressed, but for the moment he knows that they've pushed the security team too far.

"That was very moving, sir," he says when Yoshida returns. "Now may I recommend that we go back to the hotel?"[23]

# IMPERIAL HOTEL

### TOKYO
### SEPTEMBER 1, 1951

Takeo Yoshikawa reads the newspaper with moist eyes. Prime Minister Shigeru Yoshida has arrived in California to finalize the Treaty of San Francisco. He tries to hide his emotion by taking a sip of whiskey and Coke.

"I thought you might want to see that," says Gordon Prange, the chief historian on General Douglas MacArthur's occupation staff. "It's really over."

Yoshikawa has thought of this day for years, spent on the run under false names and with only sporadic trips into his village to visit his wife and child. While living as an impoverished monk and a street merchant, he's been reliving the last decade in his head and rationalizing the avoidance of his obligations to his family as self-flagellation. The Japanese

---

23. These exchanges are dramatized.

police have made an early, half-hearted attempt to locate him, but there is hardly an active dragnet. But it's easy to just run aimlessly, encouraged by pursuers that he's grateful to have as an excuse.

Now even the idea of being chased has evaporated, courtesy of the coming treaty. It's a blanket pardon and the end of his wandering traveler routine.

Seeing this happening months before, he had fetched his wife from the village outside Kyoto and headed home to Tokyo. He's been selling shave ice in public parks and biding his time. Soon he'll be able to use his own name and build an actual life around it.

But Yoshikawa's not ready to leave his role in history forgotten. His ego, pride and lack of options for the future make him ready to break his cover. In September, after seeing clues in the Japanese diplomatic cables, Prange scours Japanese Navy officers for leads. One reveals Yoshikawa's name and role in the Pearl Harbor attack. The author reaches out with a letter, and Yoshikawa agrees to an interview in Tokyo.

When they meet, the former spy tells all. By his rationale, coming forward is a way to show the American occupiers that "we Japanese are not anything like acquiescent slaves who ought to feel compelled to bow and scrape."[24]

On September 8, Japan is one of forty-nine nations that sign the Treaty of San Francisco at the city's War Memorial Opera House. Now Yoshikawa has no fear of prosecution for abuse of American POWs or his role in the Pearl Harbor attack in any criminal or civil court.

The Japanese spy at Pearl Harbor has at long last come in from the cold.[25]

---

24. Japan pays $5.4 million to the Red Cross. Article 16 bars subsequent lawsuits filed by former Allied prisoners of war against Japan.

25. When Douglas Wada read the spy had resurfaced under his real name, it made him "mad as hell." MIS Veterans Club of Hawaii interview.

# BEIJU

# DAIJINGU TEMPLE

## HONOLULU
## AUGUST 11, 1961

Hisakichi Wada watches anxiously as the temple volunteers heft the wooden shrine statue into the Daijingu temple at 61 Puiwa Road. He's wearing his best suit—a simple black jacket and tie—and the temple leader, Bishop K. Kawasaki, wears a fine ceremonial robe and tall, round hat.[1]

The statue is more than a statue; it's a four-foot-high replica of a full temple, painstakingly assembled and carved from white cedar. It's of course immaculately built in the Daijingu style, with a sharply peaked roof, dramatically curved awning and elaborately carved trim. A set of small wooden stairs leads to equally diminutive but well-adorned doors.

Kawasaki feels the man beside him tense as the workers near the shrine's main altar and offers him a smile as it's safely delivered to its home. Wada spent three years on this wooden *miyadaiku* artwork, and the date of its delivery is no accident.

Hisakichi Wada is turning eighty-eight next week, on August 16, and creating the shrine is his way of marking this important life milestone. Birthdays in Japan weren't celebrated on the day of birth, but on the first of the year, until the war ended. But even before Americanization brought personalized birthdays, turning eighty-eight was different.

It's called *beiju*, a banquet to honor a full life. The celebrant, surrounded by friends and family, eats Sekihan sticky rice colored with steamed red adzuki beans and sea bream fish dishes. As at any birthday

---

1. *The Honolulu Advertiser*, August 12, 1961.

party, the *beiju* recipient wears a special outfit: in this case, a golden *chanchanko* vest and *zukin* hat.

The placement and consecration of his woodwork shrine is more important to Hisakichi Wada than a party. It took three years to complete this work, but only after decades of relearning how to perform his craft—and demonstrate his faith—with only four fingers on his left hand. It's a feat that's not lost on *Honolulu Advertiser* reporter and photographer Jerry Chong, who's on hand to watch the delivery.

The presence of friendly media is a sign of how Honolulu has recovered. The shrines and temples of Honolulu are reviving. There are a lot fewer than before the war, and many deported priests remain in Japan. But the shadow over Shintoism and Buddhism has lifted.[2]

One of the biggest winners in the postwar spiritual scene in Hawaii is the Seicho-No-Ie. This year the sect's foundation published *Truth of Life*. Its author, Masaharu Taniguchi, is a machine of New Thought book production, already producing dozens of volumes for a growing international audience. In 1952, he coauthored a book with Fenwicke Holmes titled *The Science of Faith* that successfully promoted the budding denomination to Europe, South America and the United States. He's kept followers motivated with a steady output of writing ever since and tours the world to spread the metaphysical word.

However, the Kotohira Shrine on Kama Avenue is again being intruded on by the modern world. In 1957, the State of Hawaii announced plans to take two-thirds of the shrine's property for a highway construction project. The H-1 in downtown Honolulu, opened in 1953, is already antiquated. Making a modern freeway will require a lot more land, necessitating the use of imminent domain to force sales. The Hawaii Kotohira Jinsha must sell and can only negotiate a price. In another blow, Rev. Misao Isobe, who returned in 1952, died in April 1958.

So, Kama Lane will be changing again, this time by the intrusion of the new highway lanes. There's no way to escape life's turmoil, but it's

---

2. The same can be said of martial arts: the Mikami Dojo on Martha Street reopened in September 1945, enjoying a surge in popularity from the suppressed demand.

now again possible for an old Issei man in Honolulu to find peace and purpose.

Hisakichi Wada is making up for lost time with a quest. His days are spent with his grandchildren and Itoyo on 1042 Kama Lane, but in Wada's workshop are the designs of four more altarpieces that he plans to deliver to the surviving Shinto shrines on Oahu. The project is ambitious and will take years.

The idea makes the old man happy. Watching the grandchildren grow is like watching the wooden shrines slowly come together. They're daily reminders that his family and his faith have a future in Hawaii.

# THE CAREER OF DOUGLAS TOSHIO WADA, AND THE BIRTH OF NCIS

Douglas Wada was a trailblazer on many levels. He was the only Japanese American agent in the ONI until the late 1960s.[1] Even though he was a reservist, his civilian role in naval intelligence was also groundbreaking. This is of special interest to us, since he helped lay a cornerstone of what would become NCIS.

This all goes back to FDR's memorandum of June 1939, which directed for the first time that ONI investigate Navy cases relating to sabotage, espionage and subversive activities. Over the ensuing decades, during war and peace, the solid work done by naval intelligence agents built a foundation for independence.

This certainly includes Douglas Wada, but it's not easy to trace his contributions. Even colleagues and friends seldom got a full view of his professional life. One, Capt. Bill MacDonald, referred to him as "a man of mystery" while writing a short biography of him. Tracing his career, especially after the Tokyo Trial, is hampered by some secretive assignments and Wada's professional stoicism. He did his work and did it quietly.

Wada transferred to Japan in 1954, assigned as a liaison and interpreter to the commander, US Naval Forces, Far East. Being a "classified interpreter" for rear admirals and high-ranking officials would be part of his official job description for decades. The position brought Wada in close association with high-level Japanese intelligence officials and earned the trust of their US counterparts. He cultivated contacts with the Prime Minister's Office, Maritime Self-Defense Force, Japanese Coast Guard and National Police.

---

1. "To my recollection, up to February 1966, we had no female agents and only one non-Caucasian, Douglas Wada, in Honolulu," recalls the NIS's first director, Jack Johnson. In reality, ONI recruited an African American agent in 1965. But that's another story.

Not known for being a street agent, Wada nevertheless got involved in unorthodox field work. Soon after his arrival in Japan in 1954, a captain named Rufus Taylor ordered him to scour every bar near Yokusuka in a fruitless attempt to find out who was buying the booze appearing on the Navy base there. The dead-end assignment earned him the nickname "Bourbon and Wada."[2]

Wada's position soon evolved into more weighty intelligence operations. There's a strange reference that appears in a confidential memo in Wada's military records that summarizes his career. In February 1956, the special agent was recalled to active duty as a lieutenant commander in the Naval Reserve "and assigned to work on Project Impulse, due to his Japanese language capability." In July 1956 he was released from active duty, only to be called back to active service in January 1958 "and returned to Japan for the same project."

The memo doesn't say what Project Impulse was, and it appears in his military records and nowhere else. There is one possible candidate. Wada late in life told MacDonald that he helped Japan screen returning POWs released from China and Russia for security risks. Some prisoners had been held since World War II and had presumably been brainwashed or replaced with undercover operatives. The United States worried that the nation, still struggling to get on its feet, could be inundated with Communist infiltrators.

A confidential ONI memo from 1963 notes that Wada was the Navy's "representative in a combined collection program with the Army and Air Force. It involves preparing, levying, analyzing and evaluating . . . reports of naval interests in the Far East Communist Bloc. This program exploits the Japanese Government's most clandestine intelligence agency. It uses an elaborate apparatus to collect information from travelers, repatriates and crew members."

The mention of "repatriates" could refer to some of Wada's work with returnees from Russia and China, which seemingly expanded into

---

2. Wada himself related this anecdote to MacDonald, coauthor of "Douglas Wada Remembers," in 2007.

something more comprehensive. This could be the fruits of Project Impulse, but there's no way to be sure from available records.

Wada's usefulness to the Navy—and perhaps the CIA—only grew as his time in Japan continued. "On March 16, 1964, after protracted negotiations, another US intelligence agency turned over its collection program from the Japanese Maritime Safety Agency (Coast Guard) to the Intelligence Division, Commander US Naval Forces, Japan," the confidential 1964 memo reads. "The unique asset to accomplish this task is Douglas T. Wada. It will call for both imagination and ability of a high order to maintain historically productive relationships with an extremely shy organization which demonstrates often a xenophobic attitude toward foreign intelligence."

In any capacity, civilian or military, special agent or Navy commander, Douglas Wada was a quiet trailblazer. As the only American of Japanese descent working for ONI until the 1960s, he not only thrived but excelled.

In the United States, Wada's family also flourished. Gail Wada married Lawrence Harada on October 7, 1966, in Alameda City, California. She became a teacher and, eventually, a vice principal.

In 1975, Douglas and Helen Wada returned from Japan after twenty years. The central question is, did the Japanese community in Hawaii hold him responsible for the internments and help drive him from Honolulu?

It went that way for Gero Iwai. "Almost immediately after the war, Iwai had to bug out of there," noted Victor McPherson, a retired NCIS agent and coproducer of the agency's history project who has researched the era. "Wada stayed in Hawaii until the early fifties, and again after the war trial he had a period in there chasing Communists." But he returned to Japan, where he likely felt more useful or wanted. "You wonder if the pressure got too much for him then; people still knew who he was."

Wada's assignments abroad help shed light on his motivations for leaving Hawaii for Japan for so many years. It seems that Wada's work in Japan was urgent enough to keep him there. "Mr. Wada, recruited and trained as an investigator, has become uniquely valuable to the Navy," reads one 1964 memo from J. O. Johnson, acting chief of naval operations, arguing he be promoted under the civil service "only so long as he serves in his present assignment." His career depended on his being in Japan, and that is likely what kept him away from his beloved Hawaii for so many years.

On February 4, 1966, the secretary of the Navy created the US Naval Investigative Service as a separate entity. For the first time, NIS was divorced from the disjointed, parochial control of local District Intelligence Offices and ad-hoc security groups. ONI took on a large new responsibility outside traditional intelligence: investigative jurisdiction of major crimes throughout the Navy and Marine Corps.

Captain Jack Johnson, USNR (Ret.), the first director of the NIS, described this development in an unpublished essay:

> Mainly because of miscarriages of justice in disciplinary matters occurring during World War II, the US Congress enacted the mandates contained in the Uniform Code of Military Justice. This document placed a greater need for competent investigation of major crimes occurring among military commands on ships and ashore. Since ONI already had an investigative force for intelligence matters, it appeared logical for the task of investigating serious crimes be assigned to Naval Intelligence. Furthermore, there was frequently a relationship between security considerations and the culprits of serious crime.[3]

Johnson lauded the solid work of the generation of agents that preceded the 1966 breakthrough. "We cannot forget those hundreds of patriotic and dedicated persons, now deceased, who labored during the earlier years before NIS came into existence," he wrote. That group certainly includes the intrepid and reliable Douglas Wada.

Helen and Douglas Wada returned home when he retired from the

---

3. Accessed via NIS.org, https://ncisahistory.org/wp-content/uploads/2020/09/Capt-Jack-Johnson -memo-on-the-Gestation-of-NIS-compressed.pdf

Naval Reserve, holding the rank of commander, in July 1975. Their daughter had moved away, but they had ties in Honolulu, friends from the *haole* and Japanese communities accrued over a lifetime. Wada remained involved in youth organizations and military veterans' clubs and pursued golf and fishing with the relish of an island tourist.

On May 27, 1980, Wada and Stephen Kanda were at the Ala Wai Golf Course waiting to obtain an early tee-off time when they were robbed by clubhouse burglars, who stabbed Wada repeatedly with a pocketknife. Wada survived and sued the city of Honolulu. He lost the suit and an appeal in 1986.[4]

In 1992, an underfunded NIS reorganized and took on a new name, the Naval Criminal Investigative Service (NCIS). Two years later, NCIS was remade into a civilian-led federal law enforcement agency with fourteen field offices and operations in 140 locations worldwide. In 1995, NCIS introduced its Cold Case Homicide Unit, the first such dedicated unit in the federal government. By 2000 Congress vested NCIS civilian special agents the authority to execute warrants and make arrests. The trail blazed by Wada and his generation of agents is still being followed by multitudes.

Helen Fusayo Wada died in 2005; Douglas Wada followed her on April 2, 2007. The pair left three grandchildren and three great-grandchildren. Douglas and Helen are buried in the National Memorial Cemetery of the Pacific, in the Punchbowl Crater of Honolulu.[5] Their military marker is adorned with a small, circular flower, a faith symbol marking the grave of practitioners of Shinto.

---

4. *Hawaii Times*, May 28, 1980; *Kau v. City and County of Honolulu*, Intermediate Court of Appeals of Hawaii, February 20, 1986.
5. The Wadas' grave is located at Section C10-K, Row 300, Site 303, https://gravelocator.cem .va.gov/ngl/NGLMap?ID=7676357.

# LOOSE ENDS

# HISAKICHI WADA

The *miyadaiku* carpenter finished his quest in June 1964 when he completed construction of four decorative shrines for the Shirasaki Hachimangu, Dazaifu Tenmangu, Inari Jinja and Suitengu temples. The shrines were consecrated in a joint ceremony on July 9, 1964. He died on July 29, 1969.

# HANAKO (WADA) OTA AND ITOYO (WADA) YAMAMOTO

Hanako had three children, Craig, Ruby and Lorraine. Her husband, Tokiharu Ota, earned renown in local media for bringing palm frond brooms back to the public parks. Hanako died on November 3, 1968. Itoyo died on December 2, 1988, at age eighty-five and is buried at Nuuanu Memorial Park.

# KENNETH RINGLE

Ringle saw combat onboard the USS *Honolulu* and then as commanding officer of the USS *Wasatch*. He earned a Legion of Merit during the Battle of Leyte Gulf. After the war, he commanded a division of transport ships in China. "My sister remembers him saying that due to feeling as an inadvertent accomplice to the internment he had so fought against and loathed, he would never again speak Japanese for the US government," said his son, Kenneth Ringle Jr. "To my knowledge he never did."[1] Ringle was the architect of the naval provisions of the NATO treaty. He retired from the Navy in 1953, promoted from captain to rear admiral upon his retirement. Kenneth Ringle died of a heart attack on March 23, 1963. Margaret then married retired Navy Adm. Arthur "Rip" Struble, who directed the amphibious landing at Inchon during the Korean War and who died in 1983. Margaret Avery Ringle Struble died March 3, 1999, at age ninety-two.

# RICHARD KOTOSHIRODO

The former spy enabler became assistant treasurer of Better Brands Ltd, and his name appears in 1957 advertisements as one of the company's chief officers at a time when it had branch offices in Guam and Japan, including one at the US airbase at Kadena. His direct superior was company treasurer B. F. Dillingham II, son of the Honolulu power broker. Kotoshirodo died on July 3, 2009.

# GERO IWAI

The Army counterintelligence agent remained in Honolulu with the 401st CIC Detachment until 1949, when he was assigned to the 441st CIC Detachment in Tokyo. He returned to the US in 1954 and three years later, after twenty-six years of service, retired from the military as a lieutenant colonel. Always feeling isolated from the populace he monitored, Iwai settled in San Francisco, where he passed away in 1972. In 1993 and 1994, Douglas Wada wrote impassioned letters lobbying for Iwai's inclusion into the Military Intelligence Corps Hall of Fame, identifying him as a trailblazer for himself and others. Iwai was inducted in 1995.

---

1. Interview with the authors.

# KAZUO SAKAMAKI

The submariner spent the early days in captivity in a deep depression. However, he found incoming Japanese prisoners wrestling with suicide and became renowned in prison for assisting them. After the war he became an executive with Toyota Motor Corporation, eventually rising to president of its subsidiary in Brazil. Four years following his retirement in 1987, he returned to the United States, where he viewed the submarine he commanded during the attack upon Pearl Harbor and cried.

# MASAJI MARUMOTO

After returning to Honolulu in 1946, Marumoto resumed his law practice and in 1954 became president of the Hawaii Bar Association, the first Asian American to hold that office in the United States. President Eisenhower tapped him to become an associate justice of the Supreme Court of the Territory of Hawaii in 1956, another first. He served until 1973 and witnessed Hawaii become a state in 1959. He died on February 10, 1995.

# THOMAS GREEN

Green was promoted to the rank of major general on December 1, 1945. Green served as JAG until November 30, 1949, when he retired from the Army. Green then worked as a law professor at the University of Arizona until his death on March 27, 1971, at the age of eighty-one. For his service during World War II, Green received the Army Distinguished Service Medal with Oak Leaf Cluster and five Army Commendation Medals.

# THE STATE OF HAWAII

On August 21, 1959, President Dwight D. Eisenhower signed a proclamation admitting Hawaii into the Union as the 50th state. The new flag became official on July 4, 1960. Nisei veterans of World War II—including Masaji Marumoto—were in the vanguard of those who successfully solicited for statehood. The Nisei also helped break the traditional plantation owners' Republican lock on political power by mobilizing support for the Democratic party, which thereafter dominates the state's politics.

## TAKEO YOSHIKAWA

In the early 1960s, the spy of Pearl Harbor came forward again. He cowrote an article with Marine Lieutenant Colonel Norman Stanford, an assistant naval attaché in Japan, for the US Naval Institute's *Proceedings* magazine. He was lambasted in the Japanese media from all directions, as a traitor and a militarist. Yoshikawa lived out the remainder of his life operating a gas station, buoyed by his wife's earnings as an insurance agent. He sold appearances and articles as needed, was elected to the local town council twice after laws against veteran political involvement were lifted and died in 1993.

## THE KUEHN FAMILY

Otto Kuehn was sentenced to death, but his sentence was then commuted to fifty years of hard labor. His daughter, Susie, and wife, Friedel, also served time in prison. Dr. Bernhard Hormann, the head of the sociology department at the University of Hawaii, provided a home for young Hans Joachim Kuehn during his mother's incarceration. Susie and Friedel went back to Germany with him upon their release; Otto was deported to Germany after the war.

# CECIL COGGINS

The doctor turned spy hunter served as a guerilla fighter with the "Rice Paddy Navy" in China during World War II. During the war he also ran operations with British Secret Service Agent Ian Fleming, future creator of James Bond. One of their schemes reportedly involved radioing Japanese seamen and pilots, talking them into surrender. He was promoted to rear admiral on retirement. Coggins died May 5, 1987, in Monterey, California.

# THE *KAMAKURA MARU*

On April 28, 1943, the *Kamakura Maru* (formerly known as the *Chichibu Maru*, the passenger ship that carried Douglas Wada back to Hawaii from Japan) sailed from Manila to Singapore with 2,500 soldiers and civilians onboard. The vessel was unescorted. The American submarine USS *Gudgeon* fired a spread of four torpedoes at the Japanese vessel at 3,200 yards and sank her in the Sulu Sea. Four days later, Japanese ships rescued just 465 survivors: 437 passengers and only twenty-eight out of 176 crew.

# KOTOHIRA JINSHA

On June 26, 1962, the shrine's president, Kenichi Nakaya, finalized the sale of 30,837 square feet of shrine land to the state for $122,250. The money went into renovations of the other properties. Construction on the first new section of H-1—the Lunalilo Highway—began in 1963. On May 24, 1962, the shrine office and priest's quarters were torn down to make way for a new community hall, office and parsonage, all completed in September. The roof of the *temizusha* (absolution basin) was restored and the torii gate was repositioned. A ceremony commemorating the completion of the new shrine buildings was held on September 26, 1962. The shrine still stands at the foot of Kama Lane.

# FOLLOWING THE GHOSTS

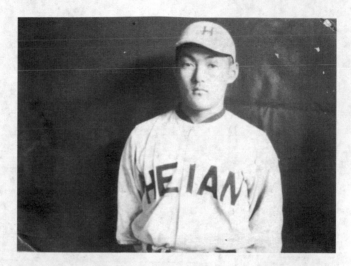

Douglas Wada in the uniform of the baseball team he played for while in Japan.
COURTESY OF THE WADA FAMILY

Douglas Wada and his University of Hawaii baseball team, the Deans, circa 1936.
COURTESY OF THE WADA FAMILY

---

## ASSOCIATION OF RETIRED SPECIAL AGENTS
## OF THE NAVAL INVESTIGATIVE SERVICE
### MEMBERSHIP RECORD

NAME: _DOUGLAS  T. WADA, CDR, USNR (RET)_

ADDRESS: _419A ATKINSON DR #308_

TELEPHONE
   HOME: _(808) 947-2934_     WORK: _NA_

DATES OF SERVICE ONI/NIS: _JAN. 1938 – JULY 1975_

TYPE OF SERVICE (SPECIAL AGENT, ACTIVE DUTY, ETC.): _SPECIAL AGENT,_

_ACTIVE DUTY_

BADGE AND CREDENTIAL NUMBERS: _#122_

LAW ENFORCEMENT/INVESTIGATIVE EXPERIENCE BEFORE APPOINTMENT TO ONI/NIS:

_UNDER COVER BEFORE APPOINTMENT_

ASSIGNMENTS: _HAWAII + JAPAN (FIRST NISEI ASSIGNED TO JAPAN)_

INTERESTING CASES/OTHER COMMENTS: _____

PLEASE COMPLETE AND SEND TO:
S. Frank Scinta, 5402 Broadmoor Street, Alexandria, VA 22315-4016—Telephone: (703) 971-4016

On his application to a naval investigative services organization, Douglas Wada listed the date of his involvement with ONI as 1938, referring to his undercover work on ships arriving in Hawaii. It was the start of a long career as an agent.
UNITED STATES DEPARTMENT OF DEFENSE

Emp. Ass'n. (a) Herbert Iamamoto, Sec., Disabled Veterans Organization. 15.(a) Kasuo Kikuta, Agr. Advisor, Waianae Develop. Co. 14.(c) Cornelius Downs, Catholic Herald. (d) William Kawahara, vegetable retailer. 15.(a) George B. Pottorff, Pub. Rel., Pan-American Airways. (b) Edward M. de Harne, Eng., Hon. Rapid Transit.

Novels, world news, movies, fishing and youth activities.

Read the local English and foreign language papers and magazine "Newsweek" to maintain broad knowledge of domestic and international affairs.

Qualified for. Considering all the activities listed under item 27, page 4, what or which do you qualify for best. List one or more.

A-4, A-10, B-5(a), B-5(b), C-10, E-8, E-9

Douglas Wada's application and appointment to a direct commission as a lieutenant in naval intelligence in 1948. His naval records are vital sources of information on his background, physical attributes, and career. Notice he was appointed January 28, 1949, but for some reason, they backdated his rank to December 28, 1948.
UNITED STATES DEPARTMENT OF DEFENSE

Douglas Wada in his naval uniform.
COURTESY OF THE WADA FAMILY

The Japanese spy at Pearl Harbor, Takeo Yoshikawa, after he revealed himself after the occupation ended. He never received official recognition for his service, and neighbors in Japan often blamed him for starting the war.
UNITED STATES WAR DEPARTMENT

Douglas Wada graduated from one of NIS's first "basic agents" classes. Formal training was a rarity prior to these sessions, and this could very well be the first class. The two men in uniform are not attendees but senior leadership, probably the director of naval intelligence and the director of NIS.
UNITED STATES DEPARTMENT OF DEFENSE

Commander Douglas Wada was in the US Naval Reserve from 1949 to 1969. He served in Japan and retired in his hometown of Honolulu.
UNITED STATES DEPARTMENT OF DEFENSE

Douglas, Helen, and baby Gail pose
with Hisakichi Wada.
COURTESY OF THE WADA FAMILY

KAZUO
SAKAMAKI
ISN HJ 1 MI

Kazuo Sakamaki after his capture as the first POW captured by US forces during WWII. He was roundly applauded for his work with suicidal POWs while in captivity, but when he returned to Japan, he also faced anonymous letters calling for his own suicide. His eldest son says he is named for his father's fallen crewman, Kiyoshi Inagaki. UNITED STATES DEPARTMENT OF DEFENSE

Sakamaki's submarine, washed ashore on the morning of December 8, 1941. NAVAL HISTORY AND HERITAGE COMMAND

A road near Ushigome Ichigaya in Tokyo in mid–
April 1945 after the bombings.
UNITED STATES DEPARTMENT OF DEFENSE

The outside of the former Japanese Ministry of War building where the Tokyo War Crimes Tribunal took place.
UNITED STATES DEPARTMENT OF DEFENSE

# OAHU

Oahu is steeped in World War II history and hosts an entire industry dedicated to telling the story of the Pearl Harbor attack. Honolulu's museums and memorials are expensive but ably done. However, there are some locations that readers of this work may want to see in person that no existing tours will visit. Here are a few places where you can walk in the footsteps of the figures in this book.

# DIAMOND HEAD BEACH PARK

It's eerie to stand exactly where Douglas Wada was fishing as the attack on Pearl Harbor unfolded. The trailhead is located on Diamond Head Road and heads down a steep, paved trail to a wave-swept beach. Wada and his friends were casting from the rocky outcrops under the Diamond Head lighthouse, which is visible when you walk to the right as you reach the beach. (Watch your step on those rocks!) The spot is popular with local surfers and squatters.

The 2023 view from Diamond Head Beach is the same as Wada's in 1941.
AUTHORS' COLLECTION

# SHUNCHORO TEA HOUSE

Takeo Yoshikawa visited this Honolulu establishment to watch the ships at Pearl Harbor. Now called "Natsunoya Tea House," it remains a traditional Japanese tea house with both sushi and warm dishes on the menu. Little changed from 1941 are the panoramic views of Honolulu and the naval base. (That big golf ball you'll see is an X-band radar built to travel like an offshore oil rig.) The tea house is located at 1935 Makanani Drive.

# CONSULATE GENERAL OF JAPAN

The nerve center of the espionage ring in Honolulu remains in the same location as 1941—at 1742 Nuuanu Avenue in Honolulu. The compound still includes residences for the diplomatic staff, as it did during Yoshikawa's time.

The consulate in 2023, as seen from the street.
AUTHORS' COLLECTION

# PACIFIC FLEET SUBMARINE MUSEUM

As people arrive to visit the USS *Arizona* Memorial and tour the USS *Missouri*, many are surprised to find the USS *Bowfin*, a Balao-class submarine, also available for a tour. With that ticket comes a visit to the Pacific Fleet Submarine Museum, a gem of a facility that covers many eras of the Silent Service. Next to the entrance is a propeller from Sakamoto's "midget" submarine, HA-19. It's still dinged and scratched from impacts with Oahu's reefs.

# BELLOWS FIELD BEACH

On the topic of HA-19, the beach where the submarine and its surviving crewman washed ashore is worth visiting. Located on the windward side of Oahu near Waimanalo, the beach is part of an active military training area. It's open to the public on weekends after noon and on national holidays. Military members and their families can access the beach on any day of the week. The beach may be closed for training, even on weekends. Yoshikawa also prowled the Waimanalo shorefront, looking for angles on land from which he could see the airfield.

Bellows Field Beach is largely ignored by tourists.
AUTHORS' COLLECTION

# KAMA LANE

The location of the Wada Camp in Honolulu remains quiet, with a distinct Japanese flavor. The Kotohira Jinsha Shrine is still in operation, with a school attached. The street is accessible from an exit off the H-1, and the shrine is also clearly visible as you drive past. If you do pull off to take a look, be aware that this is a neighborhood where the Wada family no longer lives and where uninvited visitors are coolly welcomed.

The Wada family's former house on Kama Lane in 2023. The Kotohira Jinsha still anchors the dead-end street, which has retained its Japanese roots.
AUTHORS' COLLECTION

# ACKNOWLEDGMENTS

# ACKNOWLEDGMENTS

We wish to thank:

Our steadfast partner and researcher Joe Pappalardo, a great teammate who dedicated so much time and passion to this project and was always looking out for our best interests.

Matt Parsons and Victor McPherson, whose research into Douglas Wada was invaluable in telling this story correctly. They have a trove of information and documents about the development of US naval intelligence available at the NCISA History Project website, ncisahistory.org.

Michael Smith, for his tutorials in interrogation technique, our behind-the-gates tour of Pearl Harbor and illuminating discussions about how current NCIS handles counterespionage.

Amber Barker, for helping with the field research across Oahu.

Kenneth Ringle Jr., for his time spent talking to us and his enduring interest in his father's work.

Mary Campany, of the Japanese Cultural Center of Hawaii, for her information surrounding the interview with Douglas Wada on behalf of the MIS Veterans of Honolulu, which was preserved for posterity by the JCCH.

Lori Stewart, at Fort Huachuca, for her help locating letters written by Wada that helped give more of his voice to this story.

# ABOUT THE AUTHORS

# MARK HARMON

Mark Harmon, star of screen, television and stage, is now taking on the publishing world with *Ghosts of Honolulu*.

Probably most recognized for his role as Leroy Jethro Gibbs on the hit drama *NCIS*, which he led for eighteen seasons, Harmon was also an executive producer on the show. In his other TV work, he received an Emmy nomination for Outstanding Guest Actor in a Drama Series for the critically acclaimed series *The West Wing*. Previously he earned an Emmy nomination for Outstanding Performance by a Supporting Actor in a Comedy or Drama Special for *Eleanor and Franklin: The White House Years*. He received two consecutive Golden Globe nominations for his work on *Reasonable Doubts* and received two additional Golden Globe nominations for Best Performance by an Actor in a Miniseries or Motion Picture Made for Television: one for *After the Promise* and another for his role as notorious serial killer Ted Bundy in *The Deliberate Stranger*. Along with his costars on *Chicago Hope*, he received two SAG Award nominations for Outstanding Performance by an Ensemble in a Drama Series. Further credits include HBO's *From the Earth to the Moon*, *St. Elsewhere*, *Moonlighting*, and Tennessee Williams's *Sweet Bird of Youth*.

Harmon made his feature-film debut in Alan J. Pakula's *Comes a Horseman*. Additional credits include Lawrence Kasdan's *Wyatt Earp*, *Stealing Home* with Jodie Foster, *The Presidio*, and Carl Reiner's smash hit *Summer School*. On stage, Harmon has appeared in Kevin Wade's *Key Exchange*, Bill C. Davis's *Wrestlers*, and Mark Medoff's *The Wager*. In addition, he has done several successful productions of A. R. Gurney's hit play *Love Letters* with his wife, actress Pam Dawber.

Born and raised in Southern California, Harmon excelled in sports. He quarterbacked UCLA to multiple winning football seasons and was presented the National Collegiate Football Foundation Award for All-Around Excellence. The National Football Foundation recently bestowed Harmon with their highest honor, the Gold Medal, making him the first recipient in their organization to receive both the National Scholar-Athlete Award and the Gold Medal. He is a *cum laude* graduate with a degree in communications.

# LEON CARROLL JR.

Leon Carroll Jr. is the technical advisor on the hit drama *NCIS*. A native of Chicago, Illinois, he attended Lindblom Technical High School and went on to earn a BS degree in business economics from North Dakota State University. A member of the football team, he was part of two Division II national championship teams in the late '60s. Carroll then became a commissioned officer in the United States Marine Corps, serving on active duty for six years and three years in the Marine Corps Reserves, attaining the rank of major. His duty assignments included serving in the Fleet Marine Forces and Sea Duty onboard the USS *Ogden* (LPD-5).

Following his stint in the Marine Corps, Carroll began a twenty-year career as a special agent with the Naval Criminal Investigative Service (NCIS). He served in seven different locations, including tours as a special agent afloat on the USS *Ranger* (CV-61) and as the special agent in charge of NCIS offices in the Republic of Panama and the Pacific Northwest.

Upon retirement from NCIS, Carroll was selected to be the technical advisor for the top-rated drama of the same name, holding that position for twenty seasons as of this writing. His experience in foreign counterintelligence gives him unique insight into the world in which Doug Wada operated.